VALUING EMPLOYMENT RIGHTS

This book gives new insights into employment law by analysing a neglected topic: remedies for breaches of employment rights. It explores remedies in the wider context of compliance with, and enforcement of, employment law through criminal law and other regulatory techniques.

The book argues that some of the remedies set out in statute or at common law for working people are a poor 'fit' for the employment rights they are supposed to protect. Employment rights are often undervalued in the legal system, because remedies for their infringement are subject to limitations not applicable to rights in other settings. This limits their ability both to uphold the dignity of working people and to deter breaches. Moreover, the remedies on offer do not always suggest a sensible ranking of employment rights in which fundamental rights attract stronger remedies than other kinds of rights and interests.

The book suggests why some of these problems might have arisen and makes proposals for reform. It also considers the wider implications for a system of employment law that depends so heavily for its enforcement on working people litigating to enforce their rights. Ranging widely across theory and doctrine, and analysing criminal law, contract and tort as well as statutory employment law, this book will be of interest to academics and researchers seeking a deeper understanding of the subject.

Valuing Employment Rights

A Study of Remedies in Employment Law

ACL Davies

•HART•
OXFORD • LONDON • NEW YORK • NEW DELHI • SYDNEY

HART PUBLISHING

Bloomsbury Publishing Plc

Kemp House, Chawley Park, Cumnor Hill, Oxford, OX2 9PH, UK

1385 Broadway, New York, NY 10018, USA

29 Earlsfort Terrace, Dublin 2, Ireland

First published in Great Britain 2024

A catalogue record for this book is available from the British Library.

A catalogue record for this book is available from the Library of Congress.

Library of Congress Control Number: 2024931647

ISBN: HB: 978-1-50995-526-8
ePDF: 978-1-50995-528-2
ePub: 978-1-50995-527-5

Typeset by Compuscript Ltd, Shannon

Er cof annwyl am

Edward Terence Lloyd Davies

1944–2022

ACKNOWLEDGEMENTS

This project began by accident. During the course of an email exchange with Mark Freedland, Keith Ewing and me on another matter entirely, Alan Bogg said in passing that a book on remedies might be interesting. The conversation moved on, but the throwaway remark stuck with me, and the more I thought about it, the more intrigued I became. Three years later, this is the result. I consider myself fortunate to be a part of a labour law community both in Oxford and more generally, in which colleagues are supportive of each other's endeavours and always ready to discuss and engage. I have been privileged to teach with a number of talented labour law colleagues over the years, and I am grateful for the many ways in which they have stimulated my thinking, often quite by accident.

Aspects of this book have benefited in particular from thoughtful comments from the referees engaged by Hart Publishing, participants in the Society of Legal Scholars conference in Durham in 2021, everyone involved in the *Criminality at Work* workshop and book project, and panellists and audience members in a session on remedies at the Labour Law Research Network conference in Warsaw in 2023, especially Alan Bogg, Douglas Brodie, Tess Hardy and Rüdiger Krause.

I would like to thank Hart Publishing for welcoming the project with enthusiasm when I first discussed it with them, and for their support throughout the writing and production processes. Brasenose College, Oxford, continues to provide me with a congenial working environment for which I am very grateful.

A number of people have unwittingly supported this project by distracting me from it or helping me to keep it in perspective. I cannot name everyone here, but I am particularly grateful to Bob Whorton and to Peter, Bea, Michael and Edward Groves. Last but by no means least, special thanks are due to my mother, Freda, for her unstinting love and support, and for asking every day if the book is finished yet. It is now!

The cover photograph is an image of the MG car factory in Abingdon in the 1930s. Although the MG marque lives on in a different guise, the Abingdon factory closed in 1980, and many people lost their jobs. As more recent examples have shown, large-scale redundancies are one of the areas in which the remedies on offer do little to protect working people's interests in having a voice at work and avoiding job losses wherever possible. Of course, I could have chosen any image of a factory – or perhaps a ferry – to make this point. But this particular photograph would have delighted my father, a lifelong MG enthusiast, to whose memory this book is dedicated. He taught me many things, including a great deal about dignity, one of this book's central themes.

ACL Davies
18 September 2023

TABLE OF CONTENTS

TABLE OF CASES

ECHR

CJEU

UK

TABLE OF STATUTES

TABLE OF STATUTORY INSTRUMENTS

TABLE OF INTERNATIONAL INSTRUMENTS

UNITED NATIONS

INTERNATIONAL LABOUR ORGANIZATION

COUNCIL OF EUROPE

EUROPEAN UNION

1

Overview

This book explores what can be learnt about employment law by studying the remedies that may be awarded when a person's employment rights have been infringed. For these purposes, I define a remedy in simple terms as the 'relief' a claimant can obtain from a court or tribunal.[1] Familiar examples include orders requiring the defendant employer to do something or to stop doing something, or to pay an award of compensation to the claimant.[2] Remedies can help to tell us whether the legal system takes employment rights seriously, whether it acknowledges any of the special characteristics of employment relationships, and how it ranks different employment rights against each other. For these reasons, remedies are an important subject of study, even though, in practice, many people whose employment rights are infringed never get to the court or tribunal, let alone receive an award.

This chapter lays the groundwork for the rest of the book by outlining its scope (section I) and offering a concise overview of the argument (section II). I also address some objections to the focus on remedies. I conclude with a map of the remaining chapters (section III).

I. Scope

This book considers remedies in the employment law of England and Wales. Although remedies have the potential to be an important subject for comparative analysis, there is plenty to say about these jurisdictions alone for the purposes of the present volume. Here, I make some important preliminary points about the definition of 'remedy' and the relationship between rights and remedies.

[1] AS Burrows, *Remedies for Torts, Breach of Contract, and Equitable Wrongs* (4th edn, Oxford, OUP, 2019), 3.

[2] I include declarations, a very common remedy in employment law, in this definition. Although the 'relief' involved in a declaration is limited, it may be of value to the claimant to have an official statement of their rights.

A. What is a Remedy?

As many writers have pointed out, the word 'remedy' is hopelessly imprecise.[3] It can be used in a variety of ways in common parlance, some of which are very wide-ranging. For example, the term is often used to denote any means of putting a grievance right, including the claimant's cause of action itself.[4] In an employment setting, the possibility of bringing an unfair dismissal claim might be described, loosely, as a 'remedy' for arbitrary termination of employment. But this usage includes the whole of the substantive law and does not help to identify a manageable subject of study. Following Burrows, my focus will be on remedies as awarded by courts or tribunals in the orders that they make.[5]

A definition focused on orders of the court or tribunal excludes any form of self-help, such as withholding one's labour. Although self-help is often referred to in common parlance as a 'remedy', and may be an important means of securing compliance with employment rights in particular, it does not aid me in my primary purpose of understanding the law's treatment of those rights.

Importantly, though, not every order of the court or tribunal awards the claimant a remedy. Many court orders are procedural, setting out the steps the parties must take to prepare the case for a hearing. Others are used to enforce remedies against recalcitrant defendants. For example, the procedure for 'taking control of goods' set out in Schedule 12 to the Tribunals, Courts and Enforcement Act 2007 may be used to authorise an enforcement officer to seize and sell the defendant's goods in order to pay a monetary award. Although I will discuss enforcement briefly in chapter two, the book is not generally concerned with these types of order.

B. Rights and Remedies

Employment litigation broadly conceived might involve claims brought by or against employers, working people, trade unions and public authorities. This book will focus on litigation in which the employer is the defendant. Thus, its primary focus is on civil claims brought by working people and trade unions, and (in chapter four) criminal prosecutions brought by public authorities.[6] Although both trade unions and working people may be also defendants in employment cases, the aim is to use the lens of remedies to understand employment rights,

[3] See eg R Zakrzewski, *Remedies Reclassified* (New York, OUP, 2005). Birks famously rejected the use of the term 'remedy' altogether: P Birks, 'Rights, Wrongs and Remedies' (2000) 20 *Oxford Journal of Legal Studies* 1.

[4] Birks, ibid, 10–12.

[5] Burrows, above n 1.

[6] Of course, the criminal law is not concerned with remedies for victims, but I include it because of the light it sheds on employment law's wider approach to enforcement.

which is best done by focusing on the employer as duty-bearer and defendant. Sometimes, it is instructive to compare the treatment of employers with that of trade unions as defendants in employment disputes – a well-known example is the comparison between unfair dismissal by an employer and unlawful expulsion from membership by a trade union[7] – but these issues will not be the main focus of the book.

Of course, the idea of 'employment rights' may itself require some clarification. I use this term loosely, as most employment lawyers do, to identify the substantive entitlement of a working person (usually an employee or worker[8]) that the employer does or does not do something in relation to them. At common law, rights can sometimes be difficult to identify with precision because the court's focus, when deciding a case, is on whether a remedy should be ordered, and the court's reasoning may not analyse the right in detail.[9] However, this does not mean that rights only exist when there is a remedy: there are many instances in which a claimant clearly has a substantive right but the court will not enforce it – for example, because the claim was brought out of time. Identifying a working person's substantive rights in statutory employment law is, obviously, a much less complex task, not least because they are often expressly drafted as such.[10]

Conversely, the mere existence of a substantive right is not enough to give rise to a remedy. The claimant must first establish that there is a reason for the court or tribunal to intervene: that the defendant has infringed their right in some way or is threatening to do so.[11] The claimant must prove facts giving rise to a cause of action, and this in turn generates a right that the court issues an order requiring the defendant to do something or refrain from doing something. That court order is the remedy as defined above. At the core of this book is a critical analysis of the relationship between these three elements: the claimant's substantive right, the nature of the defendant's breach (as shown by the cause of action) and the nature of the remedy on offer.

Chapter three will develop a detailed framework for this analysis, but for now, it may be helpful to give just one well-known example. An employee has a substantive right not to be dismissed in a way that is procedurally unfair. This right is clearly protected by unfair dismissal law and may also be recognised at common law where the employee has a contractual right that the employer will follow a prescribed procedure. Imagine a scenario in which the employer threatens to dismiss the employee without following any procedure at all. Smith, in a classification I will draw on in chapter three, calls this a 'rights-threat': the employer is

[7] Compare the Trade Union and Labour Relations (Consolidation) Act 1992 (TULRCA 1992), s 176, with the remedies for unfair dismissal discussed in ch 7 of this volume.

[8] Employment Rights Act 1996 (ERA 1996), s 230. I use 'working person' as a neutral, non-technical term.

[9] SA Smith, *Rights, Wrongs, and Injustices: The Structure of Remedial Law* (Oxford, OUP, 2019), 78.

[10] Eg s 94(1) ERA 1996, 'An employee has the right not to be unfairly dismissed by his employer'.

[11] Smith, above n 9, 88.

threatening to infringe the claimant's right to a fair procedure.[12] The claimant may ask the court for an injunction to restrain the threatened breach. While this remedy is available in principle at common law, it is discretionary, and in employment cases, the courts have expressed particular concern about forcing the parties to a 'personal' relationship to continue working together.[13] In the *tribunal*, however, an injunction is not an option because tribunals do not have the power to grant them, so the claimant must bring proceedings after the dismissal has taken place, and either ask for their job back by means of a reinstatement or re-engagement order, or accept an award of compensatory damages for the losses flowing from the dismissal instead. Although the employer's disregard for procedural fairness may have left the dismissed employee feeling angry and upset, this will not be reflected in the award of compensation because 'injury to feelings' is not a recognised type of loss in unfair dismissal law.[14] There is much here to discuss, both analytically and normatively, in the relationship between the right to procedural fairness in dismissal, the employer's threatened breach, and the detailed rules on what remedies the court or tribunal can order and under what circumstances.

II. The Argument in Brief

Here, I explain the three main elements of the book's argument, before discussing its methodology and identifying, for the avoidance of doubt, what the book is not about.

First, I will argue that, in some instances, there is a poor 'fit' between rights (or, more accurately, causes of action) and remedies in employment law: in other words, that the law is not always coherent. Remedies can serve a variety of different purposes.[15] Perhaps the most obvious purpose is compensation: requiring the defendant to make good the claimant's losses.[16] But there are others, including replication (forcing the defendant to do what they should have done in the first place), vindication (acknowledging that the defendant has infringed the claimant's rights) and punishment. In many cases, these purposes can work in combination: for example, a compensatory award also serves to vindicate the claimant's rights and may, occasionally, contain a punitive element. Discerning which purpose or combination of purposes any given remedy serves is a significant analytical exercise in itself. Later chapters will also identify a number of areas in which the remedy chosen is not the best fit for the right at stake. In the example given in

[12] Smith, above n 9, ch 6.
[13] Ch 6 of this volume.
[14] Ch 7 of this volume.
[15] I discuss ways of classifying remedies in ch 3 of this volume.
[16] Some regard the duty to pay compensation as a 'secondary' obligation: *Photo Production Ltd v Securicor Transport Ltd* [1980] AC 827, 849. On this view, most of the law on compensation is substantive rather than remedial. I explore this point further in ch 3.

the previous section, I showed that replicative remedies to prevent a dismissal in breach of procedures are difficult to obtain at common law and unavailable in the statute law of unfair dismissal.

Second, I will argue that the remedies available in employment law do not always reflect the subject's particular characteristics. It is often argued that employment rights are needed to uphold the dignity of working people, who cannot supply their labour without being present themselves.[17] But less attention is paid to the dignitary considerations arising in relation to remedies. I will show that remedies often fail to acknowledge that the consequences of a breach of employment rights are not always purely financial in nature and typically affect working people's social opportunities, standing in the community and life plans. Again, returning to the example given above, the law provides awards for injury to feelings (which compensate for some of these harms) in some employment cases, such as discrimination claims, but not others, notably non-discriminatory dismissals. Another significant characteristic of employment law is that, in the context of a long-term relationship, there is greater scope to deter employers from breaching the rights of working people or to force them into compliance even after a breach. But this opportunity is not always seized in the way that remedies are designed. For example, some remedies (such as the many awards of two weeks' pay applied to statutory rights[18]) are so limited that they do not suggest any serious intention on the part of Parliament that the rights in question should be enforced. As one President of Employment Tribunals has remarked, the tribunal system is often treated as a 'dustbin' for employment rights.[19]

Third, I will argue that the remedies made available by the law do not always reflect an appropriate ranking of different employment rights. Labour law protects a variety of different interests, from workers' fundamental human rights as recognised in international instruments, to less fundamental but nonetheless important interests that should be respected in a decent working environment. It is possible – albeit not uncontroversial – to identify the subject's priorities, a task I undertake in chapter three. Of course, remedies should be calibrated to reflect what has happened in a particular case: most obviously, the calculation of compensation should correspond to the losses suffered by the affected individual. However, it is also appropriate to consider the relationship between the remedy and the right. For example, is the right important enough to warrant the intervention of the criminal law, or the use of a civil penalty? Should limitations on the compensation that can be recovered be removed when particularly important rights are at

[17] Encapsulated in the International Labour Organization (ILO)'s slogan that 'labour is not a commodity'. See also P Gilabert, 'Labor Human Rights and Human Dignity' (2016) 42 *Philosophy and Social Criticism* 171.

[18] Eg a breach of the right to be accompanied to a grievance or disciplinary hearing under s 10 Employment Relations Act 1999 attracts an award of up to two weeks' pay under s 11(3).

[19] G Meeran, 'The Employment Tribunals', in L Dickens and A Neal (eds), *The Changing Institutional Face of British Industrial Relations* (Alphen aan den Rijn, Kluwer Law International, 2006), 131.

stake? The book will uncover several examples of remedies failing to reflect the law's priorities as I see them, particularly in relation to cases in which employers have breached working people's freedom of association.

It will be apparent from the above discussion that the book will adopt a two-pronged methodological approach. I will deploy traditional doctrinal methods to examine the coherence of the law on remedies in employment cases, and use normative analysis to determine whether the remedies on offer are acceptable from the perspective of the features, purposes and priorities of employment law as I define them. In some instances, I also speculate about the likely effect of particular remedies on the behaviour of employers and the litigation choices of working people, drawing on common sense understandings rather than systematic empirical analysis. These observations could, of course, be tested empirically in future research.

One obvious objection to my focus on remedies and my strategy for pursuing it is that remedies are largely irrelevant to people's lived experience of employment law. This point might take one of two slightly different forms. First, the vast majority of people who experience a breach of their employment rights never receive a remedy from a court or tribunal. Many people with a legitimate claim either do not bring proceedings or give up, because of the cost and hassle involved.[20] Even where there is litigation, cases are often settled, so that the court or tribunal never reaches the point of formally awarding a remedy.[21] Second, the remedies awarded in practice often bear little resemblance to the full range of options present in the law. For example, the average tribunal award for unfair dismissal in 2021–22 was £14,000, well below both average annual earnings and the statutory maximum.[22] But there are two reasons for pursuing a study of remedies despite their relative rarity in practice. One is that the remedies laid down in the law *do* have an influence over what happens in practice, albeit in an indirect way. For example, an employer deciding whether to settle an unfair dismissal claim would probably take advice on the maximum that could be awarded and on what a tribunal would be likely to award before making an offer to the employee. The other is that the kind of doctrinal and normative analysis deployed in the book can offer important insights about the nature of employment law as a discipline, even if it is based primarily on a study of the law 'in the books'.

Finally, it may be helpful to emphasise what this book is not about: it is not primarily about *compliance* with employment law. A book on remedies could be used to examine deterrent effects: does the prospect of a particular remedy

[20] See N Busby and M McDermont, 'Fighting with the Wind: Claimants' Experiences and Perceptions of the Employment Tribunal' (2020) 49 *Industrial Law Journal* 159.

[21] In 2021–22, ACAS achieved a conciliated settlement in 23% of early conciliation cases and 53% of Employment Tribunal cases (ACAS, *Annual Report and Accounts 2021–22* (HC 398), 23). The parties may also settle without ACAS involvement: the last SETA survey in 2018 found that 58% of cases in total were settled: Department for Business, Enterprise and Industrial Strategy, *Survey of Employment Tribunal Applications: Findings from the 2018 Survey* (BEIS Research Paper Number 2020/007), 9.

[22] Ministry of Justice, *Tribunal Statistics Quarterly, July to September 2022* (December 2022), section 10.

encourage employers to comply with the law? It could also be used to compare the effectiveness of individual litigation as an enforcement technique with other options, such as collective action by trade unions or inspection and prosecution by public agencies.[23] An effective study of compliance would require the use of empirical methods to analyse employers' awareness of, and attitudes towards, different types of enforcement activity, and to test whether changes in remedies made any difference to levels of compliance. There have been some important contributions to the debate about compliance in employment law over the years, and there are signs of a recent revival of interest in the topic.[24] But while the compliance agenda is an interesting and significant one, offering important practical insights, this book does something different. By viewing employment law through the lens of remedies, it aims to provide new theoretical understandings of the subject.

III. Structure

It may be helpful to conclude by outlining how the argument will develop through the remaining chapters of the book.

Chapter two will set the book in its broader context by examining two important practical issues: compliance generally, and enforcement through litigation specifically. Although the book is not about the pros and cons of different enforcement techniques, it is helpful to have some understanding of where litigation sits in the firmament of options open to policy-makers for getting employers to comply with their obligations. The chapter will then turn to some of the practical issues surrounding litigation itself, focusing on the accessibility of courts and tribunals and the prospects for enforcing an award if successful, drawing on the available empirical evidence and considering questions such as access to legal advice and issues around fees and costs. Although the book's main focus is on remedies from an analytical perspective, it is important to understand some of the challenges for litigants of obtaining a remedy in practice.

In chapter three, I develop the theoretical framework for my analysis of employment law from the perspective of remedies, along the lines set out above. This will generate a series of questions to be used to interrogate the remedies available for the infringement of particular employment rights in subsequent chapters. For example, does the law use replicative remedies as commonly as it should? Do the restrictions on their use – the reluctance to award specific performance

[23] For a discussion of regulatory techniques, see H Collins, 'Justifications and Techniques of Legal Regulation of the Employment Relation', in H Collins, PL Davies and R Rideout (eds), *Legal Regulation of the Employment Relation* (London, Kluwer Law International, 2000).

[24] See L Dickens (ed), *Making Employment Rights Effective: Issues of Enforcement and Compliance* (Oxford, Hart Publishing, 2012), and more recently a special issue of the *International Journal of Comparative Labour Law and Industrial Relations* (2021) vol. 37(2/3) on compliance and enforcement, edited by G Davidov.

of a contract of employment, even against an employer, for example – stand up to scrutiny? Are employees or workers fully compensated when their employer causes them a loss? Are restrictions on the recovery of compensation – statutory maximums, for example – justified? Do the remedies available in employment law sufficiently vindicate claimants' rights, or sanction the employer? Are the relative rankings of employment rights revealed by an analysis of remedies defensible? Are some remedies so trivial that they express no vindication at all?

Chapter four examines the use of criminal offences in employment law. Strictly speaking, a discussion of the use of the criminal law to punish employers does not belong in a book on remedies, since a criminal prosecution does not offer any redress to the victim. However, to ignore this issue would be to leave a gap in the analysis. Use of the criminal law implies a particularly strong interest in public condemnation of the employer's conduct, for example, in cases of deliberate or egregious breach. Thus, it can be argued that the criminal law exists on a spectrum with civil law remedies in which sanctioning the employer's wrongdoing is a significant objective. But is the line between the two drawn in the right place? Many theorists of the criminal law argue that Parliament is too quick to create new offences, particularly 'regulatory' crimes, which are not accepted by the public as 'real' or morally wrong. Moreover, the apparently strong use of the criminal law may be weak in practice if prosecutions are rarely brought. The chapter also considers whether and how redress is afforded to affected individuals where the law's principal strategy is to criminalise the employer's wrongdoing.

Chapter five considers ways in which the law seeks to punish the employer for wrongdoing but without invoking the full force of the criminal law. In some cases, the employer may be required to pay a civil penalty to the Secretary of State, as is the case under section 19A National Minimum Wage Act 1998 or under the general power to require payment of a penalty for an 'aggravated' breach under section 12A Employment Tribunals Act 1996. In others, the employer may be ordered to pay additional compensation to the claimant. Punitive or exemplary damages are potentially available in some employment cases, notably discrimination claims, though they are rarely awarded in practice. Although these forms of 'punishment' via the civil law do not carry with them the same element of public condemnation associated with a criminal conviction, they are clearly intended to single out certain breaches as particularly serious and it is worth considering the justification for this in each case. It is also helpful to examine whether the various penalties are set at levels that are sufficient to express condemnation of the employer's conduct, and how they interact with avenues of redress for affected individuals.

In chapter six, I analyse what Smith calls 'replicative' remedies.[25] These involve ordering the defendant to do something that is the same as, or similar to, the original substantive obligation. Examples include orders to pay money owed

[25] Smith, above n 9, ch 6.

(such as unpaid wages), orders for specific performance, and reinstatement or re-engagement orders. Replicative remedies are important because of their potential to secure something close to compliance for the claimant, a central concern of employment law. However, it is common to encounter a variety of more or less explicit arguments against using them in employment settings. For example, there is often a sense that it is unfair to force an employer to remain in a broken employment relationship, even where there is no objective evidence that the employee has done anything wrong. Chapter six will argue that replicative remedies are underutilised in employment law because of a lack of political will to uphold the rights of working people in the most effective way possible.

Chapter seven turns to compensatory awards. In some senses, compensation is straightforward as a remedial objective: the task is to identify and put right the losses suffered by the working person, many of which will be financial and thus relatively easy to quantify and compensate for in monetary terms. However, there are complex rules on what types of loss can be claimed, on the various deductions that must be made (in respect of mitigation or contributory conduct by the claimant, for example) and, in some cases, maximum limits on the sums that can be awarded. Several of these rules illustrate the legal system's tendency to undervalue employment rights relative to other kinds of rights.

Chapter eight considers vindicatory awards. I develop this concept to describe situations in which the financial award on offer in the event of a breach, usually of a statutory employment right, is designed to acknowledge or vindicate that breach, rather than to compensate the claimant for any losses suffered. The existence of this type of award is not usually explicitly acknowledged: they are often mislabelled either in statute or by tribunals as compensatory or punitive. I argue that a proper understanding of the nature of these awards is essential in order to determine whether they are set at an appropriate level. I also argue that in some instances, a replicative remedy may be more effective. For example, rather than providing the claimant with a sum of money when the employer does not allow them to be accompanied at a disciplinary or grievance hearing, it may be preferable to require the employer to hold the hearing again with the representative present.

Chapter nine provides an opportunity to draw together the various strands of reasoning in the book as a whole and to consider whether the law of remedies is fit for purpose. I argue that there are several areas in need of reform. First, there are a number of mismatches between rights and remedies, with many missed opportunities to achieve compliance for the claimant through the use of replicative remedies. Second, the remedies on offer often fail to achieve the specific goals of employment law – to deter breaches and to uphold the dignity of working people – because of the various limitations attaching to them. Third, while the system does sometimes recognise that a particular right is of fundamental importance, there are many inconsistencies in the way in which employment rights are ranked. While my principal focus in the book is on remedies, I also step back and consider what my findings contribute to the wider debate about the role of individual litigation as a method of enforcing employment rights.

2

Regulatory Techniques

This book is principally concerned with the conceptual analysis of remedies: it uses remedies as a lens through which to view employment rights and to understand their treatment in the legal system. From this perspective, it does not particularly matter how easy any given remedy is to obtain, or how often it is awarded. However, a purely conceptual analysis might give a rather misleading impression of the day-to-day workings of employment law. And it could not form the basis for sensible reform proposals. This chapter therefore seeks to put remedies in context.

The first part of the chapter identifies some key characteristics of litigation, the principal mode of enforcement of employment law in the UK. The aim is not to provide a comprehensive guide – there are many excellent specialist books on the topic[1] – but rather to give the reader a sense of some of the challenges litigants are likely to face in bringing proceedings. I explore the division of jurisdiction between the courts and tribunals, and the advantages and disadvantages of the tribunal system in particular. I focus on three issues: the role of alternative dispute resolution, accessibility, and effectiveness. Although tribunals are themselves an alternative to the courts (in a structural sense), recent years have seen an emphasis among policy-makers on reducing the number of tribunal claims, for example, through Alternative Dispute Resolution (ADR) mechanisms such as early conciliation under the auspices of ACAS. I consider the advantages and disadvantages of this and other ADR mechanisms. I then turn to questions of accessibility, examining how working people can access and pay for legal advice, and how rules on fees and costs may influence individuals' decisions to litigate. Finally, I consider effectiveness: academic lawyers in particular often assume that a claimant who succeeds in the tribunal receives the compensation they are awarded, whereas in practice, a surprisingly high proportion of tribunal awards are never paid.

The second part of the chapter locates litigation in the wider compliance landscape by considering some of the other regulatory techniques that can be used to enforce or promote workers' rights.[2] In English law, a small but significant group of

[1] Eg N Choudry et al, *Harvey on Industrial Relations and Employment Law* (London, LexisNexis UK, 1991, now online).

[2] H Collins, 'Justifications and Techniques of Legal Regulation of the Employment Relation', in H Collins, PL Davies and RW Rideout (eds), *Legal Regulation of the Employment Relation* (London, Kluwer Law International, 2000).

workers' rights are enforced by public agencies, a technique that is arguably more widespread in other legal systems with a single 'labour inspectorate'. I consider the advantages and disadvantages of public enforcement, particularly in comparison with litigation. I also examine some alternative routes to achieving compliance, both within and outside the public sphere, such as 'naming and shaming' schemes, statutory reporting obligations and action by a firm's shareholders.

To sum up the theme of the chapter, I can do no better than to quote Linda Dickens in an important book on compliance and enforcement in employment law:

> The enforcement landscape in Britain is the result of historical accident, political convenience and ad hoc responses to particular needs, rather than one informed by a logic of enforcement designed to make employment rights effective – by which I mean ensuring compliance with statutory standards, giving substantive effect to formal rights, reducing the likelihood of adverse treatment and promoting fairer workplaces.[3]

All too often, politicians assume that they have fixed a workplace problem by legislating to give working people statutory rights, but this is very much the beginning, not the end, of the compliance and enforcement story.

I. Litigation

Remedies as I have defined them for the purposes of this book are orders of the court or tribunal made when the claimant has won their case.[4] It is therefore helpful to have an overview of key elements of the litigation process to understand the context in which these orders are made. This section explains the respective roles of the courts and tribunals in employment law, before looking at four practical issues: access to advice, the role of alternative dispute resolution, fees and costs, and enforcement of awards. These issues are relevant to understanding the challenges claimants face both in securing an award and in ensuring that they receive what the court or tribunal has ordered. Again, while this does not affect the conceptual analysis of the role of remedies, it is important to understand these factors when making proposals for reform.

A. Overview

A strand of the argument of this book is that the remedies associated with statutory employment rights sometimes compare unfavourably with those attached to their common law equivalents. It is therefore particularly important to understand

[3] L Dickens, 'Introduction', in L Dickens (ed), *Making Employment Rights Effective: Issues of Enforcement and Compliance* (Oxford, Hart Publishing, 2012), 3.

[4] See ch 1 of this volume.

the division of jurisdiction between courts and tribunals. As creatures of statute, tribunals only have the powers assigned to them by legislation, whereas the courts have an inherent jurisdiction which can be displaced where there is another, more appropriate forum for hearing the case.[5]

Employment tribunals (originally 'industrial tribunals') were established in 1964 with a very limited jurisdiction to deal with disputes concerning industrial training levies.[6] In 1965, redundancy payments were added.[7] Their jurisdiction expanded significantly in 1971 with the introduction of the unfair dismissal legislation.[8] Since then, the tribunals' jurisdiction has continued to expand as the number of statutory employment rights has grown, and now includes certain minimum wage and unlawful deductions claims, rights to time off and leave for family reasons, working time rights more generally, discrimination and equal pay, rights for agency, fixed-term and part-time workers, and various rights relating to trade union membership.[9]

Tribunals also have jurisdiction to hear contractual claims if certain conditions are met.[10] The claim must 'arise or be outstanding' on the termination of the contract, it must be a claim for damages or for money owed,[11] but it must not exceed £25,000 in value.[12] Certain specific types of claim, such as those relating to the provision of accommodation, are excluded.[13] Although there is no requirement for the contract claim to be brought in conjunction with other proceedings before the tribunal, the provision has the clear advantage that, where the claimant *is* pursuing other proceedings, the contract claims can be heard at the same time. It has been suggested on a number of occasions that the tribunals' contract jurisdiction should be extended in various ways, not least by increasing the maximum sum that can be recovered (which is not currently index-linked so has not risen in line with inflation).[14]

It is self-evident from the very fact that there is a system of employment tribunals that they were not meant to replicate the courts. The Donovan Commission supported the creation of tribunals as an 'accessible, speedy, informal and inexpensive procedure' for the resolution of disputes.[15] As originally designed, tribunals also incorporated a lay element, with a legally-qualified chair sitting alongside lay members, one with employer expertise and one with employee expertise. I deal

[5] Employment Tribunals Act 1996 (ETA 1996), s 2.

[6] Industrial Training Act 1964.

[7] Redundancy Payments Act 1965.

[8] Industrial Relations Act 1971, Part II.

[9] Explored in detail in later chapters.

[10] ETA 1996, s 3, and Employment Tribunals Extension of Jurisdiction (England and Wales) Order 1994 (SI 1994/1623).

[11] ibid Art 3.

[12] ibid Art 10.

[13] ibid Art 5.

[14] The limit was set in 1994. See Law Commission, *Employment Tribunal Hearing Structures* (No 390, April 2020), 68–72, recommending an increase to £100,000.

[15] Report of the Royal Commission on Trade Unions and Employers' Associations 1965–1968 (Cmnd 3623, 1968), para 578.

with some issues around accessibility and cost below; here I consider the role of lay members and the question of informality.

Nowadays, although the terminology of 'employment tribunals' continues to be used, most cases are heard by a legally-qualified employment judge[16] sitting alone. The starting presumption, in section 4(1) Employment Tribunals Act 1996 (ETA 1996), is still that a three-person tribunal should hear a case. However, section 4(3) offers a long list of exceptions in which the employment judge is generally expected to sit alone. Controversially, this list includes unfair dismissal cases, a significant part of the tribunal jurisdiction. The two main types of case in which a three-person tribunal should still sit are Equality Act 2010 cases and claims regarding various types of detrimental treatment at work.[17] Under section 4(3)(e), though, an employment judge may hear a case alone if both parties consent, so the requirement to have a full tribunal for certain types of case is not absolute.

The traditional justification for the composition of tribunals was that lay members would bring to bear their workplace experience when deciding cases, particularly when applying open-textured standards such as reasonableness in unfair dismissal law. Lay members would have an awareness of how employers might react to particular types of wrongdoing or how much weight might be given to an employee's previously unblemished record. It also seems likely that representativeness is a factor, explaining why Equality Act cases should still be heard by a full tribunal: it may be preferable for difficult questions of discrimination law to be dealt with not just by a single individual, however well-qualified, so that different life experiences may inform decision-making. The government's principal explanation for reducing the use of lay members was cost and convenience: tribunal hearings are much easier to arrange for an employment judge sitting alone.[18] Moreover, it may be questioned whether there is much scope in practice for lay members to have input into decision-making, however desirable this might be. Although the reasonableness test in unfair dismissal law is often given as an example of an opportunity for lay input, it is governed by detailed legal rules which limit the ability of tribunals to impose their own views of what would have been reasonable for the employer to decide, making their workplace expertise less relevant than might appear to be the case.[19]

Another way in which tribunals are supposed to differ from courts is in their informality.[20] The intention here was that working people (and perhaps also

[16] The term 'employment judge' replaced 'employment tribunal chair' in 2007, by virtue of the Tribunals, Courts and Enforcement Act 2007, Schedule 8, para 36, inserting new s 3A, ETA 1996.

[17] At the time of writing, there are ongoing discussions about further reductions in the use of lay members: Senior President of Tribunals, *Consultation on Panel Composition in the Employment Tribunals and the Employment Appeal Tribunal* (February 2023).

[18] This change was brought about by the Trade Union Reform and Employment Rights Act 1993, ss 36–37.

[19] See *Iceland Frozen Foods v Jones* [1983] ICR 17 (EAT).

[20] Employment Tribunals (Constitution and Rules of Procedure) Regulations 2013 (SI 2013/1237), Schedule 1, rule 41.

employers) could represent themselves, without the need for costly legal advice. It remains the case that claimants can be represented by someone who is not legally qualified, such as a trade union representative, whereas in court, litigants must either be represented by a lawyer or must represent themselves. Moreover, although tribunals are adversarial in nature, they do not follow the strict rules of evidence applicable in court, and employment judges may be more inclined to ask questions to elicit the key points in the case. Again, though, as the legal regime governing the tribunals has become more complex and a body of case-law has built up, the idea of an informal dispute resolution forum has become more elusive. The parties will often need to present quite complex legal arguments and, as I discuss further below, the empirical evidence suggests that a claimant without legal representation is in fact at a significant disadvantage in the proceedings, particularly when they are facing a represented employer.

It is difficult to obtain accurate recent statistics on the work of the employment tribunals, due to problems caused by a new computer system. In 2021–22, over 70,000 people took a claim to an employment tribunal.[21] The most common claims tend to be in respect of unfair dismissal and redundancy, unlawful deductions from wages, working time and equal pay (though the statistics for the latter fluctuate as large group claims work their way through the system).[22] Only about seven per cent of these claims ultimately succeed at a hearing.[23] However, this does not mean that all the other claimants 'lose': as I explain below, significant numbers of cases are settled either through ACAS or by other means.

B. Advice and Support

As noted above, it was originally envisaged that employment tribunal claimants would be able to represent themselves. For this reason, legal aid has never been made available in tribunal proceedings. However, even if the setting is less formal than a court in some respects, the law to be applied is complex and the claimant needs to be able to present their case effectively. Employers are much more likely to be able to pay for legal representation, creating a glaring problem of inequality of arms. Trade unions, Citizens' Advice and other voluntary or pro bono organisations often help, but their resources are limited.

The 2018 Survey of Employment Tribunal Applications (SETA) found that 77 per cent of employers had representation at a tribunal hearing compared with 41 per cent of claimants.[24] The famous 1985 study by Genn and Genn found that

[21] Ministry of Justice, *Tribunal Statistics Quarterly, July to September 2022* (December 2022), Annex C.

[22] ibid.

[23] Department for Business, Energy and Industrial Strategy, *Survey of Employment Tribunal Applications: Findings from the 2018 Survey* (BEIS Research Paper Number 2020/007, July 2020), ch 5.

[24] ibid ch 3.

representation had a significant impact on a claimant's chances of success, particularly where the unrepresented claimant was up against a represented employer.[25] Problems faced by unrepresented claimants included a lack of knowledge of procedures and other rules, difficulty in working out which parts of their 'story' were legally relevant, and a struggle to stay calm and objective when trying to explain the situation.[26] A more recent qualitative study by Busby and MacDermont found that claimants typically had a very bad experience of the tribunal hearing where the employer was represented.[27] Although tribunal judges often tried to help unrepresented litigants, their need to maintain impartiality placed limits on how far they could intervene, and claimants frequently formed the impression that the employer's representative was able to communicate more freely with the judge.

It is important to state clearly the implications of these studies. A significant number of claimants whose employment rights have been infringed are unsuccessful in the tribunal because they are unable to pay for legal representation. This means that the system effectively condones significant levels of injustice and provides a better service to wealthier claimants who are able to afford a lawyer. Although there is now a high level of information about employment law available online, often expressed in relatively simple language, for example, from the government website and from ACAS, this does not tackle the underlying problem: that an individual who does not have legal training may find it extremely difficult to identify relevant facts and evidence and to apply the law in a way that will enable them to succeed in litigation. Lawyers undergo years of training to develop these skills, so it should not be a surprise to anyone that ordinary working people find it hard to acquire them for the purposes of presenting their own case.

It is not easy to identify precisely what proportion of claimants are supported by their trade union in the tribunal.[28] The official statistics show that relatively few claimants have a trade union representative before the tribunal, but it is possible that some of the legally-represented claimants are using advice paid for by their trade union. It seems likely that cost is a significant issue for trade unions in this context. Arguably, there are much greater benefits for trade unions and their members in supporting test cases, which test or develop the law on a significant point of relevance to a large number of people, than in dealing with lots of individual, fact-specific cases.[29] Prominent examples include the *UNISON* case on tribunal fees,[30] discussed in more detail below, and the challenge brought by

[25] H Genn and Y Genn, *The Effectiveness of Representation at Tribunals: Report to the Lord Chancellor* (Lord Chancellor's Department, 1989).

[26] H Genn, 'Do-it-Yourself Law: Access to Justice and the Challenge of Self-Representation' (2013) 32 *Civil Justice Quarterly* 411, 432–35.

[27] N Busby and M McDermont, 'Fighting With the Wind: Claimants' Experiences and Perceptions of the Employment Tribunal' (2020) 49 *Industrial Law Journal* 159.

[28] See Ministry of Justice, *Tribunal Statistics Quarterly, April to June 2023* (September 2023), section 7.

[29] For further discussion see T Colling, 'Trade Union Roles in Making Employment Rights Effective', in L Dickens (ed), *Making Employment Rights Effective: Issues of Enforcement and Compliance* (Oxford, Hart Publishing, 2012), especially 194–200.

[30] *R (UNISON) v Lord Chancellor* [2017] UKSC 51, [2020] AC 869.

IWGB during the pandemic to the implementation of EU health and safety directives for 'employees' rather than 'workers'.[31]

Finally, although some research has considered the implications of lack of representation before the tribunal, it is important to note the role of advice in helping people to realise that what has happened to them is unlawful and might be the subject of a successful claim. Busby and MacDermont offer a powerful account of the role of Citizens' Advice services in enabling people to identify that they have a potential claim.[32] It is impossible to quantify how many viable claims are never brought because the working person affected does not realise that their employer has infringed their rights.

C. Alternative Dispute Resolution

A clear majority of tribunal claims never reach a hearing, either because they are withdrawn by the claimant or because the parties reach a settlement.[33] The claimant may well secure some redress from the employer in these circumstances, often equivalent to the remedy the tribunal would have awarded, though it does not count as a remedy under the definition I am using.[34] On the one hand, ADR techniques can be attractive in that they save time and money, and avoid adding to the claimant's distress by having to appear before the tribunal. On the other hand, there are concerns that ADR can disadvantage claimants – who may be persuaded to settle for less than they would have received in the tribunal – and can be harmful to the wider public interest in the sense that it reduces opportunities to develop the law and set new precedents.

The Enterprise and Regulatory Reform Act 2013, section 7 made provision for an 'Early Conciliation' (EC) scheme to be operated by ACAS.[35] This applies to the jurisdictions listed in section 18(1) ETA 1996, and in practice covers the vast majority of cases before the tribunals. The claimant must notify ACAS of their intention to bring a tribunal claim.[36] ACAS will then offer conciliation. Up to six weeks is allowed for ACAS to attempt conciliation, and the time limit for bringing a tribunal claim is paused while the process takes place. If the claimant refuses conciliation, or if conciliation is unsuccessful, ACAS issues an EC certificate to confirm that the claimant notified it of the dispute. Without this certificate, the

[31] *R (Independent Workers' Union of Great Britain) v Secretary of State for Work and Pensions* [2020] EWHC 3050 (Admin), [2021] ICR 372.

[32] Above n 27, 177–79.

[33] This section does not consider the arbitration scheme operated by ACAS for unfair dismissal and flexible working claims because this is rarely used in practice. This has been in effect since 2001 under the power in s 212A TULRCA 1992.

[34] Because it is not awarded by a tribunal or court.

[35] See Employment Tribunals (Early Conciliation: Exemptions and Rules of Procedure) Regulations 2014 (SI 2014/254).

[36] The respondent can also initiate EC but this does not pause the time limit.

claimant cannot bring tribunal proceedings. It is worth noting that ACAS conciliation is always available, so even if the parties do not reach an agreement during the EC process, they may still seek ACAS's help to settle their dispute after proceedings have been issued, right up until the tribunal hears the case. Although settlements can be reached orally, ACAS-conciliated settlements are typically recorded on a form known as a COT3.[37] Detailed legal rules govern the wording and effect of settlements and, in particular, the limits that settlements place on the claimant's ability to bring other claims in the future.

The parties may also agree to settle their case themselves, without recourse to ACAS. Because this represents an exception to the general prohibition against contracting out of employment rights, certain conditions, set out in section 203 Employment Rights Act 1996 (ERA 1996), must be satisfied in order for the settlement agreement to be binding. The most important of these are that the settlement must be in writing, must relate to the proceedings in question, and that the claimant must have received independent advice from a suitably qualified adviser on the effect of the settlement. Again, there is complex case-law on the appropriate drafting of settlements and the extent to which they can effectively preclude the claimant from bringing future claims.[38]

Finally, it is also possible for a case to be settled prior to a hearing as a result of ADR conducted by the tribunals judiciary. At a preliminary hearing, the judge may give a 'judicial assessment' of the strengths and weaknesses of the case.[39] This may prompt the parties to enter into settlement negotiations, particularly where it changes one party's assessment of its own case. The preliminary hearing may also explore the possibility of judicial mediation, in which an employment judge attempts to encourage the parties to reach a settlement by mediating between them. If the mediation fails, the case proceeds to a hearing before a different employment judge.

According to SETA, 58 per cent of all tribunal claims in 2017 were settled.[40] That figure is made up of 40 per cent of claims settled by ACAS and 18 per cent settled privately. Only 17 per cent of all claims went on to a hearing, with 10 per cent of claimants losing and 7 per cent winning at that stage. However, it is worth noting that an additional 5 per cent of the total claims resulted in a default judgment in the claimant's favour. The remaining 20 per cent of claims were withdrawn or dismissed.

Settlements can be highly beneficial for both claimants and defendants. The claimant may obtain the redress they were seeking without the challenges of going to a tribunal. 40 per cent of claimants reported that they chose to settle because

[37] A COT3 can be enforced in the same ways as a tribunal award.

[38] Eg *Hinton v University of East London* [2005] ICR 1260.

[39] Employment Tribunals (Constitution and Rules of Procedure) Regulations 2013 (SI 2013/1237), Schedule 1, rule 53(1)(a).

[40] Above n 23, ch 5. It is worth noting that SETA is a survey of claimants and defendants so the figures do not correspond exactly with tribunal records, but for present purposes the survey is more helpful because it also gives insight into the parties' views.

they thought this was less stressful than proceeding with the claim.[41] While it may be questioned whether the tribunal process could be made easier for claimants, it is unlikely that it could ever be made completely free of stress. Employers typically settled in order to save time and money, and in some cases at least, this is bound to involve recognition that they had not complied with the law. However, there are at least two reasons to be concerned about the push towards ADR. One is that claimants may feel pressured into settling for less than they might have achieved at the tribunal. 55 per cent of claimants surveyed thought that they would have got a better remedy at a hearing, though it is difficult to know whether their expectations were realistic.[42] Another is that settlements are typically private, with the result that some of the significant public benefits of litigation are not realised. As Mulcahy has argued, one of the disadvantages of settlement is that the opportunity to develop the law and to set new precedents is lost.[43] Moreover, particularly where the employer has engaged in serious wrongdoing, an opportunity is lost publicly to condemn the employer and to vindicate the working person's rights. For example, settlements may be used to shield perpetrators of harassment from public condemnation in a way that allows them to repeat their bad behaviour with other victims.

D. Fees and Costs

Another important aspect of the original design of the tribunal system was that it would be less costly than taking a case to court. No fees were payable, and each party was responsible for its own costs. This meant that a working person bringing a claim would not incur the risk of having to pay the employer's costs if they lost, and of course they could keep their own costs down by getting free advice from a trade union or some other source. However, some inroads have been made into these principles.

In 2013 the government experimented with the introduction of fees as a means of reducing the number of tribunal claims.[44] It was argued that this was necessary because too many speculative or vexatious claims were being brought, thereby imposing unjustified costs on employers.[45] No evidence was provided to support this argument, and it is implausible given the many barriers to bringing a claim.[46]

[41] ibid ch 4.

[42] ibid.

[43] See L Mulcahy, 'The Collective Interest in Private Dispute Resolution' (2013) 33 *Oxford Journal of Legal Studies* 59.

[44] Added Tribunals (Employment Tribunals and The Employment Appeal Tribunal) Order 2013 (SI 2013/1892).

[45] See Department for Business, Innovation and Skills, *Resolving Workplace Disputes* (January 2011).

[46] For discussion, see eg E Kirk, 'The "Problem" with the Employment Tribunal System: Reform, Rhetoric and Realities for the Clients of Citizens' Advice Bureaux' (2018) 32 *Work, Employment and Society* 975.

The regime required claimants to pay fees at two stages in the process: issuing a claim and proceeding to a hearing.[47] Although cases were divided into two types for this purpose, with more straightforward claims attracting a lower fee, research demonstrated that in many cases, the remedy on offer would not even cover the fee paid to obtain it.[48] The number of claims dropped by around two-thirds overall, with even bigger falls in certain jurisdictions.[49] As commentators pointed out, while this certainly achieved the government's objective of reducing the number of claims, there was no real evidence to support the idea that a high proportion of claims were groundless, nor was there any connection between a person's ability to pay a fee and the merits of their claim.[50] In a powerful judgment in the *UNISON* case, the Supreme Court struck down the fees Order on the basis that it infringed claimants' common law right of access to a court, without any clear wording in the empowering legislation to indicate that Parliament intended to permit this.[51]

Despite the Supreme Court's ruling, it would not be impossible for a government to reintroduce a fees regime, and there have been occasional suggestions (not yet implemented) that this might occur.[52] Using primary rather than secondary legislation would make it impossible for the courts to strike down the fees regime, though there would still be the possibility of compatible interpretation or a declaration of incompatibility under the Human Rights Act 1998, since Article 6 ECHR also protects the right of access to the courts. It would also be possible to develop a more carefully differentiated approach to fees, making it less likely that claimants would be deterred from bringing low-value claims. Court fees have long been linked to the value of the claim, making it all the more surprising that the government adopted such a clumsy approach to tribunal fees.[53]

However, the point remains that there is no necessary connection between a person's ability to pay a fee to access the tribunal and the strength of their claim in law. There is also no necessary connection between the amount of money at stake in a tribunal claim and the 'importance' of the claim when judged in other ways. As later chapters will demonstrate, claims involving fundamental labour rights do not necessarily have a high monetary value. This may be because the remedy is an award of compensation, but the claimant did not suffer a significant loss on the facts (for example, where they were dismissed as a result of discrimination but quickly got another equally well-paid job) or because the award is a modest sum in 'vindication' of the claimant's rights. Many claimants will opt not to pursue

[47] Employment Tribunals and the Employment Appeal Tribunal Fees Order 2013 (SI 2013/1893).

[48] A Adams and J Prassl, 'Vexatious Claims: Challenging the Case for Employment Tribunal Fees' (2017) 80 *Modern Law Review* 412.

[49] ibid 416–19.

[50] ibid.

[51] Above n 30. See M Ford, 'Employment Tribunal Fees and the Rule of Law: *R (UNISON) v Lord Chancellor* in the Supreme Court' (2018) 47 *Industrial Law Journal* 1.

[52] Ford, ibid, 39–43.

[53] See, generally, Civil Proceedings Fees Order 2008 (SI 2008/1053).

litigation under these circumstances even if no fees are payable, but the reintroduction of fees would exacerbate the situation. There are other, more targeted ways of dealing with vexatious claims if they are genuinely a problem.

Of course, fees are payable in respect of the various employment-related claims that must be brought in court.[54] These include high-value breach of contract claims and tort claims in respect of personal injuries. This contributes to a class divide in employment law, in which certain types of claim – for non-payment of contractual bonuses, for example – are only ever brought by high-paid employees. It is tempting to assume that this is because contractual bonuses are confined to certain kinds of lucrative employment, such as banking. But it is important to consider the alternative possibility: that low-paid employees may sometimes also have these kinds of entitlements but the barriers to enforcement, such as court fees and the rules on costs, act as a more significant deterrent to bringing a claim. Comprehensive empirical work would be required to explore this issue further.

A different but related procedural feature of the employment tribunal regime is the power to make a deposit order.[55] Where a particular allegation or argument put forward by the claimant has 'little reasonable prospect of success', the judge may order them to pay a deposit of up to £1,000 in order to proceed with that allegation or argument.[56] Since the rule applies to each allegation or argument, it is possible for the claimant to be ordered to pay multiple deposits, though the tribunal should have regard to the proportionality and affordability of the overall total if this situation arises.[57] If the claimant fails to pay the deposit by the time specified in the order, the relevant element of the claim is struck out. Of course, a claim may alternatively be struck out where it has *no* reasonable prospect of success.[58] The deposit regime provides claimants with a strong disincentive to the pursuit of hopeless claims, which in turn reduces the costs incurred by employers in defending themselves. However, there is a risk that complex or novel legal arguments, or allegations which are difficult to prove (for example, in discrimination cases) may be inappropriately discouraged. The Employment Appeal Tribunal (EAT) has cautioned against using deposit orders in a way that would impede access to justice.[59]

A significant risk for the parties to a case in court (whether in an employment dispute or more generally) is the prospect of having to pay the other side's costs if they lose. For example, while an employee bringing a breach of contract claim against their employer might attempt to represent themselves in order to

[54] ibid.

[55] Employment Tribunals (Constitution and Rules of Procedure) Regulations 2013 (SI 2013/1237), Schedule 1, rule 39.

[56] There are costs implications if the claimant pays the deposit and proceeds with the claim but still loses, discussed below.

[57] See eg *Wright v Nipponkoa Insurance (Europe) Ltd* (UKEAT/0113/14/JOJ, 17 September 2014), [77]–[79] (HHJ Eady QC).

[58] Above n 55, Schedule 1, rule 37.

[59] *H v Ishmail* [2017] ICR 486, [11].

keep their costs down, they may be faced with a huge bill for their employer's legal representation if the claim fails. One of the ways in which tribunals were meant to be different was that each party would be responsible for its own costs. However, some inroads have been made into this principle so that tribunals may now order one party to pay the other's costs in certain circumstances. There are a variety of grounds on which such an order can be made, but two of the most important are where a party (or their representative) has acted vexatiously or unreasonably, or where the claim or response had no reasonable prospect of success.[60] Where a claimant who was subject to a deposit order pays the deposit and then loses on the relevant point for similar reasons to those given in the order, they will be deemed to have acted unreasonably in pursuing the point unless they can prove to the contrary. The deposit is paid over to the defendant and deducted from the amount of the costs order. Of course, costs orders can be made against the working person or the employer, but the prospect of them is more likely to affect the working person's calculations. Costs orders are applicable where the successful party is legally represented or has a lay representative. The tribunal may award up to £20,000 in unassessed costs, or the costs may be determined in detail by a judge or agreed between the parties.[61] Where a successful party is not represented, there is a separate power to make a 'preparation time order' to compensate them for the time spent preparing their case.[62] This order is available on the same grounds as a costs order. Costs orders remain relatively rare – in 2019–20 they were awarded to the claimant in 47 cases and to the respondent in 130 cases, with the mean award being £5,664 – but the worry is that the rule is yet another potential deterrent for a working person from bringing proceedings.[63]

The idea of tribunals as free and accessible has been somewhat compromised over the years as a result of concerns about the volume and merits of claims. These concerns have not always been backed up by robust empirical evidence. It is hard to say what the 'right' volume of tribunal claims should be, but in any event, a high volume of legitimate claims is simply an indication that employers are not complying with the law. An appropriate response to this might be a campaign of publicity and education to improve standards of employer behaviour. Where there is evidence that unmeritorious claims are being brought, steps should be taken to tackle that problem in a targeted way, for example through striking out, rather than through financial measures that disproportionately impact lower-paid workers and bear no necessary connection to the strength of a person's claim. While the deposit scheme is, arguably, justifiable, given that the judge has the discretion not to order a deposit or to order a token sum, it is at the same time important that this is not used to discourage legally creative or evidentially challenging claims.

[60] Above n 55, Schedule 1, rules 75 and 76. An award may also be made against a representative in respect of 'wasted costs' under rule 80.

[61] ibid Schedule 1, rule 78.

[62] Above n 55, Schedule 1, rules 75 and 76. The basis for calculation is set out in rule 79.

[63] *Tribunal Statistics Quarterly, April to June 2023*, above n 28, Annex C. More recent editions do not include this information.

E. Enforcement

A final point to note about the litigation process is that it should not be assumed that defendants necessarily 'pay up' when ordered to do so. This may be for a variety of reasons: some employers may genuinely have ceased trading by the time the proceedings have concluded; others may change their corporate structure to ensure that the 'employer' which was the subject of the proceedings no longer exists; or the employer may simply choose to ignore the award, taking the chance that the claimant will not initiate further enforcement action. Given the difficulties of bringing a successful claim, it is particularly concerning that the small proportion of litigants who reach this stage may not ultimately receive any redress.

Tribunal awards are generally required to be paid within 14 days.[64] However, tribunals do not have any powers to enforce their own awards. Instead, under section 15(1) ETA 1996, sums payable under a tribunal award are recoverable as if they were 'payable under an order of the county court'. The claimant must file the tribunal award at the county court and it is then enforceable as a debt through the usual enforcement methods.[65] The existence of the debt is entered into the public register used by banks and credit ratings agencies, so this may provide the employer with another reason to pay up.[66] The most likely enforcement methods in employment cases are a third-party debt order or taking control of goods.[67] A third-party debt order requires a person who owes money to the defendant to pay their debt to the claimant instead. This can be used to access funds in the employer's bank accounts, since these are, of course, debts owed by the bank to the employer. Where the claimant seeks to enforce their award by means of control of goods, a number of options are available.[68] Where the award is below £5000, it may be enforced in the county court or the High Court. Where it is over that amount, it must be enforced in the High Court. There is also a Fast Track procedure for employment cases which has been in place since 2010.[69] Under this scheme, the claimant pays a fee (currently £71) and a High Court enforcement officer will file the award with the county court, seek a writ of control from the High Court and attempt to enforce it.

A government-sponsored study in 2013 found that only 49 per cent of successful tribunal claimants were paid in full.[70] In 37 per cent of non-payment cases, claimants reported that their employer was insolvent, though half of these claimants thought that their employer had in fact continued to trade under a different

[64] Above n 55, Schedule 1, rule 66. The tribunal may prescribe a different deadline.

[65] Civil Procedure Rules 1998 (SI 1998/3132), Parts 70–73.

[66] Register of Judgments, Orders and Fines Regulations 2005 (SI 2005/3595), rules 8(1)(d) and 9A(b).

[67] Another option where the employer is a company is to file a statutory demand under s 123 Insolvency Act 1986. If the company is unable to pay, it may be wound up. Where the company is, in reality, solvent, this may provide a strong incentive to pay.

[68] Above n 65, Parts 83–84.

[69] See https://www.registry-trust.org.uk/rt-learn-ew/enforce-employment-tribunal/.

[70] Department for Business, Innovation and Skills, *The Payment of Tribunal Awards: 2013 Study* (London, 2014).

name. Of those who were unpaid for any reason, only half pursued enforcement action, and of these, only half received some or all of the money they were owed. The main reason given by claimants for not trying to enforce an award was that they did not know how to set about doing so. This illustrates the disadvantage of requiring the claimant to initiate a separate process for enforcement, rather than building this into the original claim.[71] One of the more sensible recommendations of the Taylor Review was that the government should take steps to enforce tribunal awards without requiring the claimant to pay fees, fill in extra forms or bring additional legal proceedings, but no implementation has been forthcoming.[72]

Since the research described above was conducted, the government has introduced a penalty regime for non-payment of tribunal awards. The penalty regime, which will be discussed in more detail in chapter five, is found in Part 2A ETA 1996, which was inserted in 2015. The claimant must first fill in a form requesting enforcement. The enforcement officer then gives the employer a warning, requiring it to pay within 28 days. If the employer still does not pay, the officer will give it a penalty notice requiring it to pay the Secretary of State a financial penalty of 50 per cent of the unpaid amount (subject to a minimum of £100 and a maximum of £5,000).[73] The penalty is reduced by 50 per cent if the employer pays the award and the penalty within 14 days. If the employer still does not pay, it may (in theory at least) be 'named' online by the government.[74] Although the enforcement officer may pursue the unpaid penalty as a debt, it remains the responsibility of the claimant to take enforcement action to obtain their award.

There is some suggestion that the overall level of payment of tribunal awards has improved since the 2013 study. SETA found that, in 2017, 72 per cent of claimants surveyed had received their awards.[75] Of course, some of this may be due to differences in research methodology, and it is not possible to identify the cause of any possible improvement from the SETA findings. Indeed, SETA also showed that awareness of the penalty regime, even among claimants whose awards had not been paid, was very low, at 18 per cent.[76] Although any improvement is to be welcomed, it is worth noting that 28 per cent is still an unacceptably high level of non-payment.

F. Conclusion

This section has not considered in detail the process of litigation before the courts. The reader can be expected to be familiar with key aspects of this process.

[71] For a creative, but ultimately unsuccessful, attempt to challenge this using EU law (in the context of pre-trial asset freezing), see *Anwar v Advocate General for Scotland* [2021] UKSC 44, [2022] ICR 146.

[72] Matthew Taylor, *Good Work: the Taylor Review of Modern Working Practices* (July 2017), 63.

[73] ETA 1996, s 37F.

[74] Department for Business, Energy and Industrial Strategy, *Employment Tribunal Naming Scheme Guidance* (December 2018). There is, however, no evidence of this scheme having been used.

[75] Above n 23, 65.

[76] Above n 23, 66.

If anything, the problems faced by tribunal litigants are likely to be exacerbated in court, given the more formal nature of proceedings. It is not possible to have any other kind of representative than a lawyer, and the unsuccessful claimant will *have* to pay the other side's costs. Tribunals have not been particularly successful in overcoming the difficulties faced by litigants in court, despite the differences of approach. There are at least two different conclusions that might be drawn from this. One is that the tribunal system requires a significant overhaul and injection of cash in order to be able to serve working people effectively. Without better access to advice and representation, it is hard to see how the interests of justice could ever be effectively served by the tribunal system. The idea that litigants will be able to represent themselves without disadvantage is not plausible. An alternative conclusion is that litigation is simply not suitable as a means of enforcing employment rights. However, before arriving at that conclusion it is important to consider what the other options for enforcement might be. This is the task of the next section.

II. Other Regulatory Techniques

As Collins explains, the UK has tended to treat the process of laying down a standard in law and expecting working people to enforce it through litigation as the default 'regulatory technique' in employment law.[77] But it is by no means the only option. Here, I consider two major alternatives – public enforcement and collective action – plus a group of innovative techniques which may not be sufficient on their own but may be a useful supplement to other strategies.

A. Public Enforcement

The UK is unusual, though by no means unique, in having multiple agencies tasked with the public enforcement of different elements of labour law, rather than one single 'labour inspectorate'.[78] These are the Health and Safety Executive (HSE), the Employment Agency Standards Inspectorate (EASI), Her Majesty's Revenue and Customs (HMRC) National Minimum Wage enforcement team, the Equality and Human Rights Commission (EHRC) and the Gangmasters and Labour Abuse Authority (GLAA).[79] In 2016, a new role of Director of Labour Market Enforcement was created to oversee and co-ordinate the activities of EASI, HMRC and the GLAA,[80] and more recently it has been suggested that these three bodies should

[77] Collins, above n 2, 18–20.

[78] ILO Convention 81 (1947) deals with labour inspection and there is useful information about different practices around the world in ILO, *General Survey on Labour Inspection* (2006).

[79] It is worth noting that the police and the immigration authorities may also be involved in the enforcement of certain aspects of labour law, such as crimes relating to modern slavery, or illegal working offences.

[80] Immigration Act 2016, ss 1–9.

be amalgamated into a 'single enforcement agency'.[81] However, no legislation to accomplish this has yet been forthcoming, and it would still not constitute a fully-fledged labour inspectorate, given that other public enforcement bodies, notably HSE, would not be included. The public enforcement landscape in the UK is a clear example of the problem of haphazard and unsystematic development, identified by Dickens in the quotation at the start of this chapter.[82] This section gives a brief overview of some key features of public enforcement before offering some broader reflections on the advantages and disadvantages of this approach.

In the UK at least, there is a close connection between the use of the criminal law to enforce particular employment standards and the use of public enforcement. This is not surprising: if the criminal law is to be used, a public authority is needed to investigate and possibly also prosecute, and it might reasonably be thought that a specialist authority with employment expertise is preferable to relying on the police and Crown Prosecution Service to perform these tasks. Health and safety is a good example of this.[83] A considerable degree of expertise is required to understand health and safety legislation and how its requirements should be applied in different types of workplace, and HSE is much better placed to develop this expertise than other generalist authorities.

However, the relationship between public enforcement and prosecution does not work in the other direction: in other words, it is possible to have a public agency responsible for the enforcement of the law without that law being wholly or mainly criminal. Thus, although wilful non-payment of the National Minimum Wage (NMW) is an offence,[84] the bulk of HMRC's enforcement activity is concerned with issuing notices requiring employers to pay the arrears they owe to workers and to pay a civil penalty to the Secretary of State.[85] The EHRC has various powers to conduct inquiries and investigations which have no connection to the criminal law.[86] This is an important reminder that it would be possible to make greater use of public enforcement of employment law in the UK without necessarily having to make greater use of the criminal law.

One of the central roles of the various public agencies involved in enforcement is to develop detailed guidance for employers (and working people) on their responsibilities (and rights) in the relevant area of the law.[87] For example, the detailed HMRC NMW manual, available online, offers advice on the interpretation and application of the relevant Regulations in a wide range of circumstances.[88] While this is not legally binding, and may sometimes turn out to be inaccurate if a

[81] Department for Business, Enterprise and Industrial Strategy, *Establishing a New Single Enforcement Body for Employment Rights: Government Response* (June 2021).

[82] Above n 3.

[83] Health and Safety at Work etc. Act 1974, ss 38–39.

[84] National Minimum Wage Act 1998, s 31.

[85] National Minimum Wage Act 1998, ss 17–19H.

[86] Equality Act 2006, ss 16 and 20. These powers are rarely used.

[87] This function is performed by guidance on gov.uk and the ACAS website for areas of law enforced through litigation.

[88] https://www.gov.uk/hmrc-internal-manuals/national-minimum-wage-manual.

court or tribunal interprets the Regulations differently, it performs an important function in helping employers and their advisers to understand what compliance entails. Similarly, HSE produces a vast range of materials to help employers fulfil their health and safety obligations.[89] This is particularly vital because the duties in health and safety law are, inevitably, framed in general terms, but have specific applications for different types of firm. While all employers have general duties to carry out risk assessments, the precise factors to consider will vary as between firms or parts of firms where the job entails (for example) using ladders or scaffolding to work at height, working with chemicals, or sitting at a desk using a computer. HSE produces detailed advice and tools to consider risks in each of these and many other areas. Sometimes, guidance can be given stronger legal force in the sense that non-compliance with guidance may be taken into account by a court or tribunal. Some HSE guidance takes the form of an Approved Code of Practice (ACOP).[90] If an employer is prosecuted and did not follow the ACOP, it will be found to have committed an offence unless it can show that it took other steps to comply with its legal duties.[91] Advice and guidance may also be aimed at working people to help them to understand their rights. For example, the GLAA website offers information about the rights of agricultural workers in a wide range of different languages, given the prevalence of migrant workers in this sector.[92]

In order to enforce the law, agencies obviously need to uncover violations. This typically occurs through a mix of inspections carried out by the relevant agency on its own initiative, and responses to complaints or concerns raised by affected workers. The precise balance between these two approaches is not always easy to discern from the available data. It is worth noting that the gangmasters' licensing scheme operates in a slightly different way: since a gangmaster must have a licence in order to operate, there may be an inspection prior to the grant of the licence as well as the possibility of subsequent inspections to check that the operator is still compliant.[93] The government provides an online reporting form for workers to report failures to pay the NMW, concerns about the 48-hour week and complaints about employment agencies.[94] This captures some of the most basic concerns working people might wish to report to HMRC, the GLAA, HSE or local authorities, and EASI, but it is by no means comprehensive. For example, the GLAA is not just responsible for wages,[95] and there are a variety of other limits on working time

[89] https://www.hse.gov.uk/aboutus/index.htm.

[90] Above n 83, s 16.

[91] ibid s 17.

[92] Leaflets are available in 21 different languages: https://www.gla.gov.uk/i-am-a/i-am-a-worker/workers-rights-leaflets/.

[93] See GLAA, *Code of Practice on Compliance, Enforcement, Labour Market and Modern Slavery Investigations* (October 2018), and https://www.gla.gov.uk/i-am-a/i-supply-workers/do-i-need-a-glaa-licence/inspection-information/.

[94] Available at: https://www.gov.uk/government/publications/pay-and-work-rights-complaints.

[95] Gangmasters (Licensing Conditions) Rules 2009 (SI 2009/307).

enforced by HSE or local authorities.[96] It is not particularly helpful that workers may have to find and navigate the various agencies' own websites in order to find ways of reporting other problems.

Agencies typically use a risk-based framework for the conduct of inspections. This became fashionable after a series of government reviews of regulation in the 1980s and 1990s, and reflects two linked objectives: to target scarce enforcement resources at the most high-risk employers, and to 'protect' compliant firms from 'burdensome' inspections.[97] Thus, for example, HSE targets most of its inspection activity on sectors where the risks are less well-controlled and where serious physical harm or death might occur.[98] On some levels, it is hard to disagree with the idea that inspections should be targeted: HSE does not have limitless resources and it seems appropriate to use what resources it has to tackle the most serious problems. However, risk-based regulation has its critics.[99] One problem is that firms categorised as low-risk may never encounter an inspector, with the result that they neglect their legal obligations. Another is that issues which are important to workers may not be prioritised by the agency, given the range of problems it has to tackle. For example, it is understandable that in the context of workplaces where death or serious physical injury is a real hazard, HSE does not focus its inspections on stress and mental health issues, but these are extremely serious for the people they affect.[100] Perhaps most importantly, it is difficult to determine whether risk or funding is driving the way in which the regulator categorises the risk level of different workplaces. I return to resourcing below.

Having identified infringements, either through complaints or proactive inspections, the agency must then decide what enforcement action to take. Most agencies adopt, or are directed by their empowering legislation to adopt, a version of the 'enforcement pyramid' identified by Ayres and Braithwaite.[101] In other words, they reserve their formal enforcement powers, such as prosecution, for the most serious cases, and use other strategies to deal with more minor infringements. For example, EASI rarely uses its formal powers to prosecute non-compliant agencies or to seek banning orders, but does issue a relatively large number of warning letters each year.[102] HSE has a sophisticated enforcement policy which directs inspectors as to the factors to take into account when deciding whether to

[96] Working Time Regulations 1998 (SI 1998/1833), reg 28.

[97] See eg the Hampton Review: P Hampton, *Reduction in Administrative Burdens: Effective Inspection and Enforcement* (UK Government, 2005).

[98] See eg HSE, *Enforcement Policy Statement* (October 2015).

[99] For discussion, see ACL Davies and L Rodgers, 'Towards a More Effective Health and Safety Regime for UK Workplaces Post Covid-19' (2023) 52 *Industrial Law Journal* 665.

[100] For discussion, see ACL Davies, 'Stress at Work: Individuals or Structures?' (2022) 51 *Industrial Law Journal* 403.

[101] I Ayres and J Braithwaite, *Responsive Regulation: Transcending the Deregulation Debate* (Oxford, OUP, 1992).

[102] Department for Business, Energy and Industrial Strategy, *Employment Agency Standards (EAS) Inspectorate: Annual Report, 2020 to 2021* (June 2022).

prosecute.[103] Factors pointing in favour of prosecution include where a death has resulted from the breach, where the breach was deliberate, or where there were repeated breaches, particularly after other forms of intervention by HSE. Again, there is debate about the validity of these approaches. On the one hand, it may appear that employers are 'getting away with' non-compliance in some situations, which may be particularly disappointing to any workers who raised concerns about how they were being treated. On the other hand, the point of enforcement is to secure compliance, not to make maximum use of the available powers, and this is often done more quickly and cheaply by persuasive strategies. Importantly, though, persuasion operates in the 'shadow' of the law, so the agency may need to have a credible threat that it might escalate its enforcement activities in order to get the employer to listen. As noted above in relation to inspection, there is sometimes a suspicion that an agency's enforcement policy is driven as much by resource constraints as it is by strategic considerations.

The most obvious advantage of public enforcement, particularly compared to litigation, is that it takes the responsibility away from the affected working person. Although the public enforcement landscape in the UK is somewhat chaotic, it is clear that this strategy has been adopted in areas where workers are especially vulnerable and might be unable or unwilling to enforce their rights themselves. The gangmasters' licensing regime and the NMW are key examples of this. Although a worker can complain to the relevant agency, they do not have to gather evidence, understand the law in any detail or participate in the agency's enforcement process. It is clear that, for example, a seasonal migrant worker in agriculture with little grasp of English who is only in the UK for a short time is not well-placed to take their employer to the employment tribunal.[104] But the GLAA may be able to take steps to stop that person being exploited. However, this advantage can also operate as a disadvantage. As explained above, public enforcement agencies have their own priorities and policies on inspection and enforcement, and are unlikely to be able to respond equally vigorously to all complaints. This may mean that some legitimate worker concerns are not properly addressed. Some commentators have also expressed the concern that vocal, well-resourced workers may 'capture' enforcement agencies because they are more able and willing to complain to them, leading to the neglect of more vulnerable workers who do not come forward.[105]

Another difficulty with public enforcement mechanisms is that they often neglect the obtaining of redress for the affected workers. For example, the gangmasters' licensing regime makes no formal provision for the GLAA to recover unpaid wages or other benefits from non-compliant employers, though in

[103] HSE, *Enforcement Policy Statement* (October 2015).

[104] For excellent empirical work on this topic, see eg C Barnard, A Ludlow and S Fraser Butlin, 'Beyond Employment Tribunals: Enforcement of Employment Rights by EU-8 Migrant Workers' (2018) 47 *Industrial Law Journal* 226.

[105] D Weil, 'A Strategic Approach to Labour Inspection' (2008) 147 *International Labour Review* 349, 356–64.

practice, the agency has a strong record of achieving this by informal means.[106] The HSE cannot help workers who have been injured at work to seek compensation. The only really significant exception to this is the NMW regime, in which HMRC's role includes, and indeed prioritises, securing the payment of arrears to affected workers.[107] The reasons for the neglect of redress are varied and not always entirely clear. One issue may be that the focus on the criminal law in and of itself diverts attention away from questions of redress. Another is that workers may have a range of other redress options open to them, but that these are seen as a private matter for them to pursue. For example, an injured worker may be able to claim in negligence, and the provisions on unlawful deductions may be applicable to unpaid agricultural workers.[108] The NMW example shows that these problems are not insurmountable, though it is worth bearing in mind that the NMW is relatively straightforward. The basis for a claim in negligence against an employer is somewhat different to that for a prosecution under health and safety legislation, particularly now that breaches of the legislation per se do not give rise to civil liability.[109] Thus, it may be easier to attach recovery for affected workers to public NMW enforcement than it is to other types of public enforcement.

A final problem with public enforcement is practical but profound. Public enforcement requires resources, and there is an issue, not just in the UK but across labour inspection systems worldwide, about whether states are investing enough in their public enforcement regimes.[110] Of course, there is no 'right' level of public enforcement, and the latest ILO guidance does not propose particular target numbers of inspectors (eg per 10,000 workers) because the precise nature of their activities varies from state to state.[111] Nevertheless, in the UK, there is clear and worrying evidence of cuts in relation to HSE in particular. In 2019–20, HSE employed 2,399 members of staff,[112] compared to 4,050 in 2001–2.[113] Inevitably, this significant reduction in staff numbers corresponds to a marked reduction in activity. In 2019–20, HSE conducted 13,300 inspections, issued over 7,000 notices and completed 355 prosecutions.[114] In 2001–02, HSE conducted 75,237 inspections, issued 11,162 notices and prosecuted in 1930 cases.[115] Although

[106] Gangmasters and Labour Abuse Authority, *Annual Report and Accounts 1 April 2021 to 31 March 2022* (HC 915, December 2022), 6–7.

[107] Above n 85.

[108] ERA 1996, s 13.

[109] Health and Safety at Work etc. Act 1974, s 47, as amended, Enterprise and Regulatory Reform Act 2013, s 69. An action for breach of statutory duty is now only available where the relevant health and safety regulations make express provision.

[110] Weil, above n 105, 350–53. For a recent critique of the UK position, see Resolution Foundation, *Enforce for Good: Effectively Enforcing Labour Market Rights in the 2020s and Beyond* (April 2023).

[111] ILO, *Guidelines on General Principles of Labour Inspection* (2022), 20.

[112] HSE, *Annual Report and Accounts 2019/20* (HC 442, July 2020), 13. These figures were first compiled for Davies and Rodgers, above n 99.

[113] Health and Safety Commission Annual Report and the Health and Safety Commission/Executive Accounts 2001/02 (HC 1202, October 2002), 103.

[114] Above n 112, 13.

[115] Above n 113, 75.

the proponents of risk-based regulation might defend these cuts by arguing that HSE is using its resources in a more efficient and targeted way, it is worth noting that the labour market has, if anything, become more complex in the intervening years.[116] For example, the gig economy has grown considerably during that time, and presents difficult issues in terms of getting platforms to recognise their responsibilities and to provide proper training and equipment to their workers. Arguably, cuts to HSE's budget and activities mean that health and safety law is, in effect, deregulated: inspection and enforcement activity has become so uncommon that most firms will never encounter it and may be tempted to disregard the law.[117]

All this should not be taken as a rejection of public enforcement as a regulatory technique. Rather, my point is that it is not the panacea it may appear to be. Both litigation and public enforcement require a proper investment of resources to function effectively. Both may create the impression that workers' rights are being enforced when that is not truly the case.

B. Trade Unions

Another 'enforcement' option is to rely on trade unions. This could take the form either of enabling trade unions to regulate the labour market much more comprehensively, as is the case in Scandinavian countries, or empowering them to support public or private enforcement activities in various ways. I consider each option in turn.

Relying on trade unions to regulate the labour market is not simply an 'enforcement' mechanism: it is a wholly different regulatory technique. In a country like Sweden, for example, there is no statutory minimum wage.[118] About 70 per cent of all workers are members of a trade union, and some 90 per cent have their pay and terms and conditions set by collective bargaining, which takes place primarily at industry level. Firms that do not accept the applicable collective agreement may find that they are the subject of a blockade by the unions. A variety of matters are dealt with through national legislation – unfair dismissal, for example – but, even here, the social partners may play an important role in developing proposals for the legislature to enact. Nowadays, this is also overlaid by legislation implementing the requirements of EU law. The advantage of placing more reliance on collective bargaining is that it draws on the collective strength of workers not just to set but also to enforce particular norms. It reduces the need either for workers to litigate themselves or for the state to put resources into public enforcement.

[116] Weil, above n 105.

[117] See, more broadly, M Ford, 'The Criminalization of Health and Safety at Work', in A Bogg, J Collins, M Freedland and J Herring (eds), *Criminality at Work* (Oxford, OUP, 2020); S Tombs and D Whyte, 'Reshaping Health and Safety Enforcement: Institutionalising Impunity', in L Dickens (ed), *Making Employment Rights Effective: Issues of Enforcement and Compliance* (Oxford, Hart Publishing, 2012).

[118] A Adlercreutz and B Nyström, *Labour Law in Sweden* (3rd edn, Wolters Kluwer, 2021).

However, it is difficult to see how this system could easily be transplanted to a country like the UK, in which levels of trade union membership, particularly in the private sector, are much lower.[119] Radical efforts would be required to promote trade union membership before such a move could even be contemplated. Of course, it is arguable that the prevalence of protective legislation gives individuals less of an incentive to join a union, but it would be difficult to repeal any of that legislation until the majority of the workforce had access to trade union representation instead.

Another option is for trade unions to support public or private enforcement mechanisms. In health and safety law, for example, there are formal requirements to consult working people on safety issues, which differ depending on whether there is a recognised trade union in the workplace.[120] Where there is a recognised trade union, it is entitled to appoint health and safety representatives and the employer is obliged to consult them on health and safety matters. Although this does not give them a formal role in enforcement, it is an important way of giving the workforce a voice – and one with some independence and expertise – on safety in the workplace. This may encourage employers to comply with their obligations and reduce the need for public enforcement. Similarly, there is evidence that a strong union presence in the workplace reduces the need for litigation to enforce individual rights because unions encourage employers to have more effective internal grievance procedures and support their members in using them.[121] Indeed, a plausible explanation for the overall growth in the number of tribunal claims over time is that it is linked to the decline in trade union presence in UK workplaces.[122]

Where cases do reach the tribunal, less than 10 per cent of tribunal claimants are accompanied by a trade union representative, though it seems likely that this underestimates the extent to which individuals are advised or supported in other ways by their trade union.[123] Perhaps a more productive option for trade unions is to bring test cases (either in the union's own name or supporting a particular individual, depending on the circumstances) to develop or clarify the law in a particular area. For example, the Uber drivers who successfully established that they had worker status in the Supreme Court were supported by the GMB union.[124] It is unlikely that individual workers would be able to pursue cases all

[119] Department for Business, Energy and Industrial Strategy, *Trade Union Statistics 2021* (May 2022).

[120] The Safety Representatives and Safety Committees Regulations 1977 (SI 1977/500) provide for the appointment of employees as safety representatives by a recognised trade union. Where there is no recognised trade union, the Health and Safety (Consultation with Employees) Regulations 1996 (SI 1996/1513) provide for the employer to consult with specially-elected representatives or with its employees directly.

[121] Colling, above n 29, 195–96.

[122] See Kirk, above n 46, and (more broadly) L Barmes, *Bullying and Behavioural Conflict at Work: the Duality of Individual Rights* (Oxford, OUP, 2016), ch 9.

[123] *Tribunal Statistics Quarterly, April to June 2023*, above n 28.

[124] *Uber BV v Aslam* [2021] UKSC 5, [2021] ICR 657; and see https://www.gmb.org.uk/uber.

the way to the Supreme Court without support, and this strategy can be a useful way for unions to establish points of law benefiting many thousands of workers. Although it seems unlikely to happen in practice, one way to improve the functioning of private enforcement would be for the government to allocate funds to trade unions for the *specific purpose* of supporting litigation. Given that public funds are bound to be limited, this strategy would give trade unions a role in prioritising cases likely to have the biggest impact, given the issues encountered by their members at work.

C. Alternative Strategies

For completeness, I will conclude this section by considering some other routes to securing compliance with employment law.[125] These fall into two broad groups. The first group involves encouraging, promoting or incentivising compliance in some way. These strategies are little used in the UK. The second group involves creating disincentives to non-compliance, for example, through schemes designed to create adverse publicity for firms in breach. These are somewhat more common, but still patchy in both coverage and impact. It seems unlikely that any of these alternatives would ever displace a combination of public and private enforcement, but they may play a useful supporting role.

(i) Promotional Techniques

As Collins explains, incentives such as tax breaks could be used to encourage firms to comply with employment law,[126] but there are no clear-cut examples of this in English law. Perhaps the closest analogy is with labelling or accreditation schemes. These are usually voluntary initiatives to which an employer can sign up if it meets certain criteria. An older example is Investors in People, set up by the UK government in 1991 and turned into a community interest company in 2017.[127] Firms can obtain accreditation for their staff training and development. A newer example with no government connection is the National Living Wage Foundation.[128] This organisation sets a 'living wage' which is intended to reflect the cost of living and is typically higher than the National Minimum Wage set out in legislation. Firms can badge themselves as 'Living Wage Employers' if they commit to paying the appropriate rates. In both cases, it appears that the aim is to generate positive publicity for employers which embrace good practices. This might have an impact on recruitment – since more people will want to work for a 'good' employer –

[125] See also G Davidov, *A Purposive Approach to Labour Law* (Oxford, OUP, 2016), ch 9, for a variety of interesting ideas.

[126] Collins, above n 2, 24.

[127] https://www.investorsinpeople.com/.

[128] https://www.livingwage.org.uk/.

and on customers, who may prefer to buy their goods or services from ethical sources. Although these schemes are clearly beneficial, they may also be rather niche: many firms have no significant public profile, and many consumers and jobseekers will not have the luxury of selecting among firms according to their ethical commitments.

(ii) Disincentives

Recent years have seen a trend towards the use of what might loosely be termed 'bad publicity' to give employers an incentive to comply with employment law. If certain conditions are met, an employer may be 'named and shamed' on a government website for non-compliance with the NMW.[129] The idea here is that having the firm's name published on a government website will be a significant additional disincentive to not doing what the law requires. Recent legislation has also made use of reporting requirements. For example, under section 54 Modern Slavery Act 2015, large firms are required to report on what steps, if any, they have taken to tackle slavery and other forms of forced labour in their supply chains. Under the Equality Act 2010, large firms are required to report on the gender pay gap (the difference in the average pay of women and men in the organisation).[130] There has been some discussion about introducing a similar requirement to report on pay differences between people of different ethnicities.

The impact of these measures is, of course, an empirical question. Much depends on whether journalists, trade unions or campaigners make use of the information they generate. Again, however, it is safe to assume that the impact is greatest on firms with a significant public profile, which are likely to be targeted by journalists and campaign groups if they are included on a 'naming and shaming' list or disclose inadequate efforts to tackle slavery or pay inequality. But there are other factors to consider too. One is the complexity or otherwise of compliance with the relevant standard. Non-payment of a tribunal award is a very straightforward matter; even if the defendant disagrees with the award, it is clearly payable unless a successful appeal can be launched. The other three examples are more complex. Even though non-compliance with the NMW is undoubtedly serious, there are instances in which firms have broken the law because some aspects of it are difficult to interpret. The government had to suspend enforcement in relation to 'on-call time' until after the Supreme Court's decision in the *Mencap* case because of conflicting lines of authority in the EAT about how the NMW applied to this

[129] Department for Business, Energy and Industrial Strategy, *National Minimum Wage: Policy on Enforcement, Prosecutions and Naming Employers who Break National Minimum Wage Law* (June 2022). In theory, there is a similar scheme for non-payment of tribunal awards (above n 74), but it has never been used.

[130] Equality Act 2010, s 78, and see Equality Act 2010 (Gender Pay Gap Information) Regulations 2017 (SI 2017/172). Provision for public authorities is made separately in the Equality Act 2010 (Specific Duties and Public Authorities) Regulations 2017 (SI 2017/353).

form of work, for example.[131] Where this occurs, the adverse publicity approach does not work particularly well because non-compliant firms can present reasonable explanations for their infringements and the 'shaming' effect may be much reduced.

While these various forms of publicity tend to be consumer-focused, there are ways of engaging other stakeholders in support of labour standards. These may be more powerful because of their ability to invest large sums in a particular business. One well-known example is public procurement.[132] Over the last 10 years or so, the UK government has shown increasing interest in using the procurement process to obtain additional 'social value' from contractors alongside the delivery of the main objective of the contract.[133] Terms requiring contractors to take steps to tackle modern slavery in supply chains are a common example. The idea is that the government uses firms' desire to win government business – and therefore make money – to incentivise them to improve labour standards. A bidder which fails to comply with its commitments may be excluded from future procurement exercises. Another example is ESG (environmental, social and governance) initiatives.[134] The idea here is that shareholders take into account not just a firm's profitability when making investment decisions but its broader sustainability too. A major investor, such as a pension fund, might decide not to buy shares in a particular firm because it has concerns about its employment practices.

Again, the impact of these initiatives is an empirical question. It is certainly the case that large sums of money may be at stake, either through procurement or investment, giving firms a strong motive to engage. However, it is often unclear precisely what standards firms are expected to meet or how compliance is to be investigated and judged. For example, it is difficult for a procurement official in the UK to judge a firm's efforts to combat modern slavery in the supply chain. Similarly, a common criticism of ESG initiatives is that there are no clear understandings of what the 'social' element is meant to cover. More broadly, both types of initiative involve handing over responsibility for labour law enforcement to powerful but non-expert entities (governments in their purchasing capacity, or investors) with the risk that standards are set and applied in a way that would not make sense to a labour lawyer. For example, procurement nowadays tends not to be concerned with wage levels because this would increase the cost of

[131] Department for Business, Energy & Industrial Strategy, *Government Announces Additional Support for Social Care Providers* (26 July 2017), and see *Royal Mencap Society v Tomlinson-Blake* [2021] UKSC 8, [2021] ICR 758.

[132] For an overview, see C McCrudden, 'Procurement and Fairness in the Workplace', in L Dickens (ed), *Making Employment Rights Effective: Issues of Enforcement and Compliance* (Oxford, Hart Publishing, 2012).

[133] Cabinet Office, *Procurement Policy Note 06/20 – Taking Account of Social Value in the Award of Central Government Contracts* (September 2020).

[134] Eg Companies Act 2006, s 414C; Directive 2013/34 in respect of disclosure of non-financial and diversity information by certain large undertakings and groups (currently under review).

the contract to the government, even though decent wages were historically a concern in this area.[135]

D. Conclusion

It should be apparent by now that, despite the many disadvantages of litigation as an enforcement technique, none of the alternatives offers an easy solution to the problem. Public enforcement seems attractive because it reduces the pressure on workers to enforce their own rights, but it is all too often undone by a lack of resources. And it is hard to see how any of the alternatives could provide a comprehensive enforcement regime. Trade unions would need to have much higher levels of membership and more funds before they could do anything other than sporadic enforcement, and newer alternatives such as ESG seem to be too selective in their approach.

In practice, a mixed system of enforcement is likely to be preferable. Public enforcement can be targeted where it is most needed: to help vulnerable workers who are unlikely to be able to litigate, to tackle more serious violations, or to address issues such as health and safety, requiring particular expertise. Private enforcement can be retained to allow workers the option of pursuing their own grievances where possible, ideally with more support through legal aid or trade unions so that it does not become the sole preserve of the wealthy. 'Alternative' techniques can be used to supplement these two methods by discouraging non-compliance or promoting compliance.

Finally, it is worth noting that all types of enforcement share one very fundamental problem: limited impact beyond the affected employer.[136] Lawyers often assume that employers pounce on the latest judicial decisions in employment law cases with the same enthusiasm that they themselves do, whereas the reality is much more complex. New developments in case-law – and in statute – *do* filter through to employers through their lawyers and HR advisors, particularly when the employer is contemplating a policy change for its workforce or making an individual decision about a particular employee. As chapter three explains, there is scope for employment law to have deterrent effects, but only where the employer perceives that the risk of litigation or adverse publicity outweighs the cost of compliance. The same is also true of public enforcement: employers may still decide to take the risk of non-compliance with the NMW or with health and safety rules if they think that compliance would be costly and they are unlikely to get caught. Obviously, the deterrent effect of different types of enforcement is an

[135] R Craven, 'The Legal and Social Construction of Value in Government Procurement Markets' (2020) 47 *Journal of Law and Society* 29, 46–49.

[136] See T Hardy, 'Digging Into Deterrence: An Examination of Deterrence-Based Theories and Evidence in Employment Standards Enforcement' (2021) 37 *International Journal of Comparative Labour Law and Industrial Relations* 133, and Barmes, above n 122, ch 8.

empirical question and is likely to depend on a variety of factors, but it is important to take a realistic view.

III. Conclusion

I began with a quotation from Dickens, identifying the unsystematic nature of employment law enforcement in the UK.[137] But the point can be put more strongly. As Barmes has argued, the law puts in place structures that appear to empower and protect workers, but in practice fail to do so.[138] Thus, while workers are entitled to a long list of statutory rights at work, there are significant obstacles to the enforcement of those rights at all stages of the process. The working person might not realise what their rights are or that they have been infringed. They might not feel able to pursue a case to a tribunal hearing or they might be pressured into reaching a settlement. At the hearing, they may not be able to present their case effectively and, even if they win, they may not receive the remedy the tribunal has awarded. While there are some instances in which a public agency exists to enforce the law instead, this may not be the easy solution it appears at first sight. Not all public agencies have the power to secure redress for affected workers, and their activities are often heavily constrained by resource limitations.

Although policy-makers may have acted with good intentions when enacting much of this legislation, there is something deceitful about having a system of employment law enforcement that is so ineffectual. Workers are led to believe that they will benefit from a range of rights and entitlements at work, but if their employer does not comply voluntarily, they may find that these rights and entitlements are very difficult to enforce. This is a classic example of structural injustice.[139]

But what does all of this mean for a study of remedies? It will be apparent that I do not accept the argument that it makes discussion of remedies irrelevant: important conceptual lessons can be learned from an analysis of remedies even if workers rarely reach the stage of obtaining remedies from the tribunal. The ease, or otherwise, of obtaining them is a separate field of inquiry which cannot be understood solely through doctrinal methods.

There are, however, at least two important lessons to carry through to the rest of the book. First, where possible, remedies should be designed in ways that motivate workers to seek them despite the difficulties in doing so. For example, as chapter eight will illustrate, many awards in employment law have a purely vindicatory purpose: the claimant suffers no real loss from the infringement of their rights, and the award is just an acknowledgement of the infringement. The amount is set by statute. If this amount is set too low, however, claimants may not bother to

[137] Above n 3.
[138] Barmes, above n 122, 252.
[139] V Mantouvalou, *Structural Injustice and Workers' Rights* (Oxford, OUP, 2023).

litigate, leaving the rights in question unlikely to be enforced. Second, claims about the impact of remedies on employers should be treated with a degree of scepticism. It is sometimes suggested that large compensatory awards or requirements to re-employ a dismissed person will be too costly or disruptive for employers. While this may sometimes be true of the impact of a particular award on a particular employer, it is important to be wary of this as a generalisation about the impact of employment litigation on employers as a whole. Litigation is an uncommon experience for the vast majority of employers and should not be presented as more problematic than it really is.

3

The Remedies Perspective

Although there are many practical obstacles to a claimant seeking a remedy for breach of their employment rights, a study of remedies is still important for a number of reasons. On a practical level, some claimants *do* win their cases and are awarded a remedy by the tribunal, and those who are contemplating bringing a claim (or settling a claim) may be influenced by the remedies on offer. On a more theoretical level, remedies are an important part of the architecture of employment law and have a lot to say about how different rights are ranked against each other and viewed in the wider context of the legal system as a whole. The task for this chapter is to identify and explain the three big questions about remedies which this book will address.

The first question is whether the remedy on offer fits the right. The literature identifies different types of remedy – replicative or creative, for example – and different purposes that remedies might serve (compensation, punishment or vindication). I explain these concepts in more detail below. In most cases, the question of fit between right and remedy is a technical one: compensation is an appropriate remedial purpose if the breach of the right causes the claimant loss, and is not appropriate where it does not. However, even this technical question is surprisingly neglected in employment settings. For example, there are many occasions on which the law specifies an award of compensation for breach of an employment right where it is very unlikely in practice that the breach will have caused the claimant significant loss. In these situations, courts are faced with a dilemma: disregard the ordinary principles of identifying loss, or leave the claimant without a remedy at all. But the question of fit between right and remedy may also require moral judgement. For example, although penalties or punitive damages could be attached to almost any right, the expectation is that they should only be used in relation to more serious breaches. Some thought therefore needs to be given to how to identify the appropriate level of seriousness. Section I below explores the question of fit.

The second question is whether the remedy meets the specific needs of employment law. Much of the employment law literature is devoted to explaining why particular employment rights are needed (and why the same protections cannot be delivered by individual or collective bargaining). For example, it is often argued that working time controls are needed to protect working people's health and well-being, or that the NMW is needed to give workers a basic level of dignity in their earnings. Much less attention has been devoted to explaining why, for example, the appropriate remedy for a failure to provide a rest break is payment for the duration of the missed breaks,[1] or why employers should pay a penalty to the Secretary of State as well as NMW arrears to workers.[2] The key issue here is that the factors that make employment law special need to be taken into account not just when designing rights but also when designing remedies. Section II below explains two employment law-specific factors that should be considered: dignity (because working people are inseparable from their labour) – and the importance of securing compliance wherever possible. Of course, the argument that employment law is special can cut both ways: it can be (and often is) argued that it is necessary to design remedies to protect the interests of employers, and the labour market as a whole. This claim is commonly used to explain limiting factors on remedies, such as the cap on damages for unfair dismissal.[3] Section II will consider and reject this claim.

Finally, in section III, I turn to consider whether remedies are appropriately reflective of the relative importance of different employment rights and the varying seriousness of different types of breach. For example, it might be argued that freedom of association is one of the most important rights protected by employment law. It is recognised in all the main human rights instruments and features in the ILO's Declaration of the Fundamental Rights of Workers.[4] It is central to the success of worker protection through collective bargaining. Thus, one might expect to find a particularly comprehensive remedial regime for infringements of freedom of association. It might include elements designed to vindicate the worker's rights even where no particular loss has been suffered, or punitive damages to reflect the employer's wrongdoing. Of course, within any particular right there are more or less serious breaches: a refusal to allow time off to attend a trade union meeting is less serious than the use of a prohibited list to deny a job to an otherwise qualified applicant, so the law should also reflect these kinds of differences in the remedies on offer. This book is obviously not the place for a fully worked-out theory of the relative importance of all the different rights in employment law – a matter on which opinions are likely to differ considerably – but I will offer some preliminary thoughts.

I. The Fit between Right and Remedy

This section proceeds in two parts. First, drawing on some of the more theoretical private law literature, I consider some different ways of classifying remedies and explain the terminology to be used later in the book. Second, I offer a preliminary

[1] Eg *Santos Gomes v Higher Level Care Ltd* [2018] EWCA Civ 418, [2018] ICR 1571.
[2] NMWA 1998, s 19A.
[3] Employment Rights Act 1996 (ERA 1996), s 124.
[4] ILO, *Declaration on Fundamental Principles and Rights at Work* (1998, amended 2022).

explanation of some of the technical 'fit' questions I will be examining, particularly the problem of how to provide remedies for breaches of employment rights where the claimant is unlikely to suffer any significant losses. I also examine some of the questions of 'fit' which require a greater degree of judgement: for example, does the situation reach the level of seriousness required for a punitive or replicative approach?

A. Types of Remedy

This section will explain the classification of remedies (as defined in chapter one) as either replicative or creative, and the identification of three different purposes that a creative remedy might serve: compensation, vindication or punishment. I use this classification to organise later chapters of the book. The correct treatment of compensation is a matter of considerable controversy, so I also explain the decision to regard it as creative rather than replicative.

(i) Replicative Remedies

The private law literature offers a helpful distinction between 'replicative' and 'creative' remedies[5] or 'replicative' and 'transformative' remedies.[6] Replicative remedies, discussed fully in chapter six, are those which require the defendant to do what they were originally supposed to do, and include orders to pay money owed, injunctions and orders for specific performance.[7] Creative or transformative remedies require the defendant to do something different and will be discussed more fully below.

Replicative remedies are rarely able to put the claimant into the *exact* position they would have been in had the defendant complied in the first place, for two reasons. First, the claimant incurs the additional cost and effort of going to court to get the relevant order,[8] and second, the defendant's court-ordered performance is likely to take place at a later point in time than that originally envisaged for compliance. But, with those two caveats, replicative remedies come as close as possible to ensuring that the defendant fulfils their original obligation.

One possible puzzle about replicative remedies is why they exist at all: if the defendant did not comply with the primary obligation, why would they comply with a court order? But it seems clear that, in practice, many people do just that: they ignore or even wilfully disregard the requirements of the general law, but comply when a court makes an order against them. Presumably, both the law's requirements and the consequences of non-compliance are much clearer

[5] SA Smith, *Rights, Wrongs and Injustices: the Structure of Remedial Law* (Oxford, OUP, 2019), 9–10.
[6] R Zakrzewski, *Remedies Reclassified* (Oxford, OUP, 2005), ch 5, esp 78–79.
[7] See, generally, Zakrzewski, above n 6, esp ch 7–9; Smith, above n 5, ch 6.
[8] Of course, costs may be recoverable.

at that point, giving the defendant different (and arguably stronger) reasons to comply.[9]

The availability of replicative remedies is driven largely by practical considerations. For a replicative remedy to make sense, the defendant must be engaged in what Smith terms a 'rights-threat': in other words, they must either be threatening not to fulfil their obligations or engaged in a breach of those obligations that can be described as 'ongoing'.[10] If the defendant's wrongful act is complete – they have negligently injured the claimant, for example – there is no point ordering them not to breach their duty of care. But an employer's failure to pay wages is ongoing: the debt continues to exist and can be remedied by an order to pay the working person the money they are owed.

However, in employment law, there are occasions where a replicative remedy could be made available but it is either impossible or difficult to secure in practice. Well-known examples are injunctions to prevent a wrongful dismissal or re-employment orders after an unfair dismissal. It appears that the political will to make replicative remedies work effectively is lacking in this field. I return to this point below.

(ii) What Kind of Remedy is Compensation?

At first sight, compensation appears to be a creative remedy. For example, if the defendant is under an obligation not to injure the claimant negligently, the duty to pay a sum of money in compensation is very different to the original obligation. However, there is an important school of thought that treats compensation as a replicative remedy.[11] Although it does not replicate the primary obligation (to comply with the contract or to avoid causing injury, for example) it replicates the secondary obligation arising out of that breach. In *Photo Production*, Lord Diplock stated that:

> Every failure to perform a primary obligation is a breach of contract. The secondary obligation on the part of the contract breaker to which it gives rise by implication of the common law is to pay monetary compensation to the other party for the loss sustained by him in consequence of the breach.[12]

On this view, the right to be paid compensation arises immediately the wrong is committed. Crucially, therefore, when a court orders the defendant to pay compensation to the claimant, it is simply ordering the defendant to do what they were already obliged to do: it is crystallising and replicating the secondary right.

[9] Smith, above n 5, 8–9 and ch 5. Smith's view of authority is controversial, but this need not detain us here: see A Gold, 'Rights, Wrongs, and Injustices: The Structure of Remedial Law. By Stephen A. Smith' (2020) 79 *Cambridge Law Journal* 615.

[10] Smith, above n 5, 89–90 and ch 6.

[11] See eg Zakrzewski, above n 6, ch 5 and 10; S Steel and R Stevens, 'The Secondary Legal Duty to Pay Damages' (2020) 136 *Law Quarterly Review* 283.

[12] *Photo Production Ltd v Securicor Transport Ltd* [1980] AC 827, 849.

The attraction of this view is the clarity it offers about the nature and source of the duties imposed by the law. It is the commission of the wrong that gives rise to the duty to put things right.

Smith argues that this 'continuity thesis' is implausible, for two main reasons.[13] First, on a conceptual level, it does not make sense to regard a duty not to injure someone (for example) as 'transforming' into a duty to pay compensation. A more natural reading of the situation is that once the first duty has been breached, it ceases to exist, but there is a reason for a court to make an order that compensation should be paid. In other words, what the law recognises is not a duty to pay damages but a liability to be ordered to do so. Second, many of the rules limiting damages awards, such as mitigation, do not make sense if the payment of damages is a continuation of the original obligation, where such considerations would not have arisen.

Proponents of the 'continuity thesis' criticise Smith's approach on the basis that the wrongdoer 'gets away with it' unless and until the court orders them to pay compensation.[14] However, the approach is a much more accurate reflection of what happens in the real world. Even if the 'continuity thesis' is accepted, parties in the vast majority of cases would still require the intervention of the court to resolve their dispute, because someone needs to decide how much compensation is owed by the defendant to the claimant.[15] It is much more straightforward to regard the breach as giving rise to a liability to pay compensation which can be crystallised into an obligation to pay a specific amount by means of a court order.

In employment law, the position is further complicated by the fact that many statutory employment rights are drafted so as to give the tribunal a discretion over whether to make an award of compensation. A common formulation is that, if a claim is well-founded, the tribunal 'must' make a declaration and 'may' make an award of compensation.[16] On this approach, it cannot easily be argued that the obligation to pay compensation arises when the wrong is done, since the court's role is not simply to quantify the compensation but to decide whether or not it is payable at all. Adopting the 'continuity thesis' would require me to treat discretionary awards of compensation found in employment statutes as creative remedies, and other statutory and common law awards as replicative. However, my interest is less in the nature of the duty to compensate and more in the way in which awards are calculated, so it is helpful to be able to look at statutory and common law awards together. I will therefore adopt Smith's approach and deal with awards from both sources together in chapter seven.

[13] Smith, above n 5, ch 7.

[14] Steel and Stevens, above n 11, 291.

[15] Smith, above n 5, 199–201. Critics argue that this exaggerates the impact of uncertainty on the underlying obligations: see eg Zakrzewski, above n 6, ch 5.

[16] Eg ERA 1996, s 49 (detriment claims).

(iii) Creative Remedies

A key issue with creative remedies is how to explain and justify them in the absence of the 'anchor' provided by the original obligation.[17] Private lawyers do this by focusing on the nature of the defendant's breach and the purpose the remedy is aiming to serve relative to that breach, and this approach is helpful in employment law too, provided that attention is paid to the particular characteristics of employment rights. Drawing on that literature, and Smith's work in particular, I develop a three-fold scheme for thinking about creative remedies in employment settings: punishment (for wrongs), compensation (for injustices) and vindication (for breaches).[18]

Some theorists, most famously Blackstone, regard responding to 'wrongs' as the main function of remedies in private law.[19] On this view, the vast majority of remedies, including compensation, would be regarded as responses to wrongs. However, Smith develops a novel distinction between wrongs and injustices: 'The main difference is that the concept of a wrong is used to identify undesirable behaviour, while the concept of an injustice is used to identify undesirable consequences of behaviour'.[20] He offers exemplary damages as an example of a 'wrong-responding order' and restitution and compensation as examples of 'injustice-responding orders'.[21] This distinction is helpful for employment law purposes because it helps to distinguish between different degrees of employer default. It is very tempting for employment lawyers with a strong worker-protective agenda to regard all instances of employer default as warranting punishment. But this gives rise to a real risk of devaluing the idea of punishment by using it in cases of innocent mistake. Smith's distinction helps to avoid this temptation. The idea of a wrong can be used to identify the small group of cases in which the employer's conduct warrants punishment of some kind, whereas the idea of an injustice can be used to identify the much larger group of cases in which the employer's conduct has harmed the claimant but does not require a punitive response.

Of course, punishment is typically the preserve of the criminal law, and chapter four will consider the situations in which this strategy has been invoked in employment law settings. Obviously, criminal offences are not remedies within my definition, since they do not provide any redress to the claimant, but my analysis of employment law would be incomplete without them, and there is an interesting question to address about how they interact with remedies properly so-called. Employment law also makes some use of civil penalties, for example,

[17] Smith, above n 5, ch 4; Zakrzewski, above n 6, ch 13 (though compensation is not included in this scheme).

[18] For some criticisms of Smith's approach, see S Steel, 'Remedies, Analysed' (2021) 41 *Oxford Journal of Legal Studies* 539, 555–61.

[19] See P Birks, 'Rights, Wrongs and Remedies' (2000) 20 OJLS 1.

[20] Smith, above n 5, 94.

[21] Smith, above n 5, 90–93 and ch 7.

in the rarely-used penalty for 'aggravated breach' of employment rights.[22] Again, these penalties are not remedies because they are payable to the Secretary of State and not to the claimant, but an analysis of them is necessary to build up a full picture of employment rights.

However, there are occasions on which a remedy is properly described as punitive or as containing punitive elements. For example, some of the grounds for the award of punitive or exemplary damages at common law – such as where the defendant has breached workers' rights, having calculated that its profits will outweigh any damages awarded, or has abused public power – may be applicable in employment cases.[23] It is very common for tribunals to be directed to consider the seriousness of the employer's breach when determining what would otherwise be classed as a compensatory award.[24] Smith also includes awards for pain and suffering under this heading, on the basis that it is not possible to explain them as compensation for loss.[25] They are an arbitrary response to a situation that cannot be made better by money, so it is more plausible to see them as addressing the defendant's wrongdoing.

Some private law commentators regard punitive damages as problematic because the objective of punishing the defendant is achieved by increasing the compensation payable to the claimant, with the result that the claimant gets a 'windfall' beyond the sum that is strictly necessary to compensate them for their losses.[26] The same argument may be made where damages are increased because of the employer's bad behaviour. However, these views tend to place compensation front and centre as an objective and, as I will explain, the specific needs of employment law can only partly be met by compensating the claimant for losses. Nevertheless, a key question remains, which is how to decide which infringements of employment rights constitute 'wrongs' deserving of punishment, particularly in the light of the existence of a category of vindicatory awards (discussed below) which are not compensatory either. Ultimately, this is a question of judgment and degree, which I explore more fully in chapter five.

Smith's other category of creative remedies is 'injustice-responding' orders, which are designed to deal with the harm to the claimant flowing from the defendant's breach.[27] The most obvious example is compensation. The idea of compensation is simple: the aim is to put the claimant in the position they would have been in had the wrong (the tort, breach of contract, breach of statutory employment rights) not been committed. In practice, this involves identifying the claimant's 'losses' and trying to put them right. The 'measures' of damages for contract and for tort are, of course, different: in contract, the aim is to put

[22] ETA 1996, s 12A.

[23] Though the position is very unsettled: *Virgo Fidelis Senior School v Boyle* [2004] ICR 1210.

[24] Eg ERA 1996, s 80(4)(a) (parental leave).

[25] Smith, above n 5, 218–21.

[26] For discussion, see, generally, AS Burrows, *Remedies for Torts, Breach of Contract, and Equitable Wrongs* (Oxford, OUP, 2019), ch 20.

[27] Smith, above n 5, ch 7.

the claimant in the position they would have been in had the contract been performed, whereas in tort it is to put the claimant in the position they would have been in had the tort not been committed.[28] Some employment law cases fit directly into one or other of these categories: an action for wrongful dismissal is an action for dismissal in breach of contract and the damages awarded are determined in accordance with the expectation measure (though there are particular rules applied by the courts in employment settings).[29] Claims under the Equality Act 2010, although statutory, are expressly categorised as torts, thereby instructing courts and tribunals to apply a particular set of rules when awarding compensation.[30] Other types of claim are seemingly independent of common law norms – unfair dismissal is a good example – but, in practice, courts and tribunals have often drawn on common law frameworks in order to develop principles for making awards.[31] And, of course, sometimes statute encourages this, for example, by referring to common law concepts such as mitigation when defining how awards should be calculated.[32]

As Cane helpfully explains, the law approaches 'loss' in a very particular way.[33] Thus, in a tort claim the court will consider not only losses caused directly by the defendant's wrong, but also expenses incurred as a result of the wrong, and benefits the claimant would have had but for the wrong.[34] Typically, the court or tribunal quantifies the claimant's losses some time after they have occurred, so they are divided into losses prior to the date of assessment and losses which may arise after that date. Thus, the claimant's lost earnings up to the date of assessment can be determined with some precision (assuming the claimant had not been dismissed, for example) whereas lost future earnings involve a greater degree of speculation as to how long they would have remained in the job, whether they would have been promoted, and so on.

Compensation serves an important function in employment law. It is often the case that the defendant's breach causes the claimant some loss, which should be compensated. This is so even if other actions might be taken against the defendant, such as punishment. However, there are also many statutory employment rights in respect of which compensation is not relevant because no loss is likely to be suffered as a result of breach.[35] This is why vindication, to be explored below, is so important in this context. Compensation in employment cases is generally determined in quite precise ways with relatively little discretion for the court or

[28] Burrows, above n 26, 38.

[29] Eg *Johnson v Unisys Ltd* [2001] UKHL 13, [2003] 1 AC 518.

[30] Equality Act 2010, s 119.

[31] Eg the treatment of injury to feelings: *Norton Tool Co Ltd v Tewson* [1972] ICR 501; *Dunnachie v Kingston upon Hull City Council* [2004] UKHL 36, [2005] 1 AC 226.

[32] Eg ERA 1996, s 49(4) (detriment).

[33] P Cane, *The Anatomy of Tort Law* (Oxford, Hart Publishing, 1997), ch 4.

[34] More generally, see Burrows, above n 26, ch 3.

[35] This is particularly (though not exclusively) so where the law does not allow an award for injury to feelings: above n 31.

tribunal. For example, compensation for unfair dismissal is not 'at large' but is determined by a statutory formula (for the basic award) and detailed guidance from precedent (for the compensatory award) linked closely to the claimant's earnings.[36] There is thus little force in claims sometimes made that tribunal claimants are receiving large or arbitrary payouts. Indeed, the issues in employment law are less complex than those in areas in which money is a very poor substitute for the loss suffered, such as loss of amenity damages in personal injury claims.[37] That said, there are some controversial limitations on awards of compensation in employment law, to which I will return in the next section.

Vindication is probably the least familiar of the three purposes. The idea of vindication is to acknowledge that the defendant has breached the claimant's rights. All remedies do this, even if they serve other purposes as well. The fact that the court is willing to make an order is an acknowledgment that a breach has occurred. In many cases the claimant will also have suffered losses, so the main purpose of the remedy will be to compensate for those losses. Vindication is relegated to a very secondary position. But in employment law there are many examples of remedies that are primarily vindicatory in nature.[38] The claimant is awarded a sum of money in acknowledgement that their rights have been breached even though they have not suffered any losses. These examples of vindicatory damages typically arise in relation to statutory employment rights.[39] For example, Parliament legislates to provide workers with rights to time off work in certain circumstances, and provides for a money payment to be made where the defendant employer refuses to permit the working person to take that time off.[40] Leaving aside the fact that this can sometimes be a rather lazy remedial choice, the claimant may not have suffered any loss as a result of the refusal and may not be required to demonstrate loss in order to get an award. Instead, the award is just a way of recognising that the defendant infringed the claimant's rights.

The idea of vindicatory damages is not unknown at common law.[41] In some cases, the Privy Council has considered the idea in relation to violations of constitutional rights, though the Supreme Court has rejected it for English law, memorably describing it as an 'unruly horse'.[42] It is also arguable that a version of

[36] See ch 7 of this volume for a detailed discussion.

[37] Burrows, above n 26, ch 11.

[38] See ch 8 of this volume.

[39] It seems likely that this problem is encountered primarily in relation to statutory rights because Parliament can legislate to create a right regardless of the consequences of breach, whereas the development of the common law is driven primarily (though not always) by claimants who have suffered a loss and are seeking compensation for that loss.

[40] Eg ERA 1996, s 57 (time off for ante-natal appointment).

[41] For helpful discussions, see D Pearce and R Halson, 'Damages for Breach of Contract: Compensation, Restitution and Vindication' (2008) 28 *Oxford Journal of Legal Studies* 73; JNE Varuhas, 'The Concept of "Vindication" in the Law of Torts: Rights, Interests and Damages' (2014) 34 *Oxford Journal of Legal Studies* 253.

[42] *R (Lumba) v Secretary of State for the Home Department* [2011] UKSC 12, [2012] 1 AC 245, [101] (Lord Dyson).

this idea runs through Stevens' attempt to reframe the law on remedies as valuing the right infringed by the defendant, so that compensation is not the purpose of awards but merely the practical manifestation of that value in the vast majority of cases.[43] The situations I am considering are not constitutional in nature, and while I am interested in the valuation of employment rights, I am not seeking to reframe the whole of the law in these terms. But I do think it helps explicitly to acknowledge situations in which the only thing the court can do is to value the right, even if the statutory language or the courts themselves suggest that something else, such as compensation or punishment, is the main aim of the remedy.[44] Recognising a vindicatory objective makes more sense of awards when no loss has been suffered, without having recourse to the condemnatory language of punishment, which may not always be appropriate where the breach is not particularly serious. Of course, vindicatory awards raise tricky questions of quantification, but these are much more easily addressed if they are seen for what they are, rather than trying to dress them up as compensation.

Of course, it is important to note that a single remedy may serve multiple purposes.[45] For example, a compensatory award may contain a punitive element whereby either punitive damages are available at common law, or statute provides for the possibility of taking into account the seriousness of the defendant's wrongdoing. It also makes sense to say, in most cases, that the award of a remedy by a court vindicates the claimant's rights, even if the purpose of the award is often to compensate rather than to vindicate per se. This is because the court's recognition that rights have been breached and that a remedy should be provided is a vindicatory act in itself. But it is always helpful to identify the primary aim of any given remedy, and this is the strategy I have pursued in organising the chapters of this book.

B. Questions of 'Fit'

Having identified a workable classification of different types and purposes of remedies, it is possible to turn to one of the central issues explored in the book: fit. It is not the case that, faced with a new employment right, the legislator has a completely free choice between a replicative remedy or a creative remedy pursuing the aims of compensation, vindication or punishment. Some of these options will not *fit*: they will not respond appropriately to the claimant's needs or the defendant's actions.[46] The question of fit can be considered in two senses, which can be labelled 'technical' and 'moral'.

[43] R Stevens, *Torts and Rights* (Oxford, OUP, 2007).
[44] For example, *Hasler v Tourell Precision Engineers Ltd* (Case No 11431/83, 21 June 1983) (IT), [5].
[45] See Cane, above n 33, 119.
[46] Cane, above n 33, 96.

The *technical* sense of fit is applicable where a particular remedy would simply be inapplicable to the situation. For example, injunctions only make sense where there is a 'rights-threat', in Smith's terminology: a threatened or ongoing breach for the injunction to prevent or stop.[47] In employment law, an important technical fit issue surrounds the use of compensation as a remedy for breaches of statutory employment rights. There are many awards labelled 'compensatory' in statute in circumstances where it is difficult to imagine what loss the claimant might have suffered.[48] In these situations, the courts are faced with an unpalatable choice between making an award anyway, on no proper basis, in order to ensure that the claimant's rights are vindicated, and declining to make an award because no loss has occurred, even though this will leave the claimant with nothing despite winning their case. I will argue that a number of these situations would be better dealt with by acknowledging the possibility of making a vindicatory award and quantifying it accordingly.

Another, more complex sense of 'fit' is what might be termed 'moral' fit. For the most part, the seriousness of the breach, wrong or injustice is reflected *within* the remedy on offer. For example, in discrimination cases, awards may be made for injury to feelings.[49] There are three 'bands' on the damages scale, set out in the *Vento* case, to reflect different levels of seriousness, and tribunals are able to decide which band is appropriate and where within the band to fix the award.[50] Although courts and tribunals insist that injury to feelings awards are compensatory, they are keen to take an objective approach, so while the claimant's reaction is not ignored, the level of award is set mainly on the basis of the seriousness of the defendant's wrongdoing. Similarly, although the law does not always get this right, one might expect to find different levels of vindicatory awards depending on how fundamental the right infringed might be considered to be. However, there are some questions of judgement pertaining to the choice of remedy which I will explore here.

First, there are clear questions of fit in relation to punishment, whether in relation to remedies, such as punitive damages, or civil penalties or even criminalisation. A remedy with a punitive component should only be made available in particularly serious cases; otherwise, the 'currency' of punishment will be devalued. The use of civil penalties or the creation of criminal offences involves harnessing the power of the state to condemn the employer's behaviour in a serious and public manner, often with reputational consequences. Again, this should not be done lightly. As chapter four will explain, there is a large literature on criminalisation, emphasising the need to avoid over-using the criminal law and bringing it into disrepute. In particular, it is often said that creating a criminal offence is ineffective where people generally do not believe that the wrong in question warrants

[47] Above n 5.
[48] See ch 8 of this volume.
[49] Equality Act 2010, s 119(4).
[50] *Vento v Chief Constable of West Yorkshire Police* [2002] EWCA Civ 1871, [2003] ICR 318.

criminalisation. In other words, legislating to make something a crime does not make it so on a moral level. Crimes that are not widely regarded as 'real' do not have the desired effect in terms of condemning bad behaviour. Thus, while labour lawyers may sometimes be tempted to argue for more punishment for badly-behaved employers, it is important to consider carefully when punitive measures are likely to have the greatest effect and to use them sparingly.

Second, there are questions of fit in relation to replicative remedies. These are remedies which force the defendant to do what it was originally supposed to do, or something as close as possible to that obligation. In employment law, there are a number of examples of situations in which a replicative remedy could be made available, but either Parliament or the courts have chosen not to do so. In some cases, I argue, this demonstrates a failure to take employment rights sufficiently seriously. Probably the best-known examples of this are around dismissal. At common law, it may sometimes be possible for an employee to obtain an injunction to force the employer to complete a contractual disciplinary process prior to dismissal.[51] However, there are many obstacles in the way of this type of claim, including arguments about the importance of mutual trust and confidence, which seem to be stacked against the employee. In the statute law of unfair dismissal, re-employment is theoretically available as a remedy, but it is rarely requested and even more rarely awarded.[52] Various reasons have been suggested for this, but one is the long gap between the employee being dismissed and the case coming to trial. If it were possible to bring the claim quickly or to obtain interim relief, more employees might seek re-employment. This might also be the case if the orders could be enforced more effectively. In both these cases, there is a reluctance to protect the interests of employees and undue deference to the concerns of employers, both in the courts and in the legislature.

A second example is where an employer takes a decision without following a proper procedure. Many employment rights set out procedures: the right to be accompanied at a disciplinary or grievance hearing,[53] for example, or the right to be consulted about collective redundancies.[54] Where these rights are infringed, an effective remedy would be to require the employer to take the decision again after following the correct procedure. This would ensure greater respect for the procedures themselves, and would give the affected working people the opportunity to say whatever it was they wanted to say to influence the employer's decision. This type of remedy is very common in public law. While it might be perceived as causing some delay or inconvenience, because the employer must repeat its decision, it leaves the decision in the hands of the employer and so does not infringe very greatly on managerial prerogative. However, many employment rights of a procedural kind attract a (vindicatory) financial award as the remedy. This allows

[51] Eg *Chhabra v West London Mental Health NHS Trust* [2013] UKSC 80, [2014] ICR 194.
[52] ERA 1996, s 112.
[53] Employment Relations Act 1999, s 10.
[54] TULRCA 1992, ss 188ff.

the employer simply to buy its way out of its obligations and does not meet labour law's need for compliance, a point I discuss in the next section. But there is a lack of political will to take employment rights seriously and to put the most effective remedies into place.

To sum up, it is possible to classify remedies according to the wrong they are responding to and the purpose they serve. Replicative remedies respond to rights-threats by attempting to prevent or stop them. Compensation responds to injustice by attempting to put things right for the claimant. Punishment responds to wrongs by stigmatising the defendant and applying harsh treatment. Vindication responds to breaches by acknowledging that they have taken place. Particularly in the statute law of employment, it is important that the remedy on offer fits the wrong, both in the sense of correctly identifying the problem that needs to be tackled, and in the sense of responding with an appropriate (but not excessive) degree of rigour.

II. Do Remedies Reflect What is Special about Employment Law?

In this section, I want to tackle a large but fundamental issue that underpins the rest of the book. At the heart of employment law as a subject[55] is the recognition that, in the vast majority of cases, the ordinary law of contract does not give working people the rights and protections they need in the workplace because of the inequality of bargaining power between the parties.[56] Something else is required, whether that be collective bargaining to enable working people to negotiate for themselves, or rules of employment law to give working people additional rights and protections, or a combination of these and other techniques. Much ink has been spilled debating the nature and extent of protections required and the different ways in which they might be explained and justified, given that the basic idea of inequality of bargaining power tends just to diagnose, rather than solve, the problem. But much less attention has been paid to whether employment law has specific needs when it comes to remedies and, if so, whether the remedies available meet those needs (even if, in practice, they are rarely sought or awarded in some situations).[57]

Just like the substantive law, remedies in employment law are a mix of private law remedies attached to private law causes of action, statutory remedies attached to statutory rights, and complex combinations of the two – for example, where

[55] I assume that the subject is a coherent topic of study. For discussion, see A Bogg, 'Labour, Love and Futility: Philosophical Perspectives on Labour Law' (2017) 33 *International Journal of Comparative Labour Law and Industrial Relations* 7, 9–16.

[56] P Davies and M Freedland, *Kahn-Freund's Labour and the Law* (3rd edn, London, Stevens & Sons, 1983), ch 1.

[57] This may reflect a sense that employment law should be sharply differentiated from private law, which may be true in general terms but is less helpful in the context of a claim: see Bogg, above n 55, 16–30, for an excellent discussion.

the remedy for a statutory right makes reference to common law concepts such as contributory fault or mitigation. One immediate question is whether the use of concepts from private law is simply an efficient way of specifying remedies in employment settings, avoiding any need to reinvent the wheel, or whether there are risks attached to this strategy. For example, it has often been argued that the courts' importation of common law concepts into the substantive law of unfair dismissal – such as the decision to equate constructive dismissal with repudiatory breach – has stifled its development.[58] Might the same have occurred in relation to remedies? The refusal in *Norton Tool Co* to compensate for injury to feelings is a potential example which springs immediately to mind.[59] But this is not the only issue. Even where there are employment-specific remedies, such as reinstatement or re-engagement orders, do they realise the particular purposes of employment law?

Before examining remedies in more detail, it is necessary to have some understanding of what the purposes of employment law might be. This is obviously a large topic, worthy of a book (or several) in its own right. One relatively uncontroversial approach is to suggest that employment law is principally concerned with human dignity.[60] This idea can be traced back at least to Hugo Sinzheimer,[61] and is reflected in some of the ILO's constitutional documents, such as the Declaration of Philadelphia in 1944.[62] It is true that dignity is open to many different understandings and interpretations.[63] But at a basic level, it is about treating people as people and not as means to ends. In the employment law context, this is captured in the well-known slogan of the ILO: 'labour is not a commodity'.[64] Of course, labour is a commodity in the strict economic sense, but the thrust of the slogan is that labour as a commodity cannot be separated from the human being providing the labour.[65] Thus, the dignity of the working person must be respected in the workplace.

A. Dignity and Rights

The precise requirements of dignity at work then need to be elaborated, a task which can be carried out in many different ways. One important strategy is to draw

[58] See, generally, S Anderman, 'The Interpretation of Protective Employment Statutes and Contracts of Employment' (2000) 29 *Industrial Law Journal* 223.

[59] Above n 31.

[60] See eg M Weiss, 'Re-Inventing Labour Law?', in G Davidov and B Langille (eds), *The Idea of Labour Law* (Oxford, OUP, 2011).

[61] See eg R Dukes, 'Hugo Sinzheimer and the Constitutional Function of Labour Law, in G Davidov and B Langille (eds), *The Idea of Labour Law* (Oxford, OUP, 2011).

[62] See now ILO Constitution, Annex.
https://www.ilo.org/dyn/normlex/en/f?p=1000:62:0::NO:62:P62_LIST_ENTRIE_ID:2453907:NO#declaration.

[63] See eg C McCrudden, *Understanding Human Dignity* (Oxford, OUP, 2013).

[64] Above n 4, and see P O'Higgins, 'Labour Is Not a Commodity – An Irish Contribution To International Labour Law' (1997) 26 *Industrial Law Journal* 225.

[65] H Collins, *Employment Law* (2nd edn, Oxford, OUP, 2010), ch 1.

on human rights instruments, many of which more or less explicitly have dignity at their core.[66] International statements of civil and political and economic and social rights, taken together to reflect the universality of human rights, provide fairly comprehensive statements of what is needed to protect dignity. Of course, these general rights then need to be elaborated and adapted to apply in the workplace, not least because international instruments naturally treat the state, not the employer, as the main duty-bearer. This process of elaboration may take place through national human rights instruments, detailed employment legislation and (particularly in common law systems) case-law.[67] At national level, it should be possible to give much stronger effect to vague international commitments. For example, a right to decent or dignified working conditions can be given effect through a specific minimum wage entitlement and maximum limits on working hours.

The human rights approach can be used to inform the study of remedies in two different ways. First, although there is some resistance to the idea, it is possible to identify some hierarchies within the long lists of rights found in most international or regional instruments. Some rights are just more important than others. From a labour law perspective, it might not be desirable to approach the process of prioritising rights in a traditional way. For example, civil and political rights have sometimes been treated as superior to economic and social rights, but this approach is very distorting for the subject.[68] Nevertheless, it is easy to imagine a list with certain basic entitlements, such as a dignified living wage and a right to associate, at the top. I return to this idea in Section III, below.

A second way in which a human rights approach to labour law can inform a study of remedies is through the right to an effective remedy, which is found in Article 8 of the Universal Declaration of Human Rights, Article 2 of the International Covenant on Civil and Political Rights, Article 13 of the European Convention on Human Rights, and Article 47 of the Charter of Fundamental Rights of the European Union, among others. This right sets standards for how states should secure the various substantive rights provided for in the relevant instrument to their citizens. Importantly, the right to an effective remedy typically extends beyond my definition of a remedy – an order made by a court or tribunal – to cover the process of challenging the infringement of a person's rights as a whole.

[66] Here I adopt the view that the protection of human rights is an important aim of employment law, which is somewhat separate from the (more controversial) view that human rights are the foundation of employment law. For a helpful account of this distinction, see J Atkinson, 'Human Rights as Foundations for Labour Law', in H Collins, G Lester and V Mantouvalou (eds), *Philosophical Foundations of Labour Law* (Oxford, OUP, 2018). For discussions of the latter point, see eg H Collins, 'Theories of Rights as Justifications for Labour Law' in Davidov and Langille (eds), *The Idea of Labour Law* (Oxford, OUP, 2011); P Gilabert, 'Labor Human Rights and Human Dignity' (2016) 42 *Philosophy & Social Criticism* 171; V Mantouvalou, 'Are Labour Rights Human Rights?' (2012) 3 *European Labour Law Journal* 151.

[67] See G Davidov, *A Purposive Approach to Labour Law* (Oxford, OUP, 2016), ch 2.

[68] For discussion see eg V Mantouvalou, 'In Support of Legalisation', in C Gearty and V Mantouvalou, *Debating Social Rights* (Oxford, Hart Publishing, 2010).

Thus, the right to an effective remedy under the ECHR often includes considerations such as a thorough investigation of the victim's complaint, or prompt access to justice before a state body that can issue a legally-binding decision.[69] In terms of remedies in the strict sense, the European Court of Human Rights considers both compensation to provide redress for a past violation and, in some cases, preventative measures to ensure that no further violations occur in relation to the victim.[70] More specific obligations have been developed in relation to particular rights. For example, a prompt means of challenge must be made available whenever a planned protest is banned, so that there is an opportunity for the protest to go ahead if the ban is overturned.[71] However, the Court gives signatory states a substantial margin of appreciation in respect of remedies in most cases, so there is little detailed guidance on, for example, how compensation should be calculated.

The right to an effective remedy is a long-established principle of EU law, originating in the case-law of the Court[72] and now found in Article 47 of the Charter.[73] It reflects the fact that Member States are largely responsible for the implementation and enforcement of EU laws within national systems. While they enjoy an element of autonomy to determine rules of procedure and remedies, this is qualified by the twin requirements of equivalence (on a par with the procedures and remedies available for similar claims in national law) and effectiveness. Occasionally, it may be necessary to craft a new remedy where national law offers no other means of enforcing EU law, as the *Factortame* litigation demonstrated.[74] Effectiveness is usually taken to mean a remedy that is 'proportionate and dissuasive'.[75] For example, in *von Colson*, the Court held that German law providing for a remedy of reimbursement of interview expenses where a job applicant was discriminated against was inadequate both to deter employers and to compensate claimants.[76] More recently, in *King*, a claimant who had been misclassified by the employer as self-employed and therefore denied paid holidays over a period of many years was able to rely on the principle of effectiveness to disapply limits on the recovery of back pay, including a rule prohibiting the 'carrying over' of leave from one year to the next, and a provision that holiday pay could only be recovered

[69] See, generally, C Grabenwarter, *European Convention on Human Rights: Commentary* (London, Bloomsbury Academic, 2013), Article 13.

[70] ibid 335–38.

[71] *Bączkowski v Poland* (Application no 1543/06) (2009) 48 EHRR 19.

[72] Case 33/76 *Rewe Zentralfinanz eG v Landwirtschaftskammer fur das Saarland* ECLI:EU:C:1976:188, [1976] ECR 1989.

[73] See, generally, S Peers, T Hervey, J Kenner and A Ward (eds), *The EU Charter of Fundamental Rights: A Commentary* (Oxford, Hart Publishing, 2014), Article 47; K Gutman, 'The Essence of the Fundamental Right to an Effective Remedy and to a Fair Trial in the Case-Law of the Court of Justice of the European Union: The Best Is Yet to Come?' (2019) 20 *German Law Journal* 884.

[74] Case 213/89 *R v Secretary of State for Transport, ex parte Factortame* [1990] ECR 2433; though see now Case C-583/11 P *Inuit Tapiriit Kanatami v Commission* ECLI:EU:C:2013:625, [2014] 1 CMLR 54.

[75] Case C-186/98 *Nunes et de Matos* [1999] ECR I-4883, [9]–[11].

[76] Case 14/83 *Von Colson v Land Nordrhein-Westfalen* ECLI:EU:C:1984:153, [1984] ECR 1891; and on employment cases generally see J Adams-Prassl, 'Article 47 CFR and the Effective Enforcement of EU Labour Law: Teeth for Paper Tigers?' (2020) 11 *European Labour Law Journal* 391.

for holiday in fact taken.[77] Overall, EU law has proved useful in challenging weak national remedies and removing various limitations and restrictions, some examples of which will be discussed in later chapters, but not surprisingly – given that the primary responsibility for designing remedies lies with the Member States – it has not yet provided a comprehensive framework for evaluating them.

In short, while a rights-based approach to employment law is helpful to a study of remedies in some respects, it does not offer a comprehensive theoretical approach. This is not surprising given that the main focus of rights analyses is on working out the requirements of dignity in terms of substantive entitlements, with remedies as something of an afterthought.

B. Dignity and Types of Harm

The crucial question is whether it is possible to work from the general objective of protecting the dignity of working people to more detailed principles focused specifically on the law of remedies.

One promising way to do this is to focus on the harms suffered (or potentially suffered) by a working person when their employment rights are breached. These harms are different in some important respects from the harm suffered when, for example, a commercial contract is breached. I do not suggest that employment cases are unique in this regard – other types of claim might share some of these characteristics – nor do I suggest that every employment case involves all the harms I am about to identify, but they are a significant and distinguishing feature of many employment cases. Obviously, the central form of harm in many cases is loss in the various senses identified in section I, so most working people will want to recover compensation for their losses. Here, I focus on some other less obvious, but potentially important, forms of harm.

First, in many employment cases, there is a hard-to-quantify, but important, loss of dignity when the working person's fundamental rights are infringed.[78] For example, a job applicant who is unsuccessful will often be disappointed, sometimes greatly so, but the situation is altogether different if it becomes clear that they were rejected because of their race or religion, or their trade union membership. The prospective employer has taken into account an irrelevant consideration in a way that is shocking, distressing and likely to make the person feel that they have not been treated with appropriate respect. This loss of dignity may be exacerbated where it takes place in a long-term employment relationship, where there can often be a great sense of betrayal. For example, an employee who is unfairly dismissed as a result of false allegations without having an opportunity to be heard is likely to feel particularly harshly treated if they have not been listened to or believed after many years of loyal service.

[77] Case C-214/16 *King v Sash Window Workshop* ECLI:EU:C:2017:914, [2018] ICR 693.
[78] See H Collins, *Justice in Dismissal* (Oxford, OUP, 1992), ch 1.

As later chapters will demonstrate, the law sometimes addresses this form of harm. For example, awards for injury to feelings are permitted in discrimination cases, allowing courts and tribunals to reflect the seriousness of the employer's breach of dignity when quantifying the award (on the assumption that the more serious the breach, the stronger the impact it is likely to have on the feelings of the individual).[79] However, awards for injury to feelings are not universally available: they are treated as precluded in a common law wrongful dismissal claim by the decision in *Addis*;[80] they are ruled out in the statute law of unfair dismissal by *Norton Tool Co*;[81] and there are a number of statutory rights whose remedial provisions expressly prohibit these awards.[82] Moreover, chapter eight will explore a variety of situations in which a working person's rights may be breached without any compensable loss occurring. These present particular challenges in terms of recognising and remedying the harm to the person's dignity that has nevertheless arisen.

Second, it is widely accepted that the benefits of having a job often extend well beyond the wages earned by the working person.[83] The workplace can provide significant opportunities for social interaction: work colleagues may become friends and socialise together, for example, or simply enjoy each other's company during the working day. In many cases, work itself can be a source of personal satisfaction, as the working person exercises existing skills or learns new ones, or helps other people to solve problems. For many people, there is also significant satisfaction in being able to support themselves or their family financially. A person's reputation or standing in the community often depends on their job: 'what do you do?' is a common enquiry on social occasions and many people want to be able to answer this question with a degree of pride. Conversely, problems at work – such as allegations of wrongdoing – may lead to adverse comment and isolation both in the workplace and in the wider local community. Finally, many working people view their job as one element in a wider 'career', a trajectory in which they move to positions with more responsibility and reward as they gain experience or, perhaps more commonly nowadays, transfer their skills from one sector to another in a way that brings either financial reward or personal satisfaction. A problem with one job may jeopardise a person's wider life plan.

It is important to acknowledge that no legal system could ever address all of these matters: remedies can help to put things right, but they cannot usually erase all aspects of the defendant's wrongdoing. Nor does the law typically make the defendant liable for every loss that might vaguely be attributed to the original

[79] Above n 49. Smith regards these damages as wrong-responding: Smith, above n 5, ch 7.
[80] *Addis v Gramophone Co Ltd* [1909] AC 488; *Johnson v Unisys Ltd* [2001] UKHL 13, [2003] 1 AC 518.
[81] Above n 31.
[82] Eg Part-time Workers (Prevention of Less Favourable Treatment) Regulations 2000 (SI 2000/1551), reg 8(11).
[83] Collins, above n 78.

wrong.[84] Nevertheless, it is important to consider whether the remedies on offer acknowledge to an appropriate degree the fact that the value of a person's job may be a deeply personal matter not confined to the income it generates. Of course, one way to do this is through awards designed to acknowledge feelings of hurt and upset, but these are not always made available, as explained above. Another option is to make more use of replicative remedies, which might force the employer to reconsider a decision, keep the working person in their job or require the employer to reinstate them. These remedies exist in employment law, but their availability is tightly constrained, even though they offer much better possibilities for reflecting the importance of a person's job to them than allowing the dismissal to go ahead and requiring the employer to pay compensation after the event.[85]

Third, there is a sense in which the harms suffered in employment cases often take the form of lost opportunities, not just in the career-building sense. For example, many employment rights seek to protect the individual or collective rights of working people to have their say on workplace issues that affect them, such as disciplinary matters or potential redundancies.[86] Where these rights are breached, working people lose both the right to participate itself, and the opportunity to persuade the employer to change its mind or act in a particular way. Similarly, rights to request time off for particular purposes or to request flexible working arrangements offer working people opportunities to take part in other activities of significance to them or to achieve a better work/life balance.[87] In some cases, these opportunities may be lost if the employer does not comply or only does so many months or years later, perhaps after litigation. Finally, failure to pay a person the money they are due, whether in the form of NMW infringements or unlawful deductions or denials of bonuses, may make a significant difference in terms of their opportunities to avoid falling into debt, to provide themselves with better accommodation, or to take advantage of economic opportunities.

Again, some of these harms are probably too remote for the law to contemplate: the longer-term financial consequences of not being paid appropriately are a good example. But the law's record of acknowledging even more immediate lost opportunities is patchy, at best. In unfair dismissal and discrimination claims, it is usually possible to obtain compensation for more speculative lost future earnings, such as the chance of staying at the workplace for many more years or getting a promotion with a higher wage attached.[88] Occasionally, an award may be made for career-long losses (subject to the statutory maximum where applicable).[89] But the lost opportunity of keeping one's job had redundancy consultation taken place in accordance with the law is not expressly reflected in the 'protective award' on offer,

[84] See Burrows, above n 26, 86–106.

[85] See ch 6 of this volume.

[86] Eg TULRCA 1992, s 188.

[87] Eg ERA 1996, s 80F.

[88] Eg *Griffin v Plymouth Hospital NHS Trust* [2014] EWCA Civ 1240, [2015] ICR 347; *York Trailer Co v Sparkes* [1973] ICR 518.

[89] See *Wardle v Crédit Agricole Corporate and Investment Bank* [2011] EWCA Civ 545, [2011] ICR 1290.

even though, at common law, loss of a chance is a recognised head of compensation in some circumstances.[90] More strikingly, the law rarely requires the employer to go away and take the decision again, applying the law properly, even though this would provide the precise protection envisaged.

In sum, while the law cannot provide relief for every type of harm suffered by a working person as a result of their employer's wrongs, careful thought does need to be given to specific types of harm found in the employment sphere given the inseparability of working people from their labour and the dignitarian concerns that flow from this. Measures such as more generous rules on compensation, or a greater focus on compliance may be needed to provide a more appropriate form of relief.

C. Compliance and Deterrence

Another feature of employment law worth drawing attention to is the potential for a greater focus on compliance and deterrence. This stems from the fact that, while some employment relationships (particularly nowadays) are of very short duration, many are not. Even in the gig economy, a working person may be signed up to a platform for many years, albeit that their work may be intermittent and their legal status uncertain. Legal rules can play a different role in long-term working relationships.

First, there is a real opportunity for the law to deter wrongdoing in long-term relationships.[91] Of course, on some level, deterrence is always a function of the law – there is an expectation that people will use it to guide their behaviour – but in many cases, it is rather a vague idea with limited practical effect.[92] While the criminal and civil law seek to deter bad driving, for example, it seems unlikely that a person making a poor split-second decision – to look at their phone or to overtake on a bend – spends much time considering the legal consequences of their actions.[93] By contrast, many employers contemplating a course of action in relation to their workforce will seek legal advice. In particular, they may engage in a cost-benefit analysis of their options.[94] If an employee is performing badly,

[90] Burrows, above n 26, ch 5.

[91] For an excellent overview of the complexities of deterrence in the context of 'wage theft', see T Hardy, 'Digging Into Deterrence: An Examination of Deterrence-Based Theories and Evidence in Employment Standards Enforcement' (2021) 37 *International Journal of Comparative Labour Law and Industrial Relations* 133.

[92] For a classic law and economics account, see G Becker, 'Crime and Punishment: An Economic Approach' (1968) 76 *Journal of Political Economy* 169.

[93] For examples of behavioural critiques of the classic law and economics account, see C Jolls, C Sunstein and R Thaler, 'A Behavioral Approach to Law and Economics' (1998) 50 *Stanford Law Review* 1471; P Robinson and J Darley, 'Does Criminal Law Deter? A Behavioural Science Investigation' (2004) 24 *Oxford Journal of Legal Studies* 173.

[94] Though the empirical reality is highly complex: see T Hardy and J Howe, 'Creating Ripples, Making Waves? Assessing the General Deterrence Effects of Enforcement Activities of the Fair Work Ombudsman' (2017) 39 *Sydney Law Review* 471.

should the employer give them a series of warnings and opportunities to improve, or dismiss straight away and risk a finding of unfair dismissal? A lawyer will be able to advise on the 'worst case scenario' award for unfair dismissal, so the employer will be able to compare the cost of paying that with the cost of retaining a poorly-performing employee, particularly in a senior role, and decide which is the cheaper course. In many cases, it may be possible to negotiate a settlement at even lower cost, given that many employees would prefer to avoid the difficulty and stress of trying to enforce their rights through the legal system. As later chapters will demonstrate, there are some employment rights for which the weak deterrent effect of the remedy (taken alongside the difficulties of bringing a tribunal claim) casts serious doubt on whether there is any real incentive on employers to comply.[95] By contrast, there are others for which a serious attempt has been made to generate a deterrent effect. The NMW offers a good example, because an employer in breach must not only pay the arrears owed to the affected workers, but also pay a penalty to the Secretary of State and face adverse public comment through the 'naming and shaming' scheme.[96]

Second, in a long-term working relationship, there may be more practical opportunities to use remedies to force the employer to comply with its obligations. In many situations, once a breach has occurred it cannot be undone: for example, once a negligent driver has caused an injury to another road user, all that the law can do is to require the payment of compensation. Some employment cases have similar characteristics. For example, an angry exchange between a manager and a working person involving a one-off incident of harassment by the manager can only really be dealt with through an order that the employer should pay compensation.[97] However, in other cases, the long-term nature of the relationship means that there is an opportunity to get the employer to do what it was supposed to do in the first place. For example, if the employer fails to give proper consideration to a flexible working request, it could simply be ordered to examine the matter again.[98] And provided that the working person has prompt access to a court, it is possible to obtain an injunction to force the employer to follow a contractual disciplinary procedure, an option that could be used much more widely to enforce other procedural rights.[99]

D. Economic Considerations

Thus far, the employment-specific remedial concerns I have identified – the importance of the rights at stake, the special kinds of harms that might be encountered

[95] See ch 8 of this volume.
[96] National Minimum Wage Act 1998, ss 17–19H and 31–33.
[97] Equality Act 2010, s 26.
[98] ERA 1996, s 80I(1)(a).
[99] See *Chhabra*, above n 51.

in workplace settings, and the potential for a strong focus on compliance and deterrence – are all concerned with working people and their need for protection. However, another type of employment-specific argument commonly encountered is that the remedies laid down for breaches of employment rights should take account of the needs of employers and the wider economy.[100] I interrogate this argument here.

The alleged needs of employers and the wider economy in relation to remedies are rarely spelled out with much precision, but one possible interpretation is that remedies may be a 'burden' on businesses.[101] This argument is often made in relation to employment rights more generally, but it has a strong remedial focus. Taking unfair dismissal as an example, the argument might be that the employer wishing to dismiss someone must take legal advice on permissible reasons and then invest managerial time in following the appropriate procedures. There is then a risk that the dismissed employee will sue for unfair dismissal, so that the employer incurs further legal costs defending the claim and paying compensation. In turn, so the argument goes, this makes the employer more cautious about hiring people (or perhaps hiring people and giving them employee status) which is bad for economic growth and, ultimately, for working people themselves, whose job opportunities are reduced. Arguably, this set of claims is reflected in unfair dismissal law, most obviously in the cap on the damages that can be recovered in an unfair dismissal claim (in the absence of any discrimination).[102] The effect of the statutory maximum, as it is properly known, is that even if the claimant can show that they have suffered losses (such as lost future earnings) in accordance with well-established compensatory principles, they will not be able to recover those losses beyond a year's salary or a fixed sum set out in the statute, whichever is the lower. This reduces the 'burden' on the employer by placing an artificial limit on the compensation it is obliged to pay, even if the loss its actions have caused is much greater.

Is any of this defensible? The 'burdens on business' argument has been challenged as a matter of economics. Scholars such as Deakin have argued that the labour market is constituted by legal rules, rather than having some kind of organic existence into which legal rules intrude in a potentially disruptive way.[103] Employment rights like the right not to be unfairly dismissed can bring benefits: for example, by discouraging employers from dismissing productive workers on irrational grounds, enabling more secure workers to focus on their jobs, and supporting the enforcement of other employment rights with a more direct link

[100] See Davidov, above n 67, 22–23, on how employer interests should be thought of in relation to labour law's goals.

[101] For the history of the emergence of this idea in relation to labour law generally, see P Davies and M Freedland, *Labour Legislation and Public Policy* (Oxford, OUP, 1993), ch 10.

[102] ERA 1996, s 124.

[103] See eg S Deakin, 'The Contribution of Labour Law to Economic and Human Development', in Davidov and Langille (eds), *The Idea of Labour Law* (Oxford, OUP, 2011).

to productivity.[104] Moreover, there are a variety of ways of balancing the rights of working people against the economic preferences of employers without limiting remedies. For example, the qualifying period for unfair dismissal (which is, of course, controversial in itself) provides the employer with time to judge whether it has hired the right person before incurring any liability (with exceptions).[105] Once it has been established that the employer has not complied with the law, a very strong argument is required to limit the employee's remedies. This is particularly so given that unfair dismissal compensation is not 'at large' in the sense of being a matter of discretion for the tribunal but is instead governed by a set of highly-detailed rules requiring the employee to prove their losses in accordance with established principle.[106] Thus, even without the statutory maximum, it is highly unlikely that there would be many substantial awards.

It is worth considering a couple of variants on the 'burdens on business' argument. Another version focuses on the mobility of working people within the labour market. A key example of legislation pursuing this goal is the law on redundancy payments.[107] While redundancy payments are not remedies in the sense in which I am using the term, it can be argued that their principal purpose is not to protect employees' job security (as might be expected), but rather to encourage employees to accept redundancies and to look for another job. Arguably, some elements of this idea might be seen in the law on remedies. For example, the unfair dismissal legislation also offers the possibility of reinstatement or re-engagement – indeed, these are the primary remedies before compensation is considered – but they are rarely used and weakly enforced. The legislature was reluctant to give tribunals the enforcement powers a court would have had,[108] so provided instead for an additional amount of compensation for failing to implement a re-employment order, but the sum is not large and may not have much deterrent effect.[109] Perhaps this too reflects the idea that, even in cases of unfairness, dismissed employees should be encouraged to move on to another labour market opportunity. Of course, mobility in the labour market is a good thing: working people should be encouraged to move to where their contribution is most valued, and this typically occurs through normal market mechanisms, such as the offer of higher pay to go and work for a rival firm. However, for the law to encourage this through remedies is more questionable, given all the intangible harms to the working person from losing their job detailed above. There are many situations in which the remedial regime could force the employer to reconsider or make the right decision, but instead just compensates the wronged employee.

[104] ACL Davies, *Perspectives on Labour Law* (2nd edn, Cambridge, CUP, 2009), esp ch 9.

[105] ERA 1996, s 108.

[106] See ch 7 of this volume.

[107] See Davies and Freedland, above n 101, ch 4, discussing the Redundancy Payments Act 1965. For critique, see Collins, above n 78, ch 5.

[108] Davies and Freedland, above n 101, 208–11.

[109] ERA 1996, s 117.

While this may have economic benefits, it is not clear that these outweigh the employee's less quantifiable losses.

A further variant on the argument that employment rights and their accompanying remedies are burdens on business is the argument about vexatious litigation.[110] This claim came to the fore when the government decided to introduce fees for bringing claims in the Employment Tribunal.[111] The secondary legislation setting out the fees was quashed by the Supreme Court in the *UNISON* case because it infringed the fundamental principle of access to justice, something the Lord Chancellor was not permitted by the empowering statute to do.[112] Again, the government's argument was somewhat unclear, but seemed to involve suggesting that a large proportion of tribunal claimants were 'trying it on': in other words, threatening litigation even when no wrong had been done, with the aim of securing a financial settlement from the employer. Of course, it is hardly worth pointing out the obvious logical flaw in this argument: that there is no connection between the strength of a claimant's case and their ability (or otherwise) to pay a fee to get that case before the tribunal. Moreover, work by Adams and Prassl demonstrated that there was little evidence to support the idea that there were large numbers of vexatious claims in the tribunal system.[113] Nevertheless, this argument is still used to support limits on remedies. For example, when the formula for the unfair dismissal statutory maximum was last changed, it was argued by the government that this would give employees a more 'realistic' sense of what they might be able to recover, with the clear implication that this would deter what the government regarded as frivolous claims.[114]

It is no surprise to find that the arguments sometimes made against advances in substantive employment rights are also encountered in relation to remedies. Indeed, these arguments may have more purchase in relation to remedies because the costs involved are more obvious: it is easier to quantify the basic and compensatory award for unfair dismissal for a particular employee than it is to quantify the managerial time spent observing the substantive right (issuing warnings, investigating allegations or following fair procedures, for example). But it is important to challenge these arguments. First, it is worth noting that the law often seeks to strike a balance between working people and employers in the delineation of employment rights. Continuing with the dismissal example, the law is generous in the reasons for which employers are allowed to terminate the employment

[110] See eg Department for Business, Innovation and Skills, *Resolving Workplace Disputes* (January 2011).

[111] Added Tribunals (Employment Tribunal and Employment Appeal Tribunal) Order 2013 (SI 2013/1892); Employment Tribunals and the Employment Appeal Tribunal Fees Order 2013 (SI 2013/1893).

[112] *R (UNISON) v Lord Chancellor* [2017] UKSC 51, [2020] AC 869.

[113] A Adams and J Prassl, 'Vexatious Claims: Challenging the Case for Employment Tribunal Fees' (2017) 80 *Modern Law Review* 412.

[114] Department for Business, Innovation and Skills, *Ending the Employment Relationship Consultation* (September 2012); Enterprise and Regulatory Reform Act 2013, s 15.

relationship, and applies a light touch to the assessment of the reasonableness of the employer's decision.[115] Thus, it is not easy for the employee to establish that their dismissal was substantively unfair. Careful consideration should be given to whether it is necessary to limit remedies which are relatively difficult to obtain. Second, once a right has been granted to working people, either at common law or in legislation, there is an important general interest in securing compliance with that right. Otherwise, the law is brought into disrepute. Later in the book, I will give several examples of rights that are practically unenforceable because few people would consider it worthwhile to bring proceedings in order to obtain the limited remedies on offer.[116] Third, it is worth applying some scepticism to employers' claims about the economic benefits (or even worker benefits) of limiting workers' rights. The principal benefit is to employers themselves, and given the inequalities of bargaining power in the labour market, it is essential to consider whether a powerful lobby group is simply trying to limit the impact of legislation it does not like through a rear-guard action on remedies.

E. Conclusion

To sum up, it is possible to identify some employment-specific priorities for the design of remedies. First, remedies should address the potential harms to dignity that may be suffered by working people when something goes wrong in their employment relationship. These include the basic harm of being disrespected, the loss of a wide range of intangible benefits of having a job, and lost opportunities to be heard or to have things turn out differently. As later chapters will demonstrate, the law has various strategies for remedying these harms, but they are not always used consistently or effectively in employment settings. Second, remedies should be designed to deter breaches and (where practical) to secure compliance once a breach has occurred, recognising the fact that in employment relationships there may be greater opportunities to influence the employer's behaviour than there are in some of the other legal contexts with which parallels may be drawn. Third, arguments that remedies should be limited in order to promote economic prosperity and labour market mobility, or to deter vexatious claims, should be treated with suspicion. These priorities will inform much of the discussion in the rest of the book.

[115] In a large critical literature, see eg PM Collins, 'Finding Fault in the Law of Unfair Dismissal: The Insubstantiality of Reasons for Dismissal' (2022) 51 *Industrial Law Journal* 598; A Baker, 'The "Range of Reasonable Responses" Test: A Poor Substitution for the Statutory Language' (2021) 50 *Industrial Law Journal* 226.

[116] See ch 8 of this volume. See also Adams and Prassl, above n 113.

III. Do Remedies Appropriately Reflect the Relative Importance of Different Employment Rights?

A third issue to consider is whether the remedies on offer in employment law reflect a sensible 'ranking' of employment rights. Intuitively, most people would accept that, for example, being discriminated against by their employer is more serious than not being provided with a written statement of rights within the correct timeframe, and that this should be reflected in the remedies the law makes available in each case. However, there are some conceptual and moral challenges to address in relation to this argument, and these will be the focus of this section. I will begin by explaining how a ranking might work in practice, before setting out the subject's priorities as I see them.

A. Conceptual Issues

An obvious objection to the idea of evaluating remedies from the perspective of a ranking of employment rights is that to do so focuses on the wrong thing: remedies should (and do) reflect the harm the working person has suffered rather than what the employer has done or failed to do. For example, it is generally accepted that, in a dismissal case, the damages awarded to a well-paid employee will typically exceed those awarded to a lower-paid employee, even if the employer's 'wrong' (such as failing to follow a fair procedure) is exactly the same.[117] This is because damages are intended to compensate the employees for their respective losses, rather than to punish the employer for wrongdoing. Key elements of the damages award, such as lost earnings up to the date of the hearing, and lost future earnings, are inherently linked to the claimants' respective salaries. This can also mean that a well-paid employee's 'ordinary' dismissal claim may generate a higher award of compensation than a low-paid worker's discrimination claim, for example. While the latter may be morally more serious than the former, the compensation awarded reflects the financial losses the two claimants have suffered and, again, these will reflect their earnings.

Nevertheless, there are two reasons for thinking about ranking rights, as well as harms, in employment settings. First, as I have explained, not all remedies are about providing compensation for losses suffered. In some cases, the employer's conduct is unlikely to cause loss in any meaningful sense, so the law provides the possibility of a 'vindicatory' award instead. Any attempt to evaluate these awards must involve some assessment of the nature of the employer's wrongdoing in infringing the claimant's employment rights. In other cases, the employer's wrong

[117] See Cane, above n 33, 110–12.

is seen as so serious that it warrants the attention of the criminal law (either alongside or instead of private law) and, again, the nature of the rights at stake is a relevant consideration in determining when criminalisation is warranted. Second, even where the principal remedy provided by the law is compensation for losses suffered, the nature of the right infringed can be important in determining facets of the compensation regime. For example, compensation for discrimination is not subject to the statutory maximum applicable in unfair dismissal. While this stems in practice from the intervention of EU law to require the provision of effective remedies, it is worth considering whether it can be justified by ranking the rights at stake.[118]

In most cases, whether they are concerned with the punishment for a criminal offence, a vindicatory award, a compensatory award or some other remedy, the law gives the judge a degree of discretion to match the remedy to the case at hand. This allows recognition of the fact that there are varying levels of seriousness within the same category of case. For example, the sentence for wilful non-payment of the NMW is likely to be affected by factors such as the number of workers involved and the extent of the non-payment.[119] A vindicatory award may be pitched higher up the range if the employer showed total and deliberate disregard for the employee's right, and lower if the breach was partial or technical in nature. But the task of setting the punishment or remedy in the first place, and determining the range, may be influenced by the ranking given to the right. For example, the law provides a comprehensive enforcement regime for NMW infringements, including the criminal offence just mentioned and a requirement to pay a penalty to the Secretary of State in cases of accidental infringement, as well as arrears to the workers themselves.[120] This regime suggests that the NMW is being given a particularly high ranking in the system of employment rights. It also contrasts with the many time-off rights that are remedied by a vindicatory award of two weeks' pay, or pay for the time the person would have taken off, which are clearly not rated so highly by the legislator.[121]

B. Ranking

It is not sensible to attempt a comprehensive ranking of every conceivable employment right. However, to provide some framing for the discussion in later chapters, it is helpful to identify some priority areas for the law's intervention, as a way of determining whether these do indeed get prioritised by the law in practice. I begin by addressing a couple of concerns about the ranking process, before identifying these areas.

[118] Case C-271/91 *Marshall v Southampton and South West Hampshire Health Authority* ECLI:EU:C:1993:335, [1994] QB 126.
[119] Sentencing Council, *General Guideline: Overarching Principles* (October 2019).
[120] Above n 96.
[121] See ch 8 of this volume.

One very well-known attempt to prioritise among employment rights was the ILO's Declaration of Fundamental Principles and Rights at Work, in 1998. This included freedom from forced labour, freedom from child labour, equality and freedom of association, as four 'core' rights upon which to focus the ILO's activities, particularly in terms of technical assistance. The list has since been amended to add health and safety.[122] This process proved highly controversial, with critics arguing that setting priorities would, in effect, downgrade all other employment rights to a position of insignificance.[123] This is a risk in any process of prioritisation: that public attention and funding will be directed towards the priorities, so that lower-ranked requirements effectively cease to be enforced. There is a sense in which some employment rights in English law are effectively unenforceable too. However, as discussed above, this is not a result of prioritisation per se: it is a result of not having adequate remedies for lower-ranked rights (or finding a better way than litigation to enforce them).

Another concern for many labour lawyers about prioritisation is that the wrong priorities will be selected. In international settings, for example, preference is often given to civil and political rights over economic and social ones, on the basis of questionable but familiar arguments that they are less controversial, do not require expenditure (and thus do not depend on a state's level of resources) and are simpler for courts to enforce.[124] However, this approach downgrades some very significant labour rights – such as the right to decent working conditions – and has the potential to distort the subject. The arguments for prioritising civil and political rights make considerably less sense once it is acknowledged that most employment rights (however classified) consist of a bundle of negative and positive duties on the state.[125] It is also worth bearing in mind that the task of setting international priorities is very different to that of setting priorities within a particular legal system, where issues such as level of economic development do not arise.

For the purposes of this book, I will suggest that work should have five key characteristics, reflecting different aspects of working people's dignity: it should be free and rewarded, equal, decent, participatory and reliable.[126] Any employment rights which are central to these objectives should be given particular importance, including when it comes to enforcement and the remedies made available for breach. I will explain and justify each of the five key characteristics in turn.

[122] International Labour Conference, *Resolution on the inclusion of a safe and healthy working environment in the ILO's framework of fundamental principles and rights at work* (ILC.110/Resolution I, 16 June 2022).

[123] P Alston, '"Core Labour Standards" and the Transformation of the International Labour Rights Regime' (2004) 15 *European Journal of International Law* 457.

[124] For an excellent presentation of the counter-arguments, see J King, *Judging Social Rights* (Cambridge, CUP, 2012); Mantouvalou, above n 68.

[125] See, generally, S Fredman, *Human Rights Transformed: Positive Rights and Positive Duties* (Oxford, OUP, 2008).

[126] There is some overlap with the goals of labour law identified by Davidov, above n 67, though he is concerned with identifying the subject's goals in general terms, rather than its priorities.

Although I hope that most of my choices are uncontroversial, it does not matter if there is some disagreement. My analysis of remedies in later chapters is bound to reflect my sense of priorities, and it is important to be transparent about what these are.

First, and on a most basic level, work should be freely chosen. This is so obvious that it hardly needs explanation, and is clearly reflected in international human rights instruments affording protection against slavery, servitude, forced labour and trafficking, and in core ILO conventions.[127] As chapter four will explain, this group of rights is given high priority in English law in the sense that the Modern Slavery Act 2015 criminalises the acts of holding someone in slavery or servitude, forcing them to work or trafficking them for the purposes of exploitation. This brings to bear the condemnatory force of the state, and harsh punishments, including imprisonment, on the perpetrators.

Of course, while the basic ability to resign one's job is a fundamental safeguard against exploitation, choices about work are often heavily constrained in practice by a person's economic circumstances: the need to keep a roof over their head and put food on the table. There is a significant grey area in which work may be freely chosen in a formal sense, but so problematic in other respects that it crosses the line into exploitation. There is some criticism that the Modern Slavery Act 2015 does not criminalise labour exploitation more broadly, beyond the offences identified above.[128] From the perspective of wages, minimum wage legislation has an important role to play in determining where the line between exploitation and decent work lies and protecting working people accordingly. International instruments struggle to prioritise minimum wages for two main reasons: it is impossible to set a universal minimum, given different economic conditions in different states, however undesirable that may be, and states are often reluctant to cede any control over what may appear to them to be an important source of comparative advantage over other states with higher wages. This means that a significant concern of national labour movements is often not reflected on the world stage. However, in thinking about priorities for domestic labour law, it is appropriate to give heavy emphasis to the dignity-protecting role of the NMW. Inevitably, the NMW rate is controversial. The government, acting on advice from the Low Pay Commission, is concerned to weigh workers' interests against concerns about the potential for a high rate to generate unemployment or inflationary spirals.[129] There is also a complex interaction between minimum wages and support from the social security system.[130] Organisations such as the Living Wage Foundation

[127] ILO Forced Labour Convention, 1930 (No 29) (and its 2014 Protocol); Abolition of Forced Labour Convention, 1957 (No 105); Minimum Age Convention, 1973 (No 138); Worst Forms of Child Labour Convention, 1999 (No 182).

[128] V Mantouvalou, 'The UK Modern Slavery Act 2015 Three Years On' (2018) 81 *Modern Law Review* 1017.

[129] See eg Low Pay Commission, *National Minimum Wage: Low Pay Commission Report 2022* (January 2023, CP 758).

[130] Eg K Puttick, 'From Mini to Maxi Jobs? Low Pay, "Progression", and the Duty to Work (Harder)' (2019) 48 *Industrial Law Journal* 143.

argue that higher rates are required to ensure that workers have enough to live on and, thus, that their dignity is preserved.[131] However, controversies about the rate and other substantive details of the law can be set aside when it comes to enforcement and remedies. The importance of the NMW in upholding workers' dignity warrants strong enforcement measures.

A second priority for employment law is that working people's equality rights should be respected. Again, this is a basic aspect of dignity that hardly needs explanation or justification: protected characteristics should not be used as a basis for paying particular workers or groups of workers less than others, or for treating them badly in other respects. The ILO Declaration prioritises equality and it features strongly in many international instruments, both general and more specialised.[132] Inevitably, there are conflicts and controversies within equality law. For example, there are debates about how to provide appropriate support for pregnant workers, whilst avoiding stereotyping and encouraging the sharing of parental responsibilities.[133] There are also debates about the proper place of positive discrimination or affirmative action in combatting long-standing inequalities.[134] But these need not affect a study of remedies for breaches of the law. With the exception of harassment, equality law is generally treated as a civil rather than a criminal matter, a choice that is worth interrogating. As a result, compensation for loss is the main remedy. As chapter seven will demonstrate, while it might be expected that compensation would be calculated in the same way across all types of case, there are some respects in which the law allows for more generous compensation in discrimination cases.

A third set of requirements is that work should be safe, broadly defined. This reflects the familiar point that the working person cannot provide their labour without being present themselves, with the result that some basic standards are required to protect their health and well-being. The ILO has recently added health and safety to the list of core rights in the Declaration.[135] The most obvious manifestation of a requirement that work should be safe in English law is the series of duties placed on employers under the Health and Safety at Work etc. Act 1974, which are enforced through criminal offences.[136] This suggests that a high priority is being given to health and safety concerns though, as chapter two explained, the limited resources given to HSE to enforce the law may undermine that conclusion. Working time is a complex area of regulation with a variety of different rights

[131] https://www.livingwage.org.uk/.

[132] ILO Equal Remuneration Convention, 1951 (No 100); Discrimination (Employment and Occupation) Convention, 1958 (No 111); and see eg UN, Convention on the Elimination of All Forms of Discrimination Against Women (1979); International Convention on the Elimination of Racial Discrimination (1969), among others.

[133] S Fredman, 'Reversing Roles: Bringing Men into the Frame' (2014) 10 *International Journal of Law in Context* 442.

[134] See eg S Fredman, *Women and the Law* (Oxford, OUP, 1997), ch 9.

[135] Above n 4.

[136] Section 33.

and standards, but it is important to regard at least some of these as high-priority areas in order to protect working people's capacity to take breaks from work (since rest and leisure is a fundamental right in itself[137]) and to fulfil other obligations as family members, carers or citizens.[138] The Court of Justice treats the right to paid annual leave as a fundamental social right of workers.[139] From a remedies perspective, the main focus here is on enabling workers to receive the pay they were due, with relatively generous rules on back pay. While this has an indirect impact on workers' ability to take time off, the law could place greater emphasis on facilitating exercise of the right. Another priority area in the working time context is the limit on the number of hours that can be worked in a week, which includes both rights to daily and weekly rest breaks (which can be enforced by workers themselves through the civil law)[140] and the 48-hour maximum limit on the working week (which is enforceable through the criminal law).[141] This 'mixed' approach to enforcement is confusing and often weak in practice. As with health and safety, the use of the criminal law creates an impression of priority which may be undermined by the reality of enforcement. Where workers are able to enforce rights for themselves, it may be more effective to use replicative remedies instead of compensation to force employers to limit working time.

Fourth, working people should be empowered to protect their own interests at work through collective bargaining and action. Freedom of association is widely recognised in international human rights instruments and in the ILO Declaration, and there is now much greater recognition that freedom to associate is of limited value unless it is accompanied by rights to bargain and to strike.[142] Although the most obvious benefit of freedom of association is to give workers the option to bargain over pay and other conditions, other significant benefits include the possibility of democratising the workplace (giving workers the opportunity to voice their views on issues affecting their day-to-day lives)[143] and dealing with grievances without the need for litigation.[144] Both of these benefits can help to ensure that workers' dignity is more fully respected at work. Chapter seven will demonstrate that the law *does* prioritise freedom of association to some extent, for example, through minimum compensatory awards where a worker is dismissed on trade union grounds.[145] However, there is a missed opportunity to use replicative

[137] Universal Declaration of Human Rights, Article 24.
[138] Working Time Regulations 1998 (SI 1998/1833).
[139] Case C-151/02 *Landeshauptstadt Kiel v Jaeger* ECLI:EU:C:2003:437, [2003] ECR I-8389, [47], [66]–[71].
[140] Above n 138, regs 10, 11, 30.
[141] ibid, regs 4 and 29.
[142] ILO Freedom of Association and Protection of the Right to Organise Convention, 1948 (No 87), Right to Organise and Collective Bargaining Convention, 1949 (No 98). See also *Demir and Baykara v Turkey* (Application no 34503/97) (2009) 48 EHRR 54; *Enerji Yapi-Yol Sen v Turkey* (Application no 68959/01), 21 April 2009.
[143] Eg Davidov, above n 67, 56–57.
[144] See ch 2 of this volume.
[145] TULRCA 1992, s 156.

remedies to force employers to consult workers before taking major decisions affecting them. For example, the remedy for a failure to consult on collective redundancies is a monetary award, which I argue is vindicatory in character, whereas an injunction to stop the redundancies until the employer has carried out a proper consultation would be much more effective in securing participation rights.[146] I develop this argument more fully in chapter six.

Fifth, work should be reliable.[147] This may be particularly hard to defend as a priority, for two reasons: it is not well-recognised internationally, and it goes against the trend towards more flexible forms of work. Indeed, there may be a sense that working people who have a degree of job security are already in a position of considerable privilege. However, it is possible to counter both of these objections. The lack of international recognition for job security rights reflects, in part at least, the complexities of international negotiations. For example, an attempt by the ILO to give priority status to Convention 158[148] was blocked by the employer group, which objected to greater regulation in the area.[149] The trend towards flexibility, while undoubtedly a very strong one, driven both by employer preferences and technological advances, should be subject to questioning and challenge. The goal of most workers is to have a job that is reasonably stable, which brings in a steady income. This allows the worker to plan their life, for example, by making financial or family commitments. Although it is often said that workers value flexible working as a way of fitting work around their other obligations, it is important not to be too readily seduced by this idea.[150] Some workers do value flexibility, particularly when they have other substantial commitments in their lives and are not wholly reliant on work (such as students seeking extra income), but this is not usually the case for workers with families to support. Of course, while unfair dismissal legislation is often seen as the main mechanism for protecting job security, this may not be the only option, and there may be ways of promoting reliable work alongside a greater degree of flexibility, for example, by requiring employers to give flexible workers a set period of notice of a shift or a cancellation.[151]

Again, however, my concern here is not with the details of the substantive law, but with remedies. Where the law *does* provide working people with a degree of protection for their ongoing working relationship, this should be regarded as an important benefit, with appropriately powerful remedies provided in the event of breach. Just because not all working people enjoy this right is no reason to limit

[146] TULRCA 1992, s 189.

[147] Davidov, above n 67, 64; M Freedland and N Kountouris, *The Legal Construction of Personal Work Relations* (Oxford, OUP, 2011), 379–82.

[148] ILO, Termination of Employment Convention, 1982 (No 158).

[149] ILO, Final report of the Tripartite Meeting of Experts to Examine the Termination of Employment Convention, 1982 (No 158), and the Termination of Employment Recommendation, 1982 (No 166) (Geneva, 18–21 April 2011) TMEE/C.158-R.166/2011/2.

[150] Eg S Fredman, 'Women at Work: the Broken Promise of Flexicurity' (2004) 33 *Industrial Law Journal* 299.

[151] Eg Directive 2019/1152 on Transparent and Predictable Working Conditions, Article 10.

the remedies on offer for those who do. For example, I will argue in chapter six that the re-employment remedy in unfair dismissal law should be reformed to make it more practical and effective, to reflect the importance to employees of being able to keep their job and the limited value of compensation as an alternative. I will also challenge the obstacles to obtaining an injunction in wrongful dismissal cases, and the limits on unfair dismissal compensation.

To sum up, the core priorities of employment law should be to ensure that work is freely chosen and appropriately paid, that work is safe and healthy, that working people are treated equally, that their rights to associate are respected, and that their job security is protected. There are a number of respects in which the substantive law falls short of fully realising these goals, but my focus will be on whether they are properly reflected in the law on remedies. Of course, the priorities themselves are broadly framed, and many of the more detailed rights and duties found in employment law, particularly in legislation, can be traced back to these priorities. Indeed, one of the challenges that employment lawyers face is that their ability to move from objectives to details and back again through interpretation is carefully honed, with the result that almost any detailed obligation can be traced back to an important goal or right. However, this urge must be resisted if there is to be any chance of drawing up a sensible list of priorities for the subject. Moreover, duties not included in the subject's central goals are still important and should be properly enforced; otherwise, the law risks falling into disrepute.

IV. Conclusion

In this chapter, I have sought to set out a framework for thinking about remedies in employment law, with three elements. First, I have argued that the remedy should 'fit' the wrong done to the working person. For example, if the employer's conduct has caused loss, the remedy should be concerned with repairing that loss through an award of compensation. Although 'fit' is typically a conceptual question, I also noted that, in some cases, there is a need for political will to provide the most effective remedy for the situation. In employment law, there are a number of examples of situations in which a replicative remedy could be provided to put things right for the working person, but in practice a vindicatory or compensatory award is provided instead. I will interrogate the reasons for this elsewhere in the book. Second, I have argued that remedies in employment law should reflect what is special about employment situations. In particular, I argued that working people may suffer certain kinds of harm or loss that are less likely to be present in, for example, ordinary commercial transactions. These include harm to career plans and loss of social opportunities or standing in the community. The law sometimes reflects some of these less obvious considerations but rarely does so in a systematic way. Another employment-law-specific consideration is that there may be greater scope both to bring employers into compliance even after a breach, because employment is often a long-term relationship, and to deter breaches in the first place, because many employers take advice before making employment decisions. This set of considerations is rarely acknowledged. Third, I have argued that, when evaluating remedies in employment law, it is vital to consider whether the most effective remedies are attached to the most important rights. While it is appropriate that remedies should reflect the employer's wrongdoing or the harm done to the working person in the individual case – for example, by providing compensation to reflect losses actually suffered – the nature of the right infringed is also an important consideration. This can help to determine whether private law remedies should be replaced with, or supplemented by, criminal or civil penalties, or to decide how to pitch an award of vindicatory damages. While the law *does* broadly reflect the priorities I have identified for the subject, it does not do so in a particularly systematic way and there are flaws in the treatment of freedom of association, unfair dismissal and working time rights in particular.

4

Criminal Offences

Strictly speaking, a discussion of the criminal law does not belong in a book on remedies.[1] Prosecuting the employer for committing a criminal offence does not, in itself, provide any 'relief' to the working person harmed by the employer's wrongdoing. However, in theory at least, the decision to criminalise a particular act is the strongest possible form of condemnation society can offer, so an understanding of the role of the criminal law in the employment sphere is essential in order to gain a more complete picture of the way in which employment rights are ranked and valued.

This chapter will consider six main areas of law[2] in which there are criminal offences applicable to employers in respect of wrongs done to their workers: modern slavery, gangmasters' licensing, agency work, health and safety, the National Minimum Wage (NMW) and working time.[3] Employers may also commit offences under immigration legislation, but I have omitted these because my focus is on employers' *treatment* of their workers.[4] Immigration offences seek to co-opt employers as enforcers of the wider immigration regime. The criminal law also plays an important regulatory role in relation to working people. For example, there is extensive regulation of industrial action through the criminal law.[5] However, since my focus is on working people's rights against their employers, I will not discuss these examples here.

[1] This chapter has benefited greatly from my participation in the 'Criminality at Work' project, with many of the contributions to that project being cited in this chapter: A Bogg, J Collins, M Freedland and J Herring (eds), *Criminality at Work* (Oxford, OUP, 2020).

[2] Harassment is also a criminal offence which can be committed in an employment context, but its principal relevance to employers (unless the employer is a natural person guilty of the offence) is through damages claims based on vicarious liability: Protection from Harassment Act 1997, ss 1 and 3, and see *Majrowski v Guy's and St Thomas's NHS Trust* [2006] UKHL 34, [2006] ICR 1199.

[3] For completeness, it is worth noting that there are a number of 'supplementary' offences – such as obstructing an officer in the course of their duty – which might be committed by an employer who is under investigation by HMRC or HSE, for example. Since these are only indirectly related to the treatment of workers they will not be examined in detail here.

[4] Immigration, Asylum and Nationality Act 2006, s 21. There is also a system of civil penalties. For discussion, see A Aliverti, 'Doing the Dirty Job: Labour at the Intersections of Criminal Law and Immigration Controls', in A Bogg, J Collins, M Freedland and J Herring (eds), *Criminality at Work* (Oxford, OUP, 2020).

[5] A Bogg, KD Ewing and A Moretta, 'The Persistence of Criminal Law and Police in Collective Labour Relations', in A Bogg, J Collins, M Freedland and J Herring (eds), *Criminality at Work* (Oxford, OUP, 2020).

The first section of the chapter will consider the question of 'fit': when is criminal punishment an appropriate response to an employment law wrong? This requires engagement with the extensive literature on the justifications for criminalisation. While some employment-related offences, such as slavery or trafficking, are clearly moral wrongs (*mala in se*), others (such as operating without a gangmaster's licence) are *mala prohibita*, offences because the law designates them as such.[6] In recent years, an important strand of argument against 'over-criminalisation' has been developed by some leading criminal law scholars, which presents particular challenges for crimes in the latter group. However, there are good reasons for retaining some *mala prohibita* offences, and I argue that the concerns and values of employment law can often provide a justification for criminalising non-compliance with regulatory regimes in the field.

The second section of the chapter examines how the various criminal offences work in practice and whether they meet the particular needs of employment law as explored in chapter three. A key question is whether they are likely to have a deterrent effect on employers when considering how to behave in relation to their workers. Of course, deterrent effect is an empirical question, and some may be sceptical of its very existence, but it is possible to offer some hypotheses based on the available evidence. To the extent that a deterrent effect applies, it is likely to involve a calculus based on the sanctions involved and the social stigma attached to a conviction, set against the likelihood of prosecution. The latter obviously depends on the resources available to enforcement agencies to pursue prosecutions, but it can also be influenced by the design of the relevant offence and the ease of proving the various elements to the criminal standard. The discussion will demonstrate that levels of prosecution of employment-related offences are generally very low. This may not matter where the criminal offence sits at the apex of an effective enforcement regime which also includes civil sanctions and other measures, but this is not always the case in practice.

The third section of the chapter examines how the criminal law intersects with redress for working people affected by the employer's criminal wrongdoing. Obviously, the criminal law is not itself primarily concerned with redress, so in each case it is necessary to consider what other routes are open to affected workers for securing a remedy. In some cases, notably the NMW, the statutory regime has been designed so that redress sits comfortably alongside the criminal process, whereas in others, redress has largely been overlooked. It seems particularly problematic that some of the agencies operating in the field, notably the Gangmasters and Labour Abuse Authority (GLAA) and the Employment Agency Standards Inspectorate (EASI), do not have formal powers to secure redress for workers, even though they have been set up because workers in the relevant sectors are thought to be particularly vulnerable.

[6] A Bogg and M Freedland, 'Criminality at Work: A Framework for Discussion', in Bogg, J Collins, M Freedland and J Herring (eds), *Criminality at Work* (Oxford, OUP, 2020).

Finally, in the fourth section of the chapter, I assess whether the use of the criminal law in employment settings reflects an appropriate ranking of employment rights as against each other. The law has developed in a somewhat haphazard way over time, and it is possible that there are some equally important rights that do not attract a criminal sanction. For example, a case has been made by Mantouvalou for the blacklisting by employers of trade unionists to be made a crime,[7] and by Green for fraud offences to be used in relation to 'wage theft'.[8] I evaluate these claims and suggest avenues for reform.

I. When is the Use of the Criminal Law Appropriate?

Creating a criminal offence is the most serious step Parliament can take, so it is generally accepted that this should only be done where there is a strong justification for criminalisation as opposed to any other strategy, such as creating a civil wrong or discouraging the conduct through taxation or education.[9] Critics have expressed concern that creating new offences has become Parliament's 'go-to' approach, even when this risks duplicating other offences or undermining the deterrent effect of the criminal law.[10] Here, I examine some of the arguments about criminalisation before assessing how they apply to the various offences in the employment field.

Feinberg's version of Mill's well-known 'harm principle' is a useful starting-point for justifying the creation of a new criminal offence:[11]

> It is always a good reason in support of penal legislation that it would be effective in preventing (eliminating, reducing) harm to persons other than the actor (the one prohibited from acting) and there is no other means that is equally effective at no greater cost to other values.[12]

This places the focus on the prevention or reduction of harm, which may be done by criminalising not only acts that cause harm but also acts that create an (unjustified) risk of harm. This explains why it is appropriate to criminalise, among other

[7] V Mantouvalou, 'Human Rights, Labour Rights, and Criminal Wrongs', in A Bogg, J Collins, M Freedland and J Herring (eds), *Criminality at Work* (Oxford, OUP, 2020).

[8] S Green, 'Wage Theft as a Legal Concept', in A Bogg, J Collins, M Freedland and J Herring (eds), *Criminality at Work* (Oxford, OUP, 2020).

[9] See, generally, AP Simester et al, *Simester and Sullivan's Criminal Law: Theory and Doctrine* (6th edn, Oxford, Hart Publishing, 2016), ch 16.

[10] Some of the leading contributions to a large literature are A Ashworth, 'Is the Criminal Law a Lost Cause?' (2000) 116 *Law Quarterly Review* 225; RA Duff, *Answering for Crime* (Oxford, Hart Publishing, 2007); D Husak, *Over-Criminalization. The Limits of Criminal Law* (New York, OUP, 2008); AP Simester and A von Hirsch, *Crimes, Harms and Wrongs: On the Principles of Criminalisation* (Oxford, Hart Publishing, 2011).

[11] JM Robson (ed), *The Collected Works of JS Mill*, Vol XVIII (London, Routledge, 1977), 223.

[12] J Feinberg, *The Moral Limits of the Criminal Law: Harm to Others* (Oxford, OUP, 1984), 26.

things, attempts to commit an offence, such as murder, as well as the underlying offence itself.

The harm principle does not offer a sufficient justification on its own, though, because it is liable to be too broad and too narrow at the same time. Two additional requirements are needed. First, the harm must be wrongful: it is not justified to criminalise every harmful act.[13] For example, it is harmful to a competitor's business to outbid them for goods in short supply, or to sell goods more cheaply to their customers, but these are normal market behaviours and are not generally seen as wrongful. The harm in question must deserve the public condemnation and stigma associated with the commission of a crime. Second, as the quotation explains, it is still necessary to weigh up the advantages and disadvantages of criminalisation even in relation to clear-cut examples of wrongful harm.[14] Factors to consider include the seriousness of the harm and the likelihood of it occurring, and any positive value attaching to the harmful conduct. For example, there are many ways in which speech may harm others, but the value of freedom of expression is a strong counterweight to criminalisation outside of extreme cases, such as the incitement of hatred.[15]

From this starting-point, it is straightforward to justify criminalising the act of subjecting another person to slavery, forced labour or trafficking.[16] The harm is clear: the victim is deprived of any choice in relation to the performance of work. The harm is also wrongful: the victim is not treated with the dignity and respect due to another human being. This is further reinforced by the mental element: the slavery and trafficking offences require that the defendant knew or ought to have known that the person was being held against their will or trafficked.[17] Thus, the offences are concerned with the deliberate violation of a person's dignity. And there are obvious advantages to criminalisation: the conduct involves serious harm to the individual and the state should take every possible step to deter and discourage it. Of course, the criminalisation of forced labour and related offences is not without its critics: it is often pointed out that the 'bad apples' explanation – that forced labour occurs because of the wrongful actions of a small group of offenders – is an oversimplification.[18] The labour market structures put in place by governments can also contribute significantly to the problem. For example, the complexities of migration law can be exploited by unscrupulous employers to force workers into an irregular situation, making them more vulnerable to forced labour and less likely or able to seek help from the authorities. However, these issues are more to

[13] Simester et al, above n 9, 665.

[14] ibid 665.

[15] Public Order Act 1986, Parts 3 and 3A.

[16] Modern Slavery Act 2015, ss 1 and 2.

[17] ibid ss 1(1) and 2(4).

[18] Eg B Anderson, 'Migration, Immigration Controls and the Fashioning of Precarious Workers' (2010) 24 *Work, Employment and Society* 300; M Freedland and C Costello, 'Migrants at Work and the Division of Labour Law', in C Costello and M Freedland (eds), *Migrants at Work: Immigration and Vulnerability in Labour Law* (Oxford, OUP, 2014); Mantouvalou, above n 7.

do with how the criminal offences in this context sit within the wider enforcement landscape and with how victims are treated. They do not amount to a convincing argument of principle against having a forced labour offence.[19]

It is also possible to justify some employment-related crimes as *mala in se* even though they are closely linked to a regulatory regime. For example, while health and safety legislation contains a number of *mala prohibita* offences – breach of the duty not to charge employees for protective equipment or safety measures is a good example[20] – it is arguable that some health and safety crimes are *mala in se*.[21] It is an offence under section 33(1)(a) of the Health and Safety at Work etc. Act 1974 (HSWA) to 'fail to discharge' the general duty under section 2(1) of the Act: 'It shall be the duty of every employer to ensure, so far as is reasonably practicable, the health, safety and welfare at work of all his employees.'

Starting with the harm principle, it is not an element of the offence that an employee should have been injured by the employer's breach, though harm will often be a factor influencing the decision to prosecute.[22] However, the harm principle may also be satisfied by creating a *risk* of harm. Here, the employer's failure to take reasonable steps to protect employees' health and safety will, in most cases, create a risk that they will be harmed.[23] There is also a strong argument that the risk of harm is wrongful, for two reasons: the employer is usually much better placed than employees to ensure that working conditions are safe and healthy, and the employer derives profit from the work. Taken together, these two factors place a compelling moral obligation on the employer to ensure that it is not profiting from a dangerous situation it could reasonably have taken steps to prevent.

Although some employment-related offences are properly regarded as *mala in se*, the vast majority are *mala prohibita*, offences which would not constitute wrongful harms if the law did not designate them as such. As a result, they cannot be justified using the framework set out above. Commentators concerned with the problem of 'overcriminalisation' are exercised by the proliferation of these offences,[24] and the Law Commission has produced an important report exploring how they might be streamlined and systematised.[25] However, from an employment law perspective, at least some of the *mala prohibita* offences in the field can be seen as valuable tools to enforce important regulatory regimes intended to protect the rights of vulnerable workers. Duff, an eminent criminal lawyer, has argued that these types of offence may be justified where the regulatory regime in question pursues the common good and where it would be a public wrong to

[19] Bogg and Freedland, above n 6, 12–13.

[20] Health and Safety at Work etc. Act 1974, ss 9 and 33.

[21] Bogg and Freedland, above n 6, 9.

[22] HSE, Enforcement Policy Statement (October 2015), 10.

[23] Law Commission, *Criminal Liability in Regulatory Contexts* (Consultation Paper No 195, 2010), paras 4.33–4.34.

[24] See the works cited in n 10, above.

[25] Above n 23.

breach the requirements of the regulatory regime.[26] I turn now to consider this approach in relation to offences concerning the NMW, gangmasters' licensing and agency work.

Deliberate non-payment of the NMW is an offence under section 31(1) of the 1998 Act:

> If the employer of a worker who qualifies for the national minimum wage refuses or wilfully neglects to remunerate the worker for any pay of reference period at a rate which is at least equal to the national minimum wage, that employer is guilty of an offence.

Although non-payment of the NMW causes harm to the affected workers, it is difficult to argue that this harm would exist in the absence of a statute specifying what constitutes an acceptable minimum level of pay.[27] Applying Duff's approach, though, the offence is relatively easy to justify. The NMW legislation pursues the public good by requiring employers to remunerate their workers at what society regards as a decent rate. Not every instance of non-compliance with the regulatory regime warrants criminal punishment. The NMW (despite the government's efforts to make it straightforward) is complex and, in some situations, the employer may accidentally miscalculate the worker's entitlement. Civil penalties apply in these cases. However, the offence is to 'refuse or wilfully neglect' to pay the wage due, and it is this deliberate refusal to comply with the regime that requires the intervention of the criminal law.[28] It is confined to extreme cases in which the employer has chosen to disregard both the applicable law and the dignity of its workers.

A more obviously 'regulatory' offence is the strict liability offence under section 12(1) Gangmasters (Licensing) Act 2004 of providing labour in a regulated sector (acting as a 'gangmaster') without holding a licence under section 6. This tackles two situations: someone operating in the sector in disregard of the regulatory regime, and someone whose licence has been removed for breaches (a sanction in itself) but who continues to operate in defiance of the law. The harm principle is not satisfied in the normal way by these offences: there is no harm or risk of harm *inherent* in operating as a gangmaster without a licence, and indeed a person could conceivably be running their business in a fair and proper way.[29] Not having a licence is a sign that the gangmaster does not care about the law, which does not bode well for the workers' wellbeing, but workers are only harmed or put at risk of harm by other independent acts of the gangmaster, such as withholding pay or using unsafe transport.

Again, though, it is possible to justify this offence using Duff's approach.[30] There is a strong case for saying that agricultural workers work in circumstances

[26] See A Duff, *The Realm of the Criminal Law* (Oxford, OUP, 2018), 313–22.

[27] There might be a general sense that very low wages are inappropriate, but requiring someone to work for little or no pay may constitute a forced labour offence.

[28] See Law Commission, above n 23, paras 4.41–4.61.

[29] ibid, para 4.35.

[30] Above n 26.

of particular vulnerability, and that it is therefore justified for Parliament to put in place a licensing system to protect them.[31] Agricultural workers are typically short-term seasonal migrants who are reliant on employers for accommodation as well as work, and therefore face particular difficulties in enforcing their rights through the tribunal. Anyone who is prepared to operate as a labour provider in the sector in disregard of the licensing system is creating a risk of harm to those workers in a broader sense by ignoring the legislation that is intended to protect them. The work of the GLAA in running the licensing regime would, arguably, be much harder if the worst that could happen to a non-compliant operator was a civil penalty, which could be seen as no more than a tax on doing business.

However, there are some offences in employment settings that are open to debate. One example is breach of the regulations governing the proper conduct of an employment agency under section 5 Employment Agencies Act 1973. The regulations in question cover a wide variety of different infringements, including failing to agree terms with a work-seeker, failing to vet the work-seeker, withholding pay without justification, and subjecting a worker to detriment for accepting a permanent contract with the end user.[32] But while these are all important elements of protection for agency workers, who are often vulnerable, they are no different to other 'ordinary' employment rights, breaches of which are seen as private wrongs to be tackled through litigation by the affected individuals, rather than public wrongs with which the state should be concerned. There are obvious parallels with the gangmasters' licensing regime (and indeed, agencies themselves were subject to a requirement to hold a licence until this was repealed[33]), but there is an important moral difference between breaching some aspect of a detailed set of employment regulations and ignoring or defying a whole regulatory regime. In practice, prosecutions for offences under the 1973 Act are extremely rare, because EASI is under-resourced, and it is unlikely that a trivial infringement would be pursued, but it would be preferable for the law to contain more clearly focused offences. Indeed, the Act itself already provides for the possibility of a prohibition order to stop a person who has breached the Regulations from running an agency for a period of time,[34] and it is obviously appropriate that there is an offence, under section 3B, of running an agency in breach of a prohibition order.

One response to this discussion might be to say that it is overly influenced by the concerns of criminal law theory. The idea of 'overcriminalisation' is focused on preserving the liberty and autonomy of individuals, and on ensuring that what is criminalised in law is largely confined to what the ordinary person in the street would regard as morally wrong.[35] Different considerations operate in the

[31] ACL Davies, 'Migrant Workers in Agriculture: A Legal Perspective', in Costello and Freedland (eds), *Migrants at Work: Immigration and Vulnerability in Labour Law* (Oxford, OUP, 2014).

[32] Conduct of Employment Agencies and Employment Businesses Regulations 2003 (SI 2003/3319).

[33] Employment Agencies Act 1973, ss 1–3, as originally enacted, repealed by the Deregulation and Contracting Out Act 1994.

[34] Employment Agencies Act 1973, s 3A.

[35] See the works cited in n 10 above.

employment law context.[36] Employers are in a position of power vis-à-vis their workers, and their exercises of power need to be regulated in various ways. They can also be expected to find out what rules are applicable to the particular activity of employing people and to comply with them. From an employment law perspective, it may seem entirely appropriate to harness the full force of the criminal law to deter bad behaviour and to punish it when it occurs. However, there are two reasons for being cautious about pressing this argument too far. One is the concern that if the criminal law is invoked too regularly in employment settings it will lose its impact. Employers will be able to present offences as 'technical' infringements for which a fine is paid, rather than as serious moral wrongs deserving society's condemnation. This is reinforced by a second, more practical consideration: while the creation of a criminal offence in legislation may suggest that a problem is being taken seriously, that offence will only have an effect on behaviour if there is a reasonable chance of its being enforced. As the next section will show, lack of enforcement is a significant problem for many of the offences already applicable in employment settings.

II. Offences and the Prospects for Deterrence

In this section, I set myself the difficult task of assessing the various employment-related offences for their capacity to deter employers from behaving in the ways they prohibit. A full answer to this question would require detailed empirical research, to investigate employers' awareness of the applicable criminal offences, their use of legal advice in decision-making, and their calculus about the risks and rewards of particular courses of action. Findings would no doubt vary according to factors such as the size of the employing entity and the sector in which it operated. It is also important to acknowledge that the deterrent effect might be limited or non-existent in some, or even many, cases. However, deterrence factors are worth considering. In chapter three, I argued that one of the distinctive characteristics of employment law is that employers often make decisions in a considered way, after taking legal or other advice. This opens up some space in which the law might perform a deterrent function. And if it is obvious, even on limited evidence, that a particular offence is unlikely to have much of a deterrent effect, that suggests that the use of the offence should be reconsidered.

In simple terms, deterrence can be thought about as a function of the penalty (and the associated stigma of a criminal conviction) and the chance of being caught and prosecuted. Most employment-related offences attract fines, though

[36] For a thought-provoking alternative account, see GR Sullivan, 'Workplace Welfare and State Coercion', in A Bogg, J Collins, M Freedland and J Herring (eds), *Criminality at Work* (Oxford, OUP, 2020).

there are examples of custodial sentences, for example, for slavery and trafficking offences.[37] The stigma attaching to a custodial sentence is obviously much higher, and there is always a risk that fines could be seen by employers as a 'cost of doing business' rather than as a serious criminal punishment, despite the accompanying conviction. This latter problem is particularly likely to arise where the offence itself is *mala prohibita* – part of a regulatory regime – rather than *mala in se*. For example, it is not clear that a fine for deliberate non-payment of the minimum wage adds much to the overall regime, which also includes civil penalties.

One obvious issue with punishment and stigma in the employment context is that, although employers are often spoken about as if they are real human beings, in practice, most people are employed by a legal entity. As a result, what is at stake for the 'employer' in criminal proceedings is damage to the firm's reputation and the financial cost of any fines rather than personal stigma or harsh treatment of an individual. Some legislation addresses this by providing for the prosecution of directors or others who have been responsible for the commission of an offence by the legal entity, as well as the entity itself.[38] The classic formula is found in section 37(1) HSWA:

> Where an offence under any of the relevant statutory provisions committed by a body corporate is proved to have been committed with the consent or connivance of, or to have been attributable to any neglect on the part of, any director, manager, secretary or other similar officer of the body corporate or a person who was purporting to act in any such capacity, he as well as the body corporate shall be guilty of that offence and shall be liable to be proceeded against and punished accordingly.

According to the House of Lords in *R v Chargot*, the officer's 'consent or connivance' is easier to establish 'if the circumstances under which the risk arose were under the direction or control of the officer. The more remote his area of responsibility is from those circumstances, the harder it will be to draw that inference.'[39] Thus, individuals may also be at risk of criminal prosecution, which is liable to increase the deterrent effect.

Of course, sanctions themselves are insufficient to generate a deterrent effect if those subject to the law deem it unlikely that their wrongdoing will be identified or punished. It is therefore helpful to review the statistics on prosecution levels, where available, to get some sense of how often different types of employment-related crime are prosecuted. Interpreting the statistics is not without its challenges. The right level of prosecution to achieve a deterrent effect – given that the extent of any given type of offending is unknown and not every offender can be prosecuted – is impossible to specify. Regulatory agencies, in particular, often rely

[37] For simplicity, I focus on maximum sentences, though of course only the most serious offenders will receive the maximum. Further research would be required to analyse sentences actually handed down.

[38] Gangmasters (Licensing) Act 2004, s 20; Employment Agencies Act 1973, s 11; National Minimum Wage Act 1998, s 32; Working Time Regulations 1998 (SI 1998/1833), reg 29B.

[39] *R v Chargot Ltd (t/a Contract Services)* [2008] UKHL 73, [2009] ICR 263, [34].

on the argument that prosecution should be seen as a last resort when other, less serious, forms of intervention have failed. This has a sound basis in regulatory theory, which proposes an 'enforcement pyramid': using educational or persuasive techniques for non-compliant but well-meaning firms, warnings and civil sanctions for those who need more pressure, and prosecution for those who refuse to comply or engage with the regulator.[40] However, the 'last resort' argument can also be used to explain away very low levels of prosecution when the reality is that the agency has insufficient resources to do its job.[41] Thus, a low level of prosecution is not necessarily a problem, but it is a sign that further investigation is required. This is particularly so when combined with evidence that a regulator's resources are limited (relative to the size of the labour market) or have been cut.

A further factor in decisions to prosecute is the ease of proving the offence to the criminal standard. Most regulators follow a similar approach to that found in the Code for Crown Prosecutors, which requires there to be a 'reasonable prospect of conviction' and that it be in the public interest for the prosecution to go ahead.[42] While the chances of securing a conviction turn partly on the available evidence, another important factor is the definition of the offence itself and any applicable defences. For example, the offence of operating as an unlicensed gangmaster is relatively easy to prove, given that it is a strict liability offence with no mental element, whereas corporate manslaughter is notoriously difficult to establish because of the need to show the involvement of 'senior management'. However, the picture is not straightforward because there is sometimes a suggestion that strict liability offences are more 'regulatory' in nature and less worthy of the stigma attaching to so-called 'real' crimes. Without the need to prove a mental element, the public impact of the conviction may be reduced.

The remainder of this section explores the main offences relating to employment with these themes in mind. It necessarily involves brief coverage of each offence, and the reader is referred to specialist works for more detail. But it is helpful to see all the offences together because a pattern emerges of relatively low levels of prosecution, with a strong preference for other methods of enforcement where available. This raises several questions and concerns about the role of these offences to which I return in the conclusion.

A. Slavery and Trafficking

The Modern Slavery Act 2015 contains two principal offences, one dealing with slavery, servitude and forced or compulsory labour, and the other dealing with

[40] I Ayres and J Braithwaite, *Responsive Regulation: Transcending the Deregulation Debate* (Oxford, OUP, 1992).

[41] See eg ACL Davies and L Rodgers, 'Towards a More Effective Health and Safety Regime for UK Workplaces Post COVID-19' (2023) 52 *Industrial Law Journal* 665; M Ford, 'The Criminalization of Health and Safety at Work' in A Bogg, J Collins, M Freedland and J Herring (eds), *Criminality at Work* (Oxford, OUP, 2020), 430.

[42] Crown Prosecution Service, *The Code for Crown Prosecutors* (October 2018).

trafficking.[43] The Act was an attempt to consolidate older offences, to bring them into line with applicable international standards, including the Palermo Protocol,[44] ILO,[45] ECHR[46] and EU[47] norms, and to increase the applicable penalties.

The offence under section 1 is knowingly[48] holding 'another person in slavery or servitude' or knowingly requiring 'another person to perform forced or compulsory labour'. It is expressly provided in section 1(2) that these terms are to be construed in accordance with Article 4 ECHR prohibiting slavery and forced labour. This means that there is potential for the meaning of the offence to develop over time as the ECtHR's interpretation of Article 4 – which itself relies on a variety of other instruments, including ILO materials – evolves,[49] though a disadvantage (particularly acute in the context of the criminal law) is the uncertainty that this may generate.[50] According to the Court's decision in *Siliadin*, slavery is to be construed relatively narrowly, with the emphasis on ownership, and servitude is treated as closely linked to slavery, with a focus on coercion.[51] Forced labour is defined by the ILO as 'all work or service which is exacted from any person under the menace of any penalty and for which the said person has not offered himself voluntarily'.[52] In *Rantsev*, the ECtHR held that: 'For forced or compulsory labour to arise … there must be some physical or mental constraint, as well as some overriding of the person's will'.[53] In relation to all three possibilities, the trial court is required to have regard to all the circumstances, including any vulnerability on the part of the individual (such as age or illness). Under section 1(5), the offence may still be committed where the person has consented to the defendant's actions, effectively creating a presumption that any purported consent is not genuine.

In practice, a key interpretive challenge is to draw a boundary around the criminal offence of subjecting someone to 'forced or compulsory labour'. This offence clearly extends beyond obvious forms of coercion, such as physical violence. The

[43] For helpful overviews, see J Fudge, 'Why Labour Lawyers Should Care about the Modern Slavery Act 2015' (2018) 29 *King's Law Journal* 377; V Mantouvalou, 'The UK Modern Slavery Act 2015 Three Years On' (2018) 81 *Modern Law Review* 1017.

[44] UN Protocol to Prevent, Suppress and Punish Trafficking in Persons Especially Women and Children, supplementing the United Nations Convention against Transnational Organized Crime (November 2000), General Assembly Resolution 55/25 of 15 November 2000.

[45] ILO Convention No. 29, Forced Labour Convention (1930); No. 105, Abolition of Forced Labour Convention (1957).

[46] Article 4, on which see ECHR, *Guide on Article 4 of the European Convention on Human Rights* (August 2022).

[47] Directive 2011/36/EU on preventing and combating trafficking in human beings and protecting its victims, [2011] OJ L 101/1.

[48] This includes situations in which the defendant ought to have known.

[49] *Siliadin v France* (Application no 73316/01) (2006) 43 EHRR 16, [115]–[121].

[50] Mantouvalou, above n 43, 1024–25.

[51] Above n 49, [122]–[124].

[52] ILO Convention No. 29, Forced Labour Convention (1930), Art 2(1).

[53] *Rantsev v Cyprus and Russia* (Application no 25965/04) (2010) 51 EHRR 1, [276].

courts may also take into account work performed in circumstances of 'exploitation' as defined in section 3. Under section 3(5), this includes the use of 'force, threats or deception designed to induce' the person to perform work. For example, in *Siliadin*, threats and deception were used to force the young victim to work: she was initially promised that she would be educated and her immigration status regularised, and later left at risk of the exposure of her (still irregular) immigration status to the authorities.[54] However, both the ECtHR and the UK courts have been clear that not all kinds of exploitative working practices, such as long hours or very low pay, are sufficient to constitute unfree labour. For example, in *Tibet Mentes v Turkey*, the claimants had signed contracts requiring them to perform 24-hour shifts, and were threatened with dismissal if they refused, but the Court held that they had consented to the hours and that the threat of dismissal did not amount to a 'penalty' within the meaning of Article 4.[55] Similarly, in *Rooney*, the Court of Appeal noted that exploitative working conditions such as low pay or breaches of health and safety law were not sufficient to constitute the offence.[56] Rather, the central question was whether the alleged victim 'had offered himself voluntarily for [the] work'.[57]

The trafficking offence under section 2(1) is committed 'if the person arranges or facilitates the travel of another person ("V") with a view to V being exploited'. Under section 2(4), this last phrase is satisfied where the person committing the offence intends to exploit V or where that person 'knows or ought to know that another person is likely to exploit V'. Exploitation is further defined in section 3 to include anything that amounts to an offence under section 1, and exploitative work within section 3(5) as noted above.[58] The offence must have a connection to the UK where the defendant is not a UK national,[59] but may be committed by a UK national in respect of trafficking anywhere in the world.[60] Although most trafficking *does* involve crossing national borders, it is important to note that the offence may be committed where a person is trafficked wholly within the UK, a point clarified by section 2(5)(c).

The maximum sentence for the sections 1 and 2 offences is life imprisonment on conviction on indictment, and 12 months' imprisonment or a fine or both on summary conviction.[61] A person who commits a second offence under section 1 must receive a life sentence, under the Sentencing Act 2020.[62] The offences are to

[54] Above n 49.

[55] *Tibet Mentes v Turkey* (Application nos 57818/10, 57822/10, 57825/10, 57827/10 and 57829/10) (2018) 67 EHRR 13.

[56] *R v Rooney* [2019] EWCA Crim 681, [2019] 4 WLR 89, [56].

[57] ibid [54].

[58] The offence also addresses non-work-related wrongs such as organ harvesting, which are not discussed here.

[59] Modern Slavery Act 2015, s 2(7).

[60] Section 2(6).

[61] Section 5(1).

[62] Sentencing Act 2020, Schedule 15, para 1.

be treated as 'very serious crime' and long sentences are appropriate even where there is no serious physical violence involved.[63]

It is important to note that Article 4 ECHR imposes a number of positive obligations on signatory states to investigate and prosecute slavery and related offences.[64] Thus, from the perspective of compliance with the Convention, appropriately-drafted offences with severe penalties are insufficient unless they are properly enforced. This has proved to be much more of a challenge for the authorities, as a number of reports have found. For example, the Independent Anti-Slavery Commissioner has raised concerns about the low level of prosecutions under the 2015 Act and related offences. In 2020–21, there were 451 prosecutions in respect of the principal offences in the Act,[65] against a background of over 12,000 referrals for support (explained below).[66] The pandemic may have affected these figures, both because of the greater difficulty of detecting modern slavery offences during periods of lockdown, and because of the backlog of criminal cases before the courts. However, the Commissioner has suggested various steps that might help to increase the level of prosecutions, such as investigation by specialist officers, better support for victims within the criminal justice system, and greater emphasis on gathering a variety of different types of evidence (not just victim testimonies) to bolster the prosecution case.[67]

International law also places positive obligations on the state to ensure that victims are provided with appropriate protection and support.[68] This aspect of the 2015 Act and the wider context in which it operates have been strongly criticised by commentators, not least because it risks undermining victims' willingness to come forward and to seek help from the authorities.[69] Once a victim receives the final determination that they have been enslaved or trafficked, known as the 'conclusive grounds decision', the financial and practical support available through the National Referral Mechanism (NRM), known as 'move on support', ceases after 45 days.[70] The victim may be entitled to other forms of state assistance, for example, through the benefits system, but this is complex to navigate. A further, related problem is that many victims are not UK nationals and do not have the right to remain in the UK. While they may be given temporary leave to remain in the UK for the purposes of assisting a criminal investigation or prosecution, seeking compensation or recovering from physical or psychological harm, even this is not automatic, so victims often find that they are liable to be deported (and potentially

[63] *R v Bariana* [2021] EWCA Crim 967, [19]. See also Sentencing Council, *Sentencing Guidelines: Modern Slavery* (October 2021).

[64] The leading case is *Rantsev*, above n 53.

[65] Independent Anti-Slavery Commissioner, *Annual Report 2021–2022*, 28. https://www.antislaverycommissioner.co.uk/media/1796/iasc-annual-report-2021-2022.pdf.

[66] ibid 12. For obvious reasons, it is difficult to assess the full extent of the problem.

[67] ibid ch 2.

[68] Council of Europe Convention on Action Against Trafficking in Human Beings (2005).

[69] Fudge, above n 43, Mantouvalou, above n 43.

[70] Home Office, *Modern Slavery: Statutory Guidance for England and Wales and non-Statutory Guidance for Scotland and Northern Ireland* (30 January 2023), para 8.27.

ineligible for various kinds of state assistance pending deportation).[71] This can have the effect of putting them back into a position where they are vulnerable to being 're-trafficked'. Once the Illegal Migration Act 2023 comes into force, a person who is in receipt of a 'positive reasonable grounds' decision that they may be a victim of modern slavery, but has entered the UK illegally as defined in that Act,[72] will no longer be eligible for support during the recovery period and will only exceptionally be granted temporary leave to remain, thus making the position considerably worse.[73]

The slavery and trafficking offences are, in themselves, relatively well-designed and attract suitably severe penalties. The problems with them are two-fold. First, there has not been enough effort to investigate and prosecute these offences. This means that any deterrent effect generated by the penalties is instantly undermined by the fact that people engaged in these abhorrent practices are unlikely to be caught or convicted. Second, the statutory scheme neglects the situation of victims, who may find it difficult (in the case of victims who are also migrants) to avoid a cycle of deportation and repeated trafficking. These two problems are, arguably, connected, in the sense that investigation and prosecution of perpetrators usually require the co-operation of victims, but this is unlikely where they are afraid of the consequences of coming forward. As commentators have argued, the government's strong focus on immigration control in this context may be getting in the way of providing effective solutions.[74]

B. Gangmasters' Licensing

The legislation on gangmasters is intended to ensure that labour providers in the agriculture, shellfish and food processing industries comply with a set of detailed worker-protective standards.[75] It does this by requiring labour providers to hold a licence issued by the Gangmasters and Labour Abuse Authority (GLAA).[76] Importantly, the principal sanction for a gangmaster who does not comply with the relevant standards is refusal or revocation of the licence.[77] The criminal offences in this area play a secondary, reinforcing function.

The principal offence under the Gangmasters (Licensing) Act 2004, section 12(1) is to act as a gangmaster without holding a licence. This is a strict liability offence.

[71] With effect from 30 January 2023, the relevant regime is found in s 65 Nationality and Borders Act 2022 and Immigration Rules, Appendix, Temporary Permission to Stay for Victims of Human Trafficking or Slavery.

[72] Illegal Migration Act 2023, s 2.

[73] ibid ss 22–29.

[74] Fudge, above n 43; Mantouvalou, above n 43.

[75] Gangmasters (Licensing Conditions) Rules 2009 (SI 2009/307); GLAA, *Licensing Standards* (October 2018). https://www.gla.gov.uk/media/9590/licensing-standards-october-2018-final-reprint-jan-2020-v22023.pdf.

[76] Gangmasters (Licensing) Act 2004, s 6.

[77] Or granting it subject to additional conditions.

It is also an offence under section 12(2) to possess a document knowing or believing it to be 'false' or 'improperly obtained', or belonging to someone else, 'with the intention of inducing another person to believe' that the individual in question is a licensed gangmaster. On conviction on indictment for a section 12 offence, the individual may be imprisoned for up to 10 years, or fined, or both.[78] The intention behind these penalties is clearly to deter labour providers from operating outside the regulatory regime.[79] The licensing system is further reinforced by virtue of section 13, which makes it an offence to enter into an arrangement to obtain workers from an unlicensed gangmaster. It is a defence for the end user to show that it took reasonable steps to satisfy itself that the gangmaster had a valid licence. The intention is to encourage end users to check gangmasters' licences as a way of making it difficult for unlicensed gangmasters to remain in business. This offence carries a maximum sentence of 51 weeks' imprisonment or a fine, or both.[80]

Of course, levels of investigation and prosecution are also crucial to securing any potential deterrent effect. Successful prosecutions under the Act are very rare: there was one conviction under section 12 in 2021–22, none in 2020–21 and eight in 2019–20.[81] The last conviction under section 13 was in 2013–14.[82] Given that these offences perform a reinforcing role, the number of licence refusals and revocations may be a more relevant statistic: the most recent figures are 12 refusals and two revocations in the year to March 2022, and six refusals and 17 revocations in the year to March 2021.[83] The GLAA has also made modest use of the power to seek a Labour Market Enforcement Undertaking (LMEU), typically to restrain a person from attempting to supply workers without a licence.[84] These are ultimately backed up by criminal penalties. All these figures should be set against a background of just over 1,000 active licences at any given time.[85] One possible explanation for these relatively low figures is that the GLAA's remit has been expanded without any significant corresponding increase in its funding, making it difficult for the organisation to juggle its competing responsibilities.[86]

[78] Gangmasters (Licensing) Act 2004, s 12(4), and see s 12(3) for summary conviction.

[79] Note that the GLAA can also use Labour Market Enforcement Undertakings (LMEUs) and Labour Market Enforcement Orders (LMEOs) under the Immigration Act 2016, which are backed by criminal offences.

[80] Gangmasters (Licensing) Act 2004, s 13(4).

[81] https://www.gla.gov.uk/our-impact/conviction-totals/.

[82] ibid.

[83] Gangmasters and Labour Abuse Authority, *Annual Report and Accounts 1 April 2021 to 31 March 2022* (HC 915 2022), 83. https://www.gla.gov.uk/media/8947/glaa-annual-report-and-accounts-2021-22-web-version.pdf. For a longer time series, see https://www.gla.gov.uk/our-impact/revocations-results/.

[84] The regime is contained in Immigration Act 2016, ss 14–30. For examples, see GLAA Press Release, 'New labour market powers used in consecutive months in Shropshire', 24 January 2019, available at: https://www.gla.gov.uk/whats-new/press-release-archive/24012019-new-labour-market-powers-used-in-consecutive-months-in-shropshire/.

[85] Above n 83, 83.

[86] E Guild and AM Barylska, 'Decent Work for Migrants? Examining the Impacts of the UK Frameworks of Gangmasters Legislation and Modern Slavery on Working Standards for Irregularly Present Migrants' (2021) 1 *Global Public Policy and Governance* 279.

Concern that the GLAA may not be sufficiently active (or may not have sufficient capacity) is reinforced by evidence of the problems faced by migrant agricultural workers in particular. A recent Home Office-led investigation found that many workers brought into the UK on a temporary seasonal work scheme were subjected to serious abuse and ill-treatment at work, even though the scheme itself was a pilot being closely monitored by the authorities.[87]

The gangmasters' licensing regime is not without its strengths, the most important of which is its potential to secure compliance with a wide range of worker-protective standards for a particularly vulnerable group of workers. Indeed, some commentators have called for it to be extended to other sectors in which similar vulnerabilities exist, such as construction, care and hospitality.[88] However, even taking into account the secondary position of section 12 offences in the system, the level of prosecution remains low.

C. National Minimum Wage

I explained above that it is an offence to refuse or wilfully neglect to pay the NMW under section 31(1) of the 1998 Act. Somewhat confusingly, given the mental element, there is a defence in section 31(8):

> it shall be a defence for the person charged to prove that he exercised all due diligence and took all reasonable precautions to secure that the provisions of this Act, and of any relevant regulations made under it, were complied with by himself and by any person under his control.

It is difficult to understand how a person could simultaneously refuse to pay the NMW and exercise 'all due diligence', and it seems likely in practice that this defence is more relevant to the record-keeping offence under section 31(2), to which it also applies. The offence attracts a fine.[89]

Government data from 2023 indicates that, since 2007, 18 employers have been convicted of this offence.[90] This number is obviously tiny relative to the size of the economy and the estimated size of the problem of underpayment.[91] However, the criminal offence does at least sit at the top of a comprehensive enforcement regime.[92] Where HMRC successfully pursues an employer for arrears, a penalty is

[87] ACL Davies, 'Problems Continue in the Horticulture Sector: the Seasonal Workers Pilot Review 2019' (2022) 51 *Industrial Law Journal* 494.

[88] K Poinasamy and A Bance, *Turning the Tide: How Best to Protect Workers Employed by Gangmasters, Five Years after Morecambe Bay* (Oxfam 2009), available at: https://policy-practice.oxfam.org/resources/turning-the-tide-how-best-to-protect-workers-employed-by-gangmasters-five-years-114054/.

[89] National Minimum Wage Act, s 31(9).

[90] Department for Business and Trade, *National Living Wage and National Minimum Wage Government evidence on enforcement and compliance 2021/2022* (April 2023), 15.

[91] Low Pay Commission, *Compliance and Enforcement of the National Minimum Wage* (September 2023).

[92] Civil penalties are explored in more detail in the next chapter.

also payable to the Secretary of State. 696 penalties were issued to non-compliant employers in 2021–22 and 575 in 2020–21.[93] HMRC also has the power to issue LMEUs in respect of serious or persistent breaches, which are backed up by criminal sanctions. This option was used in 40 cases in 2021–22.[94] These provide 'escalating' enforcement options, leaving prosecution as the last resort for the most serious cases. This is confirmed by the applicable enforcement policy, which indicates that prosecution is more likely where the employer has failed to comply in the long term or where there is evidence that the employer has committed other criminal offences, such as slavery or trafficking.[95]

The NMW offers a good example of how a criminal offence can be a useful element in employment law where it forms part of a carefully-thought-out and comprehensive enforcement regime. The legislation provides for civil penalties to fill the gap between 'mere' employment breaches and the criminal offence. Although, as chapter five will explain, civil penalties are not without their problems, they do help to overcome the issue that a purely criminal approach can sometimes seem too harsh for the circumstances, with the result that no legal action is taken at all. But the legislation also retains the possibility of prosecution for offenders who do not respond to other measures and as a general deterrent to non-compliance. The only significant element of concern is whether the prospect of a fine (albeit with no maximum limit) is a sufficient deterrent. By contrast, the maximum sentence for theft is seven years' imprisonment.[96]

D. Agency Work

The Employment Agencies Act 1973 contains three principal criminal offences: breach of the regulations governing the proper conduct of employment agencies, charging a working person for the use of the agency's services, and running an employment agency in breach of a prohibition order. All three are punishable by a fine. It is worth noting that the Act, as originally passed, created a licensing regime, and it was a criminal offence to run an agency without having a licence in place. This regime was repealed in 1995.

Section 5(1) of the 1973 Act empowers the Secretary of State to make regulations 'to secure the proper conduct of employment agencies and employment businesses and to protect the interests of persons availing themselves of the services of such agencies and businesses'. The current Regulations are the Conduct of Employment Agencies and Employment Businesses Regulations 2003.[97] Under section 5(2), 'any person who contravenes or fails to comply with any regulation

[93] Above n 90, 14.
[94] ibid 15.
[95] Department for Business and Trade and HMRC, *National Minimum Wage: Policy on Enforcement, Prosecutions and Naming Employers who Break National Minimum Wage Law* (June 2022), para 4.2.
[96] See, generally, Sentencing Council, *Theft Offences: Definitive Guideline* (2016).
[97] SI 2003/3319.

made under this section shall be guilty of an offence'. This is a strict liability offence and covers a wide range of different obligations set out in the Regulations. Examples include failing to agree terms with a work-seeker, failing to vet the work-seeker, withholding pay without justification, supplying workers to do the work of people who are on strike, and subjecting a worker to detriment for accepting a permanent contract with the end user. In practice, there is little danger of over-zealous prosecution under this provision because the enforcement authority, currently the Employment Agency Standards Inspectorate (EASI), has very limited resources.[98] However, it seems inherent in the design of this offence that great reliance is placed on prosecutorial discretion to ensure that the provision operates fairly in practice.

Under section 6 of the 1973 Act, it is an offence to 'request or directly or indirectly receive' a fee for finding someone work. This is subject to a (controversial) exception in regulation 26 of the Regulations for agencies finding work for people in the entertainment industry, as models or in professional sport. The Regulations also supply further detail, for example, in regulation 5, which prohibits an agency or employment business from making the supply of work-finding services (for which no fee can be demanded under section 6) conditional on the use of other services provided by the agency or business for which a fee can be charged, such as help with CV-writing. This aims to close off an obvious route for evading section 6.

Under section 3A, an employment tribunal may make a 'prohibition order' barring a natural or legal person or a partnership from carrying on an employment agency or business altogether, or a specified type of agency or business, or may make the person's involvement subject to conditions. The prohibition order can last for up to 10 years. The tribunal must be satisfied that 'on account of his misconduct or for any other sufficient reason, [the person is] unsuitable to do what the order prohibits'. Where the order is based (as it typically will be) on evidence that the person has been involved in running an employment agency or business improperly in the past, under section 3A(7) the person 'shall be deemed to have been responsible for what happened unless he can show that it happened without his connivance or consent and was not attributable to any neglect on his part'. It is a criminal offence under section 3B to fail to comply with a prohibition order 'without reasonable excuse'. This qualifier is not present in other offences under the Act and its inclusion here seems slightly odd since it is difficult to imagine what might constitute a 'reasonable excuse' in this context, though it is possible that there may be some scope for interpretive misunderstandings where the prohibition order does not take the form of an outright ban.

In 2020–21, the total number of complaints received by EASI was 1,827, leading to 147 warning letters being issued and five prosecutions.[99] It is clear from

[98] Employment Agency Standards Inspectorate, *Annual Report 2020–2021* (June 2022), 7.
[99] ibid 10–11.

EASI's annual reports that prosecutions and prohibitions are a relatively small part of its role because of the difficulty of securing sufficient evidence to meet the threshold set by the Crown Prosecution Service to bring a prosecution. At the time of writing, four individuals are subject to prohibition orders.

In the previous section, I questioned whether there was any need for criminal offences in the context of agency work, other than to enforce prohibition orders. Here, I focus on deterrence. It seems unlikely that the offences under the 1973 Act constitute an effective deterrent, because levels of prosecution are so low. Even if those levels could be increased, there would be a problem about stigma: where an offence is insufficiently targeted at serious wrongdoing, there is a risk that criminalising it does not have the desired effect of condemning and stigmatising the behaviour. This is because the offence may come to be seen as a crime that is 'administrative' or not 'real' in character.[100] If there is a desire to continue with specific regulation of employment agencies – an issue which is beyond the scope of this chapter – it might be preferable to re-introduce a licensing regime, and to reserve the criminal offences for unlicensed operators.

E. Health and Safety

Health and safety is a highly complex, specialised area of law. The principal Act is the Health and Safety at Work etc. Act 1974, but there are numerous regulations made under the Act, and other important pieces of legislation governing hazardous substances and other topics.[101] The principal regulator is the Health and Safety Executive (HSE), though local authorities have responsibility for certain sectors, including retail, offices, hotels and hospitality.[102] There are also some specialist regulators, for example, for nuclear installations. It is possible only to give the briefest of overviews here.[103]

The 1974 Act, section 33(1), creates the main health and safety offences:

> (1) It is an offence for a person—
>
> (a) to fail to discharge a duty to which he is subject by virtue of sections 2 to 7;
>
> (b) to contravene section 8 or 9;
>
> (c) to contravene any health and safety regulations or any requirement or prohibition imposed under any such regulations …

The content of the offences thus created obviously turns on the precise drafting of the duties, requirements or prohibitions they contain. In broad terms, the offences

[100] For discussion of this phenomenon in the context of corporate health and safety crimes, see P Almond and S Colover, 'Mediating Punitiveness: Understanding Public Attitudes towards Work-Related Fatality Cases' (2010) 7 *European Journal of Criminology* 323.

[101] Eg Control of Substances Hazardous to Health Regulations 2002 (SI 2002/2677).

[102] Health and Safety (Enforcing Authority) Regulations 1998 (SI 1998/494).

[103] For detail, see eg *Tolley's Health and Safety at Work Handbook 2023* (London, LexisNexis, 2022).

can be divided into those which involve contravening an absolute requirement of the Act or regulations, and those which are subject to a 'reasonable practicability' standard. I will examine some examples of each.

One absolute requirement under the Act is the ban on charging for safety measures under section 9: 'No employer shall levy or permit to be levied on any employee of his any charge in respect of anything done or provided in pursuance of any specific requirement of the relevant statutory provisions.' It is only necessary to demonstrate that there was a charge levied or authorised by the employer in order to prove that this offence has been committed.

Similarly, under the Provision and Use of Work Equipment Regulations 1998,[104] regulation 5(1): 'Every employer shall ensure that work equipment is maintained in an efficient state, in efficient working order and in good repair.' This is another absolute requirement, though there is obviously some scope for debate about what constitutes an 'efficient' or 'good' state of repair in relation to any particular type of equipment. In both cases, there is no opportunity for the employer to argue that it could not reasonably comply with the requirements, for example, because it could not afford to provide safety equipment or to get work equipment checked.

Other offences are subject to a 'reasonable practicability' standard. This includes the general duty under section 2(1): 'It shall be the duty of every employer to ensure, so far as is reasonably practicable, the health, safety and welfare at work of all his employees.' This is then further specified in a series of duties under section 2(2). For example, section 2(2)(e) requires: 'the provision and maintenance of a working environment for his employees that is, so far as is reasonably practicable, safe, without risks to health, and adequate as regards facilities and arrangements for their welfare at work.' Section 40 puts the burden of proof on the employer to satisfy the 'reasonably practicable' requirement:

> In any proceedings for an offence under any of the relevant statutory provisions consisting of a failure to comply with a duty or requirement to do something so far as is practicable or so far as is reasonably practicable, or to use the best practicable means to do something, it shall be for the accused to prove (as the case may be) that it was not practicable or not reasonably practicable to do more than was in fact done to satisfy the duty or requirement, or that there was no better practicable means than was in fact used to satisfy the duty or requirement.

As the House of Lords explained in *R v Chargot*, the effect of this provision is to require the prosecution merely to prove that the employer did not achieve or prevent a result, before the burden shifts to the accused to establish that they had done everything 'reasonably practicable' to protect against the risk.[105] For example, in *Chargot* itself, an employee was killed when a dumper truck he was driving at work overturned, in circumstances that were unclear. The task for the prosecution

[104] SI 1998/2306.
[105] Above n 39, [17]–[21].

was to show that the employer had failed to prevent a risk of injury arising out of the use of the truck. That risk was evidently non-trivial because it had resulted in the employee's death. But the prosecution did not need to identify specific precautions that the employer ought to have taken. Instead, the burden was on the employer to show that it had taken all 'reasonably practicable' steps to prevent the accident from occurring. In some cases, the foreseeability of the injury can play an important role in determining whether the precautions taken by the employer met the required standard.[106] In *Davies*, a challenge that the reverse burden of proof was incompatible with the ECHR was rejected, because of the importance of the safety objectives being pursued by the Act.[107]

A longstanding criticism of the health and safety regime is that, particularly in cases of avoidable deaths at work, the health and safety offences do not correctly 'label' the employer's wrongdoing or attract the appropriate level of social stigma.[108] The offence of corporate manslaughter under section 1 Corporate Manslaughter and Corporate Homicide Act 2007 was intended to provide a way of signalling the seriousness of the employer's culpability in appropriate cases. The offence is defined as follows:

> (1) An organisation to which this section applies is guilty of an offence if the way in which its activities are managed or organised–
>
> (a) causes a person's death, and
>
> (b) amounts to a gross breach of a relevant duty of care owed by the organisation to the deceased …
>
> (3) An organisation is guilty of an offence under this section only if the way in which its activities are managed or organised by its senior management is a substantial element in the breach referred to in subsection (1).

There is widespread criticism of the 'senior management' element under section 1(3).[109] This was intended to be easier to establish than the common law offence of gross negligence manslaughter in a corporate case, which required a particular director to be guilty of the offence in order for the firm itself to be guilty, under what was called the 'identification' doctrine.[110] However, while there is no need for 'senior management' to be grossly negligent under the statutory offence, there is still a difficulty of proving senior management involvement in the series of events leading up to a workplace death, particularly in larger firms. This is reflected in

[106] Eg *R v Tangerine Confectionery Ltd* [2011] EWCA Crim 2015, [36].

[107] *Davies v Health and Safety Executive* [2002] EWCA Crim 2949, [2003] ICR 586.

[108] For a helpful analysis, see V Roper, 'The Corporate Manslaughter and Corporate Homicide Act 2007: a Re-Evaluation 10 Years on from the First Case' [2022] *Criminal Law Review* 290.

[109] See eg J Gobert, 'The Corporate Manslaughter and Corporate Homicide Act 2007 – Thirteen Years in the Making but was it Worth the Wait?' (2008) 71 *Modern Law Review* 413; D Ormerod and R Taylor, 'The Corporate Manslaughter and Corporate Homicide Act 2007' [2008] *Criminal Law Review* 589.

[110] See *Tesco Supermarkets Ltd v Nattrass* [1972] AC 153; [1971] 2 WLR 1166. The Corporate Manslaughter and Corporate Homicide Act 2007, s 20, abolished the offence of gross negligence manslaughter as it applied to corporations.

the fact that, although firms of varying sizes have been prosecuted for corporate manslaughter, most of those convicted are small firms, where 'senior management' involvement is easier to establish.[111]

An offence under section 33(1)(a) HSWA (which includes the employer's general duties) attracts a fine or a sentence of imprisonment of up to two years, or both, as does an offence under section 33(1)(c) (breaches of regulations).[112] Charging employees for safety measures under section 9 and section 33(1)(b) is punishable by fine.[113] Corporate manslaughter – as a specifically corporate offence – is punishable by a fine,[114] though the use of this offence does not preclude the prosecution of responsible individuals in their own name for gross negligence manslaughter, which could attract a substantial prison sentence.[115] In practice, the vast majority of health and safety-related offences attract fines, though in some cases these can be substantial. Roper demonstrates that a high proportion of firms convicted of corporate manslaughter ceased to trade, though of course this may be as much for reputational reasons as for financial ones.[116] But it is no objection to a substantial fine that the firm involved may go out of business.[117]

In terms of the overall framework of health and safety regulation, it is worth noting that, in addition to the informal persuasive tactics used by most regulators, HSE has access to two 'intermediate' measures to attempt to secure compliance without resort to prosecution: 'improvement notices' and 'prohibition notices'. Under section 21 HSWA, an inspector may serve an improvement notice where they are of the opinion that a person is in breach of a duty under the Act. The notice must give a deadline for compliance and cannot impose ongoing duties, such as requiring the person to refrain from future breaches. Under section 22, an inspector may serve a prohibition notice, requiring a person to put a stop to an activity which involves a risk of serious personal injury. A prohibition notice may also be served where the person is in breach of statutory duties. Failure to comply with either type of notice is an offence.[118]

In 2022–23, HSE issued some 6,000 improvement notices and 2,000 prohibition notices, and brought 216 prosecutions with a 94 per cent conviction rate.[119] Prosecutions for corporate manslaughter are relatively rare, with just over 40 since the Act was passed.[120] This may be explained, in part at least, by plea bargains in which firms plead guilty to health and safety offences instead of manslaughter, or by decisions to prosecute only for health and safety offences, which are easier

[111] Roper, above n 108, 296–300.
[112] HSWA, Schedule 3A.
[113] ibid.
[114] Corporate Manslaughter and Corporate Homicide Act 2007, s 1(6).
[115] Sentencing Council, *Sentencing Guidelines for Gross Negligence Manslaughter* (November 2018).
[116] Above n 108.
[117] Sentencing Council, *Sentencing Guidelines for Corporate Manslaughter* (February 2016).
[118] HSWA, s 33(1)(g).
[119] Health and Safety Executive, *Annual Report and Accounts 2022/23* (HC 1599, July 2023), 11.
[120] Roper, above n 108, 297.

to prove.[121] Rodgers and I have argued elsewhere that the overall level of health and safety enforcement is low relative to the size of the economy as a whole, and in particular when compared with HSE's past performance when it had a much larger budget.[122] Critics, notably Ford and Almond, have argued that health and safety is effectively 'deregulated' because the likelihood of facing a prosecution is so low.[123] A more charitable view might be that the characteristics of workplaces have changed, as the economy has shifted away from manufacturing towards services. However, while this may have reduced the risk of death and physical injury to some extent, other risks have become more prominent, such as mental ill-health caused by stress and overwork.[124] A regime driven by prosecution has not, so far at least, proved to be particularly effective in addressing these newer risks.[125]

Prosecution – for manslaughter, corporate manslaughter or health and safety offences – clearly has an important role to play in cases in which an employer's failure to provide a safe working environment for its employees has led to death or serious injury. These are precisely the kinds of situations in which the full force of state condemnation and harsh treatment should be brought to bear on an employer. However, the available evidence gives cause for concern about the overall level of investigation and prosecution, particularly in less obviously serious cases. Even the system of improvement notices is quite driven by the requirements of the criminal law: the person on whom the notice is served must be given clear objectives and a deadline for compliance.[126] Proposing a full overhaul of health and safety law is, obviously, beyond the scope of this book, but it is clear that more could be done to enhance the deterrent effect of this body of legislation by increasing HSE's budget and capacity, and by locating prosecutions at the apex of a more flexible enforcement regime.

F. Working Time

The Working Time Regulations 1998 (WTR) adopt a two-pronged approach to enforcement, in which workers are able to enforce some provisions themselves through the tribunal system, but others – typically breaches of limits on working time – are handled through the criminal law.[127]

The WTR offence is set out in regulation 29(1) but it refers to any breach of the 'relevant requirements' as defined in regulation 28. Thus, it is necessary to

[121] Roper, above n 108, 303–4.

[122] Above n 41.

[123] P Almond, 'Workplace Safety and Criminalization: A Double-edged Sword', and M Ford, 'The Criminalization of Health and Safety at Work', both in A Bogg, J Collins, M Freedland and J Herring (eds), *Criminality at Work* (Oxford, OUP, 2020).

[124] ACL Davies, 'Stress at Work: Individuals or Structures?' (2022) 51 *Industrial Law Journal* 403.

[125] Davies and Rodgers, above n 41.

[126] ibid.

[127] SI 1998/1833.

examine each of the 'requirements' in turn in order to understand the content of the various offences under the Regulations. These can helpfully be grouped into three main categories for the purposes of analysis: strict liability offences, strict liability offences with an evaluative element, and offences which are only committed where the employer has failed to take reasonable steps to achieve a particular result. Under regulation 29(4), all these offences are punishable with a fine.

A key example of a strict liability offence is regulation 6A: 'An employer shall ensure that no young worker employed by him works during the restricted period.' Thus, it is an offence to require a young worker to engage in night work. Another group of offences follows a similar pattern but with greater scope for argument about their exact requirements, because of the use of evaluative language. For example, regulation 8 attempts to implement the principle of the 'humanisation' of work[128] by creating a criminal offence of uncertain application:

> Where the pattern according to which an employer organizes work is such as to put the health and safety of a worker employed by him at risk, in particular because the work is monotonous or the work-rate is predetermined, the employer shall ensure that the worker is given adequate rest breaks.

In addition to the lack of clarity surrounding the concept of a 'risk-inducing' pattern of work, the idea of providing 'adequate' rest breaks opens up scope for argument unless the offending employer has provided no breaks at all. Similarly, it is a criminal offence to fail to provide compensatory rest in accordance with regulation 24 in situations where the worker is exempted from the regulation 6 limits on night work, but this applies 'wherever possible', and alternative 'protection' may be offered instead.

A third group of limits incorporate a reasonableness component. These are the average 48-hour limit on the working week (for those workers who have not opted out[129]), the 40-hour week and eight hours per day limits on the working time of a young worker,[130] and the average limit of eight hours in every 24 for non-hazardous night work by an adult.[131] All three adopt the same formulation of the employer's duty:

> to take all reasonable steps, in keeping with the need to protect the health and safety of workers, to ensure that the limit specified … is complied with in the case of each worker employed by him in relation to whom it applies.

Obviously, the crucial question – which would depend on the circumstances – is what steps it would have been reasonable for the employer to take.

Detailed evidence of the number of prosecutions of these offences is hard to obtain, not least because HSE's published reports do not differentiate working time prosecutions from those under health and safety legislation, but it seems unlikely

[128] A term often attributed to B Bercusson, *European Labour Law* (London, Butterworths, 1996), 332.
[129] Under WTR, reg 4(1).
[130] WTR, reg 5A.
[131] WTR, reg 6.

that extensive use has been made of any of these offences.[132] One obvious reason emerges from the above analysis of the provisions themselves: outside the context of the strict liability offences, it is difficult to say with certainty when an offence has been committed, given the various qualifications they contain. Prosecuting authorities are unlikely to invest time and resources in bringing a prosecution unless they feel relatively sure of getting a conviction. The more uncertain the offence, the less likely this will be. Of course, in the working time context, flexibility is seen as necessary to accommodate the fact that this is a 'one-size-fits-all' piece of legislation, covering a huge variety of different sectors of the labour market and types of employment.[133] But this does not sit comfortably with the criminal law, either on a practical level or as a matter of principle. Another obvious reason is that one of the main limits to be enforced through the criminal law, the 48-hour limit on the working week, is subject to the individual opt-out. Evidence suggests that a high proportion of workers have signed an opt-out, so that this limit is no longer applicable to them.[134]

The logic behind the use of the criminal law to enforce certain aspects of the working time regime is its clear link to health and safety, where this approach also prevails. For example, given that it is regarded as unsafe for young workers to be engaged in night work, it would not be appropriate to give them a civil claim for compensation or a vindicatory award in respect of having been required to engage in such work. The objective of deterring this type of work from happening at all is more likely to be served by making it a criminal offence. However, the effectiveness of this strategy is cast into doubt if prosecutions are rare. For adult workers, in particular, it might be worth exploring replicative alternatives, enabling workers themselves to seek a court order prohibiting work in excess of the permitted hours. The courts have taken some tentative steps in this direction through the use of declarations at common law.[135] Greater use of this approach – or the formalisation of a statutory equivalent – would empower workers to protect themselves.

G. Conclusion

Reviewing these six areas of law – modern slavery, gangmasters' licensing, agency work, NMW, health and safety, and working time – a pattern emerges. Criminal offences are enacted (often, though not always, with the possibility of a substantial fine or a custodial sentence) but prosecutions for those offences seem relatively rare. This suggests that they are unlikely to be having the intended deterrent effect

[132] See eg HSE, above n 119. Local authorities also have enforcement responsibilities in the sectors they regulate for health and safety purposes: above n 22.

[133] C Barnard, 'The Working Time Regulations 1998' (1999) 28 *Industrial Law Journal* 61.

[134] R Hobbs, C Barnard and S Deakin, 'Opting Out of the 48-Hour Week: Employer Necessity or Individual Choice? an Empirical Study of the Operation of Article 18(1)(b) of the Working Time Directive in the UK' (2003) 32 *Industrial Law Journal* 223.

[135] *Barber v RJB Mining (UK) Ltd* [1999] ICR 679, discussed in ch 6 of this volume.

on employers, complex and uncertain though deterrent effects might be. However, as I noted at the outset, one response to this in the regulation literature is to point to the fact that prosecution should be used as a last resort for the most serious cases, for example, where the employer is a repeat or deliberate offender. On this view, an apparently low level of prosecutions may be a sign not that the system is in trouble, but that it is working as intended. All the regulators discussed in this section – the GLAA, EASI, HMRC and HSE – use advisory or persuasive techniques to various degrees to get employers to comply.

But there are two important caveats. First, modern slavery offences do not have a single 'regulator' and, as serious offences in breach of victims' fundamental rights, are not an appropriate subject for persuasive strategies. Low levels of prosecution here, as identified by the Independent Anti-Slavery Commissioner, are a serious cause for concern. Second, it is worth asking whether, in the other regulatory regimes, prosecution *does* sit at the apex of a functioning system with a range of lesser alternatives, or whether low levels of prosecution are a sign of low levels of activity more generally. One issue here is system design: for example, although EASI now has access to LMEUs, the agency regime might work more effectively if agencies were required to be licensed. This would give EASI an opportunity to identify and inspect agencies before granting a licence, and the threat of revocation would act as a deterrent to poor practice in itself. Similarly, although HSE can use improvement and prohibition orders as measures short of prosecution, it might also be able to make good use of a system of civil penalties. Very little coherent or systematic thought has been given to the design of regulatory regimes or the updating of older regimes in the light of modern developments in regulatory practice. Another issue is resources: no doubt an argument could be made that any or all of the agencies under discussion here are under-funded, but the problem seems particularly acute in relation to EASI, and cuts to HSE funding over the years have been clearly documented.

III. Redress

Another characteristic of employment law identified in chapter three is its concern with the dignity of working people. Where an employer's wrongdoing is dealt with through the criminal law, the dignity of affected workers is upheld in a moral sense because they have the satisfaction of knowing that the full force of the state has been brought to bear to address their employer's bad behaviour. However, this may not be of much comfort where the worker has, for example, suffered significant financial or other harms as a result of the employer's offending. It is therefore worth exploring what forms of redress are available to workers where the criminal law forms a major part of the relevant regulatory landscape.

Although the primary function of the criminal law is to punish wrongdoing, not to provide redress, section 133 Sentencing Act 2020 *does* provide for the sentencing court to make a compensation order requiring the offender 'to pay compensation for any personal injury, loss or damage resulting from' the offence. Although the making of such an order does not affect the calculation of compensation in any subsequent civil proceedings, there is provision against double recovery in section 144. In contrast to civil proceedings, the offender's means are relevant to the assessment of any compensation payable, by virtue of section 135(3). From an employment perspective, the key limitation on compensation orders as a means of securing redress is the courts' view that they should only be made in straightforward cases.[136] If there is any need to make complex enquiries to determine the extent of the offender's liability, the matter should be left to be determined in civil proceedings. Thus, it seems likely that, in many cases, victims of criminal offences in employment settings may still need to find another way of securing redress.

A first point to note in this regard is that the law has largely moved away from the position that the employer's commission of a criminal offence can also be treated as a breach of statutory duty giving rise to a civil law claim for the worker. This possibility still exists under regulation 30(1) Conduct of Employment Agencies and Employment Businesses Regulations 2003. Any breach of the 1973 Act or 2003 Regulations by an employment agency or business is expressly made actionable in the civil courts as a breach of statutory duty if it causes 'damage'. A similar provision in the Health and Safety at Work etc. Act 1974 was repealed as part of a government 'deregulation' initiative in 2013.[137] And while the Modern Slavery Act 2015 might have been an obvious candidate for the creation of a civil claim, the government suggested that this was unnecessary because victims would be able to bring other types of action, such as a tort claim or employment tribunal proceedings.[138] Section 8 of the 2015 Act provides for a 'slavery and trafficking reparation order' in the victim's favour, but this is only available where the defendant has been convicted of an offence under the Act and is the subject of a confiscation order.[139]

This leads neatly to the second point: the worker will typically need to 'reframe' what has happened to them as a tort claim or an employment law wrong and bring separate proceedings in court or in the tribunal in order to seek redress. For example, the employer's failure to take steps that were 'reasonably practicable' to fulfil its duties under health and safety legislation, thereby leading to an injury to an employee, is also likely to amount to the tort of negligence, giving rise to a damages claim. Indeed, some commentators have suggested that the removal of the action for breach of statutory duty has made little difference in this area.[140] In other cases, though, the 'reframing' is a more complex process. For example, a worker who is

[136] *R v Stapylton* [2012] EWCA Crim 728, [2013] 1 Cr App R (S) 12.

[137] Section 47, as amended, Enterprise and Regulatory Reform Act 2013.

[138] Lord Bates, HL Deb 23 February 2015, col 1464.

[139] See Baroness Hale's comments on the weaknesses of this remedy in *Onu v Akwiwu* [2016] UKSC 31, [2016] ICR 756, [34].

[140] SF Deakin and Z Adams, *Markesinis and Deakin's Tort Law* (8th edn, Oxford, OUP, 2019), ch 18.

required to work very long hours by an employer in breach of the 48-hour limit would only be able to bring a claim in tort if they suffered actionable damage as a result. Although long hours of work can sometimes result in physical harm to the worker, a more likely consequence is stress and mental ill-health, but the law tends to be more restrictive about tort liability for these kinds of harm.[141]

In other cases, particularly those involving victims of modern slavery or workers who have been engaged by an unlicensed gangmaster or improperly-run agency, the claims are most likely to be for unpaid wages or holiday pay, though of course any number of employment wrongs may have been committed.[142] The most likely route is therefore to bring a claim in the tribunal for unlawful deductions or breach of the WTR (or a NMW claim, to which I return below). One problem facing many workers in these kinds of cases is that they are migrants with a limited right to remain in the UK. For example, many agricultural workers are migrants on short-term, seasonal visas, making it impractical for them to bring lengthy tribunal proceedings. There is a discretion to allow victims of modern slavery to remain in the UK while they seek redress, but they can still be deported where the government deems it possible for them to continue to seek redress from their home country.[143] Another, more profound problem is that the worker may be an irregular migrant. This means that they are at risk of a court or tribunal striking out any claims for money owed or for compensation, on the ground of illegality.[144] Recent years have seen the emergence of a more sympathetic approach in the case-law, in which the courts will now balance the rights of the worker against the public policy reasons for not allowing claims based on illegal working relationships,[145] but these positive developments in the case-law may have been undermined by the creation, in 2016, of a specific offence of illegal working.[146]

This leads to a third issue: the presence of regulators with no powers to intervene. It might be expected that, where an expert regulator has investigated a situation and identified wrongdoing, potentially leading to a prosecution, it would also be able to secure redress for affected workers. However, most of the agencies under discussion have no formal powers to do this, and only a few seek to do so informally. The main examples of the latter are the GLAA and EASI. In 2021–22, the GLAA recovered some £78,922, mostly consisting of unpaid holiday

[141] Davies, above n 124.

[142] For a creative approach, see *Antuzis v DJ Houghton Catching Services Ltd* [2019] EWHC 843 (QB), [2021] EWHC 971 (QB).

[143] Above n 71.

[144] For detailed analysis, see A Bogg and S Green, 'Rights are not just for the Virtuous: What *Hounga* Means for the Illegality Defence in the Discrimination Torts' (2015) 44 *Industrial Law Journal* 101; A Bogg, '*Okedina v Chikale* and Contract Illegality: New Dawn or False Dawn?' (2020) 49 *Industrial Law Journal* 258.

[145] *Allen v Hounga* [2014] UKSC 47, [2014] ICR 847; *Okedina v Chikale* [2019] EWCA Civ 1393, [2019] ICR 1635.

[146] Immigration Act 2016, s 34.

pay, for victims.[147] EASI recovered over £130,000 in 2020–21, usually in cases in which agency workers had not received the pay due to them.[148] But neither agency has formal powers either to seek redress directly or to support victims to bring legal action to secure redress. While it would perhaps be undesirable for there to be too many agencies with overlapping powers, this does seem like a missed opportunity.

Against this background, the NMW regime stands out. The decision to prosecute an employer who has refused to pay the NMW does not, in itself, result in any recovery for the affected workers. However, this is not particularly concerning because HMRC also has powers to seek arrears for the affected workers, albeit via separate proceedings.[149] Indeed, in most cases, the agency's starting-point is to seek redress (which is accompanied by civil penalties in any event[150]) with prosecutions reserved for the most serious cases.[151] HMRC may also be able to take over where informal approaches from EASI or the GLAA have not been successful.

It would be too simplistic to conclude from this that all regulatory regimes in employment law should operate in the same way as the NMW. For example, most claims for workplace injuries are relatively straightforward and are met by the employer's insurers, an insurance policy being required by statute.[152] It might not be the best use of HSE's time to help with these claims. Moreover, even when there is a clear need for working people to have support from a regulator, it is worth remembering that the NMW is much simpler to enforce than other regimes. The GLAA imposes a wide variety of standards on licence-holders, so it would be a much more challenging task for it to help working people get redress for the full range of infringements. Instead, the key point to take away from the discussion is that the creation of a criminal offence might sound like the strongest possible way of upholding the rights of working people, but in practice, may feel like a hollow victory. Nowhere is this more true than in slavery and trafficking cases, where vulnerable victims are largely left to fend for themselves. Remedies should be considered carefully in the design of any regulatory regime which is supposed to protect working people.

IV. Ranking

I turn finally to consider whether the criminal offences in use in employment law reflect an appropriate ranking of employment rights. The preceding discussion has already highlighted some areas in which the criminal law is not playing a

147 Above n 83.
148 Above n 98, 13.
149 National Minimum Wage Act 1998, s 19.
150 ibid s 19A.
151 Above n 95.
152 Employers' Liability (Compulsory Insurance) Act 1969.

particularly useful role and should be reconsidered, so I will not repeat that analysis here. Instead, I will explore whether there is any scope for the expansion of the criminal law. This may seem odd against the background of theoretical concerns about overcriminalisation and practical concerns about weak enforcement. But it is still a question worth considering, not least because the existing criminal offences have been enacted over a long period of time in response to different political imperatives and social concerns, so they can hardly be described as a coherent and well-thought-out selection. I consider two possibilities here: serious examples of labour exploitation or wage theft, and serious infringements of the freedom to associate.

One proposal for criminalisation advanced by Mantouvalou in an important contribution to the debate is blacklisting.[153] The compilation of a prohibited list is an obvious breach of Article 11, since the aim is to identify trade union members or activists in order to discriminate against them because they have exercised their right to associate. As Mantouvalou explains, this is particularly serious in cases where the list is shared among multiple employers because of the risk that the worker will not be able to secure employment at all in their chosen trade or profession, thereby leading to broader harmful consequences such as poverty and social exclusion.[154] The requirements of harm and wrongfulness for criminalisation are relatively easily made out in this context.

The central question then becomes whether the advantages of criminalisation outweigh the disadvantages. At present, the law addresses prohibited lists primarily by civil means, under the Blacklists Regulations.[155] Under regulation 3, 'no person shall compile, use, sell or supply a prohibited list'.[156] Under regulation 13, a working person may seek compensation for losses suffered by means of an action for breach of statutory duty, or bring proceedings in respect of refusal to hire, detriment or dismissal because of their inclusion on such a list.[157] Regulation 13 also contains an important power for the court to make an order 'restraining or preventing the defendant from contravening' the regulation 3 prohibition. Failure to comply with an injunction prohibiting any further dissemination of a prohibited list could, of course, result in criminal proceedings for contempt of court. It is open to debate whether these provisions are sufficient to tackle the problem. On the one hand, the criminal law has the potential to offer a much more powerful deterrent to the compilation and use of prohibited lists by stigmatising those who engage in these practices.[158] On the other hand, it is not clear whether the use of such a list is so significantly worse than other forms of discrimination against trade unionists to warrant the use of the criminal law, when it is not seriously suggested

[153] V Mantouvalou, 'Human Rights, Labour Rights and Criminal Wrongs', in Bogg A Bogg, J Collins, M Freedland and J Herring (eds), *Criminality at Work* (Oxford, OUP, 2020), above n 1.

[154] ibid 219.

[155] Employment Relations Act 1999 (Blacklists) Regulations 2010 (SI 2010/493).

[156] ibid.

[157] ibid.

[158] Mantouvalou, above n 7, 223–24.

that all such discrimination should be criminalised. The debate is finely balanced. My own view is that criminalisation would be beneficial alongside the existing civil remedies for individuals, but that it should be used sparingly to capture cases in which affected individuals were deprived of any meaningful work opportunity over a significant period of time.

Another example to consider is 'wage theft'.[159] This non-technical label is used to cover a range of exploitative labour practices that result in working people not being paid the money they are due. Examples include non-compliance with the NMW or the right to paid holidays, using deductions of various kinds to reduce the wages apparently owed to the working person, and wrongly classifying the working person as self-employed in order to avoid employment rights such as NMW entitlements. As Green persuasively argues, the existing offence of theft is not a particularly good fit for these scenarios, since this requires that the property in question already belongs to the victim before being wrongfully appropriated by the offender.[160] In 'wage theft' cases, the employer's wrongdoing typically means that the employer is not taking the working person's money from them, but rather denying that they are owed the money in the first place.

Green suggests that fraud by abuse of position may be a better match for this type of wrongdoing.[161] This is defined in the Fraud Act 2006, section 4(1), as follows:

> A person is in breach of this section if he:
> (a) occupies a position in which he is expected to safeguard, or not to act against, the financial interests of another person,
> (b) dishonestly abuses that position, and
> (c) intends, by means of abuse of that position:
>   (i) to make a gain for himself or another, or
>   (ii) to cause loss to another or to expose another to risk of loss.

Although there has been some debate in the context of implied terms about the employer's financial duties towards its employees, the employment relationship can arguably be seen as an example of the type envisaged in sub-paragraph (a), at least in the sense of an expectation on the employer not to act against the financial interests of its employees or workers.[162] The gain and loss elements are also relatively easy to make out, in the sense that the underpaying employer will increase its profits at the expense of the working person who could have expected to receive more in pay. Importantly, there is no requirement for the gain or loss to manifest in practice in order for the offence to be committed. It appears, then, that the central question would be the dishonesty element in sub-paragraph (b). According to the

[159] For an important discussion, see S Green, 'Wage Theft as a Legal Concept', in A Bogg, J Collins, M Freedland and J Herring (eds), *Criminality at Work* (Oxford, OUP, 2020).
[160] ibid 135–46.
[161] ibid 146–50.
[162] See eg *Scally v Southern Health and Social Services Board* [1992] 1 AC 294.

Supreme Court in the *Ivey* case (albeit obiter), this requires that the defendant's conduct be judged against the 'standards of ordinary decent people'.[163] Importantly, then, the offence can be committed even if the defendant does not believe that their conduct was dishonest.

Thus, there is potential to prosecute at least some of the employer wrongdoing characterised in common parlance as 'wage theft' as fraud. The more profound question is whether or in what circumstances that would be an appropriate use of the criminal law. This is particularly challenging because fraud is a relatively serious offence with a strongly stigmatising effect, so convincing justifications are required. One problem is drawing a clear boundary between conduct that is ordinary – if unattractive – market behaviour, and conduct that ought to be characterised as wrongful harm. Misclassifying a working person as self-employed rather than a worker or an employee is a case in point. It is very tempting from an employment law perspective to argue that this behaviour is, indeed, wrongful, because it deprives working people of their employment rights. However, employers might reasonably argue that it should not be an offence to try to carry on their business in the way that is cheapest or most convenient for them, or that classifying a working person as self-employed might have benefits for that person too. Another problem is the definition of dishonesty: when should the employer be regarded as lying or cheating as opposed to just trying to minimise its liabilities? This is a particularly challenging area because the employer's own belief in the honesty or otherwise of its actions is not relevant as a result of the decision in *Ivey*, so the employer could be criminalised for behaviour it thought was legitimate.[164] It is true that some employers go to considerable lengths to misclassify their workers, but it is hard to say precisely when elaborate contract drafting shades over into dishonesty.

Even if it is accepted that some instances of 'wage theft' constitute wrongful harm, it is still necessary to consider whether the benefits of criminalisation would outweigh the disadvantages. Again, this requires consideration of the potential deterrent effect of criminal offences and the associated stigma, and the risk of bringing the law into disrepute by over-using the criminal law in ways that do not fit with most people's moral compass. It is important to disentangle different types of 'wage theft' for these purposes. The practice of making deductions for the provision of uniforms or equipment, or charging for the use of facilities, can be unfair where it significantly reduces the 'headline' rate of pay promised by the employer to its workers. It is regulated in various ways: by the ordinary law of contract, by the unlawful deductions regime, where the employer has no power to make the deduction,[165] and it may be caught by NMW legislation where the deductions take the worker below the required NMW rate. But there is considerable scope to improve (for example) the unlawful deductions regime, to offer

[163] *Ivey v Genting Casinos UK Ltd (t/a Crockfords Club)* [2017] UKSC 67, [2018] AC 391, [74].
[164] ibid.
[165] ERA 1996, s 13.

some substantive protection to working people before seeking to engage the criminal law to regulate these practices. For example, employers could be required to provide uniforms or equipment (as they are with safety equipment) or limited as to the charges they can make. In relation to misclassification, a different kind of argument might be made. It is only relatively recently that the courts have fully grasped the problem of misclassification, in the *Uber* decision, and have adopted a well-reasoned and effective strategy for dealing with it.[166] This may, in itself, act as a significant deterrent: there is no point in drafting elaborate contract documents pointing towards self-employment if tribunals are liable to conclude that the reality of the situation is that the working person ought to be protected by employment legislation. On this view, it may be premature to resort to criminal sanctions to try to address a problem which the courts may already have resolved. Finally, of course, one example of wage theft – deliberate non-payment of the NMW – is already a criminal offence.[167] As I argued above, this provides an important way of dealing with employers who wilfully disregard their workers' basic right to a decent level of pay, and sits within a carefully-thought-out enforcement regime which provides for lesser penalties for inadvertent violations and ensures redress for affected workers.

Farmer offers a useful reminder that the criminal law is a product of its time: although it is tempting to think in terms of universal values, it is bound to reflect what people think is important and worth protecting under particular social conditions.[168] Thus, it is possible that views may change and poor treatment of working people by their employers may come to be seen as less tolerable than it is at present. This may strengthen the argument for greater use of criminalisation in some areas of employment law. It is certainly important to keep the position under review, and to avoid the assumption that the only direction of travel in the employment sphere is away from the criminal law.

V. Conclusion

This chapter has sought to set the scene for the discussion in the remainder of the book by highlighting some of the issues with using the criminal law to enforce the duties of employers and others towards working people. The criminal law clearly has a place in employment law. Some offences, most obviously those relating to modern slavery, deal with serious infringements of individuals' fundamental rights and clearly warrant the intervention of the state to condemn and punish. Other employment-related offences, although not *mala in se*, play a key role in helping

[166] *Uber BV v Aslam* [2021] UKSC 5, [2021] ICR 657.
[167] National Minimum Wage Act 1998, s 31(1).
[168] L Farmer, *Making the Modern Criminal Law: Criminalization and Civil Order* (Oxford, OUP, 2016), ch 7.

to enforce regulatory regimes, such as the NMW and health and safety, which pursue valuable public goals. There may even be scope for adding new offences to the list, to deal with some of the more egregious abuses of workers' rights, such as blacklisting.

However, while the use of the criminal law can be justified as a matter of principle, there are two important practical questions to address. First, it is essential that sufficient resources are provided for the investigation and prosecution of offences, and (particularly in regulatory regimes) that the regulator is not solely reliant on the criminal law but has a menu of lesser enforcement options to choose from. If these measures are not in place, there is a real risk that the creation of a criminal offence will do nothing to solve the problem: employers will not regard it as a deterrent because it will be so rarely invoked. Second, redress for workers should always be considered. Many of the factors that point in the direction of creating criminal offences and special regulatory regimes – that serious, wrongful harm is being suffered by vulnerable workers, for example – also point towards a need for easily-accessible remedies for those workers. But the creation of a criminal offence often seems to be accompanied by unrealistic assumptions about the capacity of workers to bring proceedings or to reframe their problem under a different legal category.

5

Penalties and Punitive Awards

This chapter considers situations in which an employer's breach of an employment right may result in a court order, the sole or main aim of which is to punish the employer for its actions. Punishment in this context has the usual meaning of harsh treatment meted out by an authority in response to wrongdoing. Although punishment is typically associated with the criminal law, there are several examples of non-criminal punishments in employment law, and these will be the focus of this chapter. All these punishments involve the payment of money by the employer.

Punitive orders can take one of two different forms, depending on who is the recipient of the money the employer has to pay. One is an order to pay a penalty to the Secretary of State. Civil penalties have the advantage of being easier for the authorities to obtain than a criminal conviction, but by the same token, they may not carry the same level of stigma. The other is an order to pay a sum of money to the affected worker. This may take the form of an award of punitive or exemplary damages at common law or, more commonly, an award of a sum of money under the statute which is not normally labelled as punitive but cannot be explained by any other purpose, such as compensation or vindication. These kinds of awards are often criticised for providing the recipient with a 'windfall', but this criticism only makes sense if compensation is regarded as the sole legitimate function of an award. Of course, there are important conceptual differences between civil penalties and punitive awards to claimants: only the second of these is a 'remedy' strictly so-called, but it is difficult to obtain a rounded understanding of the law without considering both.

Another important distinction which it is useful to draw at the outset concerns the reason for ordering the employer to pay a penalty or a punitive award. There are three main situations in which such awards can be made: non-compliance with a particular employment right, such as the worker's entitlement to the NMW; non-compliance with a tribunal order, such as an order to reinstate an employee or to conduct an equal pay audit; and (loosely) where the manner of the employer's breach of an employment right has aggravating features which are thought to render the employer deserving of punishment. The chapter will be organised around these three different situations.

Although this chapter touches on some big debates in related areas of law – the regulation literature on the role of civil penalties, for example, and the debate on punitive damages in private law – my focus will be on the three core questions identified in chapter three. First, I will argue that some examples of penalties in employment law are a poor fit for the rights they purport to enforce. In particular, they are often used where a replicative remedy would be more appropriate, or where tribunals lack the enforcement powers that a court would have. Second, I will consider whether penalties or punitive awards serve the particular purposes of employment law in an effective way. Deterrence is an important consideration here, since one might expect penalties to have a strong deterrent effect. However, this is not necessarily the case for a variety of different reasons, including lack of awareness among employers (a particular issue for the tribunal's power to order a penalty for an 'aggravated breach' of employment rights), poor system design (as is the case with the NMW), or simply the low level of the award (often true of awards made when the employer has not complied with a previous tribunal order, such as for re-employment). Third, I will consider whether the most important employment rights are sufficiently prioritised. The somewhat random approach to the availability of punitive damages is a particular problem here.

A final word of caution: grouping the various penalties and punitive awards found in employment law together risks creating the impression that there is a clear system or set of guiding principles explaining and justifying their use. Nothing could be further from the truth, as the discussion will demonstrate.

I. Non-Compliance with Particular Employment Rights

A. National Minimum Wage

Perhaps the most well-known example of a civil penalty in use in employment law is that found in section 19A National Minimum Wage Act 1998 (NMWA 1998).[1] Where an HMRC enforcement officer determines that an employer has failed to pay the NMW, they may issue a 'notice of underpayment' under section 19, requiring the employer to pay the affected worker or workers what they are owed. Under section 19A, the notice must also include a requirement on the employer to pay to the Secretary of State a penalty of double the amount owing to each affected worker, subject to a minimum of £100 and a maximum of £20,000 per worker. The penalty is payable within 28 days, but if the employer pays within 14 days, it may discharge its obligation to pay the penalty by paying half.

This use of a penalty reflects a strong commitment by the state to treat the NMW as a fundamental right and to impose serious consequences on employers

[1] There are also penalties under the Information and Consultation of Employees Regulations 2004 (SI 2004/3246) and the Occupational and Personal Pension Schemes (Disclosure of Information) Regulations 2013 (SI 2013/2734), but I do not consider these in detail here.

in respect of a breach. The fact that the cost of non-compliance is so high should incentivise employers to consider carefully whether they are paying the NMW.

However, there are two difficulties with this stringent regime. First, by making the penalty payable at the same time as the arrears, the government has removed an element of escalation from the original design of the system. The Act as originally passed provided for the employer to be served with an 'enforcement notice' requiring it to pay arrears owed to workers in the first instance.[2] If the employer did not comply within 28 days, the enforcement officer could then issue a 'penalty notice' requiring it to pay the Secretary of State a penalty of twice the NMW hourly rate per worker in respect of each day of non-compliance.[3] Thus, the penalty was used as a means of incentivising employers to pay their workers what they owed. If the employer did not pay promptly, its liability would increase. This reflected the 'enforcement pyramid' approach, introduced in chapter four, in which sanctions escalate for more serious offenders.[4] The current regime punishes from the outset.

Second, the penalty applies regardless of whether the employer's failure to pay the NMW was deliberate or accidental. The use of a penalty in respect of accidental breaches is unusual and makes a particularly strong statement about the importance of NMW compliance. However, as with all forms of strict liability, there is some risk of undermining the condemnatory effect of the penalty.[5] This is particularly so in situations in which the law is open to different (legitimate) interpretations, rendering the employer's obligations unclear. It is noteworthy that the government had to intervene to direct HMRC not to take enforcement action during a period of uncertainty surrounding the correct NMW treatment of so-called 'sleep-in' shifts because of the potential unfairness of punishing employers who were faced with conflicting lines of authority in the courts.[6] This is a recognition that penalising employers risks bringing the law into disrepute if it is unclear what they need to do in order to comply.

As chapter four explained, deliberate non-payment of the NMW is a criminal offence, so there is the possibility of further escalation beyond the penalty regime for employers who wilfully flout the law.[7] In that limited respect, penalties still sit somewhere in the middle of the sliding scale. The use of a civil penalty in respect of accidental breaches is obviously less controversial than the use of a strict liability criminal offence of non-payment of the NMW would be.

[2] NMWA 1998, s 19, as originally enacted. The change in approach was effected by the Employment Act 2008.

[3] NMWA 1998, s 21, as originally enacted.

[4] I Ayres and J Braithwaite, *Responsive Regulation: Transcending the Deregulation Debate* (New York, OUP, 1992).

[5] This issue also affects the 'naming and shaming' scheme, discussed in ch 2 of this volume, which operates alongside the legal regime.

[6] Department for Business, Energy and Industrial Strategy, *Enforcement of the National Minimum Wage in the Social Care Sector* (July 2017). The issue was resolved, albeit not in a worker-protective way, by the Supreme Court in *Royal Mencap Society v Tomlinson-Blake* [2021] UKSC 8, [2021] ICR 758.

[7] NMWA 1998, s 31.

In sum, the NMW adopts a particularly stringent approach to enforcement in which employers are punished even for accidental infringements. The government defends this by pointing to the importance of the NMW as a right and by emphasising the employer's responsibility to find out what its obligations are and to comply with them. However, while infringing the NMW is now very costly for employers, the indiscriminate use of penalties does not seem to have added to the stigma of non-compliance.[8] A more targeted approach, like the one originally used in the Act, might be preferable.

B. Expanding the Role of Civil Penalties?

Although there are issues with the design of civil penalties currently in use, it is worth considering whether there is a role for (well-designed) civil penalties in other areas.

One example is in the field of health and safety. As chapter four explained, health and safety rules are enforced primarily through the criminal law, with breaches of employers' duties under the legislation constituting criminal offences.[9] This is the case whether the consequences of the employer's breach caused death or serious injury, or merely created a risk of minor injury or illness. In practice, HSE's enforcement policy dictates that prosecution is much more likely in the event of a breach leading to death or serious injury.[10] This has significant consequences. On the one hand, it corresponds much more closely to the situations in which prosecution might be expected, and helps to target limited resources at the most serious cases. On the other hand, it means that there are many day-to-day health and safety infringements which are unlikely ever to result in prosecution and are, effectively, deregulated. Giving HSE access to civil penalties could help to bridge the gap between cases warranting prosecution and cases which should not be ignored completely.[11] For example, poor practices relating to working time, stress and burnout are unlikely to result in prosecution, but can have serious consequences for those dealing with them.[12] Of course, careful thought would need to be given to the design of the system, and to ensuring that HSE had enough resources to implement it – both of which are issues beyond the scope of the present chapter – but it is clear that HSE's current enforcement regime is far too blunt.

[8] A point presciently made by B Simpson when the changes were made: B Simpson, 'The Employment Act 2008's Amendments to the National Minimum Wage Legislation' (2009) 38 *Industrial Law Journal* 57.

[9] Health and Safety at Work etc. Act 1974, s 33(1). Some duties under the Act and accompanying regulations are absolute, though many are subject to a 'reasonable practicability' standard.

[10] HSE, *Enforcement Policy Statement* (October 2015), 10.

[11] ACL Davies and L Rodgers, 'Towards a More Effective Health and Safety Regime for UK Workplaces Post COVID-19' (2023) 52(3) *Industrial Law Journal* 665.

[12] ACL Davies, 'Stress at Work: Individuals or Structures?' (2022) 51 *Industrial Law Journal* 403.

II. Non-Compliance with Tribunal Orders

Penalties or punitive awards (albeit often not labelled as such) are much more common in situations in which the employer has not complied with a tribunal order. These fall into two broad groups. First, there is a civil penalty regime for employers who do not pay tribunal awards. This is designed to address the problem, noted in chapter two, that many workers who are successful in the tribunal never receive the compensation they were awarded, by adding to the employer's cost of non-compliance. Second, there are many examples of tribunal orders which, if not complied with by a certain date, may result in either a penalty payable to the Secretary of State or, more commonly, the award of additional 'compensation' to the working person. An example of the former is the obligation to conduct an equal pay audit. Examples of the latter include orders to reinstate or re-engage an employee after an unfair dismissal, or orders to comply with tribunal recommendations after a breach has been identified.

All these examples raise, in different ways, the problem of the ineffectiveness of the tribunal system. Even when a claimant wins their case, the employer may choose simply to ignore the tribunal's award against it, relying on the complexity of the enforcement process to deter the claimant from taking matters further. Other types of order, such as re-employment orders or recommendations, can be ignored because the worst that can happen is that a small, additional sum of money becomes payable. There are serious deficiencies in the deterrent effect that should be a significant feature of the system of employment law. Moreover, although in some cases the claimant obtains an additional payment as a result of the employer's default, there is a real risk that this is not a benefit but an infringement of the claimant's dignity. Instead of the legal system securing the employer's compliance, all it can provide is a token financial gesture.

A. Non-Payment of Tribunal Awards

Tribunal awards are generally required to be paid within 14 days.[13] However, tribunals do not have any powers to enforce their own awards. Instead, under section 15(1) Employment Tribunals Act 1996 (ETA 1996), sums payable under a tribunal award are recoverable as if they were 'payable under an order of the county court'. The claimant must file the tribunal award with the county court and can then, on payment of a fee, initiate one of several different enforcement procedures, such as taking control of the defendant's goods or seeking a third-party debt order.[14]

[13] Tribunal Rules 2013 (set out in Schedule 1 to the Employment Tribunals (Constitution and Rules of Procedure) Regulations 2013 (SI 2013/1237)), rule 66. The tribunal may prescribe a different deadline.

[14] Awards can also be enforced via the High Court, and employment tribunal claimants have access to a special fast track procedure for this purpose. A fee is also payable for using the fast track procedure.

In 2015, a new Part 2A was inserted into ETA 1996 to create a penalty regime.[15] The claimant must first fill in a form requesting enforcement. The enforcement officer then gives the employer a warning under section 37E, requiring it to pay within 28 days. If the employer still does not pay, the officer will give it a penalty notice requiring it to pay the Secretary of State a financial penalty of 50 per cent of the unpaid amount (subject to a minimum of £100 and a maximum of £5,000).[16] The penalty is reduced by 50 per cent if the employer pays the award in full and the penalty within 14 days.[17] If the employer still does not pay, it may (in theory at least) be 'named' online by the government.[18] Although the enforcement officer may pursue the unpaid penalty as a debt, it remains the responsibility of the claimant to take enforcement action to obtain their award.

From a practical perspective, this has the advantage for claimants that it is free and relatively straightforward to use. However, the deterrent effect is limited, for at least two reasons. First, where the award itself is small, the penalty will be small too. For example, an award of £500 in unpaid wages, while highly significant to the claimant in many cases, will only attract a penalty of a further £250. Second, the maximum of £5000 limits the impact of the provision in relation to some of the larger awards that might arise in unfair dismissal or discrimination claims. Employers who are determined not to pay an award are unlikely to be motivated to comply by being fined these relatively modest sums.

A government statement in 2020 explained that, since April 2016, 'a total of £1,343,941.96 was recovered for 231 workers after only issuing a warning notice. A total of £1,222,472.23 was recovered for 225 workers after issuing a penalty notice'.[19] Although this is obviously positive for the workers involved, the overall level of use of the scheme seems relatively low. SETA found that only one in five claimants who had not used the scheme knew about it, though the finding is based on data from 2016–17, when it was relatively new.[20]

The penalty provisions seem to be a 'sticking plaster' solution to a much deeper problem: that the system for enforcing tribunal awards is too cumbersome, costly and complex. Simple reforms, such as giving tribunals their own enforcement powers, or at least streamlining the process of passing awards on to the courts to enforce so that the claimant does not have to initiate enforcement, would be much more effective. Given how vulnerable many employment claimants are, it would also be preferable to recover the fee for enforcement from the employer, rather than to require payment up front by the claimant.

[15] Department for Business, Energy and Industrial Strategy, *Employment Tribunal Naming Scheme Guidance* (December 2018).

[16] ETA 1996, s 37F.

[17] ibid, s 37F(8)–(10).

[18] Above n 15. This scheme has never been used, for reasons which are not clear.

[19] Kelly Tolhurst (Undersecretary, Department for Business, Energy and Industrial Strategy), parliamentary written answer, 3 February 2020.

[20] Survey of Employment Tribunal Applications, *Findings from the 2018 Survey* (BEIS Research Paper Number 2020/00765-66), 12.

B. Equal Pay Audits

Another non-compliance situation in which the law makes use of penalties is in relation to equal pay audits. Under the Equality Act 2010 (Equal Pay Audits) Regulations 2014, the tribunal must order an equal pay audit where the employer has been found to have discriminated on grounds of sex in relation to pay.[21] There are various exceptions, including one for small businesses and for businesses that had been in operation for less than a year prior to the infringement.[22] The tribunal must set a deadline for the audit that is not less than three months from the date of the order.[23]

When the tribunal receives the audit, it must decide whether it complies with the various substantive requirements of regulation 6. These include, for example, an action plan for tackling unequal pay in the workplace. If it does not, the tribunal must give reasons and fix a date for a hearing at which the employer can make representations.[24] The tribunal may consider making an order for a penalty under regulation 11 if it is found that the audit is not compliant.[25] A penalty may also be considered if the audit is not provided at all or is not provided by the deadline.[26] The penalty may only be ordered if the employer has 'no reasonable excuse' for breach. The penalty is subject to an upper limit of £5,000 and the tribunal must have regard to the employer's ability to pay.[27] However, it is possible to order more than one penalty to be paid, for example, if the employer repeatedly fails to produce the audit.

The Regulations are unusual because they give the tribunal a 'regulatory' function. The original claimant is no longer involved in the case, but the tribunal has an ongoing role (acting of its own motion) in making sure that the employer takes steps to prevent future breaches. A penalty regime seems to be the obvious choice because there are no easily identifiable 'beneficiaries' of the equal pay audit, since they could include the employer's future as well as current workers. Reform of this regime could go in either of two contrasting directions. On the one hand, it could be strengthened by giving tribunals the power to grant injunctions, backed by contempt powers. This would overcome the problem that the sums involved are small, particularly for larger firms. On the other hand, it could be argued that it would be preferable for ongoing obligations to be enforced by a regulator, which could support and supervise the employer's compliance, with the option of returning to the tribunal only in the event of breach. This might be more productive of genuine change than ramping up the penalties available.

[21] SI 2014/2559, reg 2.
[22] ibid regs 3–4.
[23] ibid reg 5.
[24] ibid reg 8.
[25] ibid reg 8(4).
[26] ibid reg 8(5).
[27] ibid reg 11(3) and (4).

C. Re-Employment

In chapter six, I explore the reinstatement and re-engagement orders which may be awarded in a successful claim for unfair dismissal. Here, I consider what happens if the employer does not comply with those orders.

Under section 117(1) ERA 1996, the tribunal must order the employer to compensate the employee if a re-employment order is not fully complied with. This award is genuinely compensatory, in the sense that it focuses on losses caused by the employer's partial failure. Under section 117(3)(b), if a re-employment order is not complied with at all,[28] the tribunal must order the payment of compensation in the ordinary way for the original unfair dismissal, plus an 'additional award' of between 26 and 52 weeks' pay.[29] The concept of total non-compliance has been interpreted broadly to include situations in which the employer purported to re-employ the claimant but, in practice, did not do so properly, for example, by demoting them or offering a job a long way away from their original workplace.[30] The 'additional award' is clearly not compensatory: it is subject to a minimum, and there is no need to prove loss.[31] Since it is applicable where the employer has failed (without excuse) to comply with the tribunal's order, it is appropriate to regard it as punitive.[32] This is reflected in the way in which tribunals determine the level of award to make. In *Mabirizi*, the Court of Appeal put the point as follows:

> An employer's conduct is the most obvious factor to be taken into account and a finding of a deliberate refusal without any reasoned justification to support it will doubtless in most cases warrant an award at or near the top of the scale.[33]

Of course, implicit in that statement is the possibility that the employer may be able to supply an acceptable explanation for the failure to re-employ. This means that even though, *ex hypothesi*, it has been found that it was practicable to re-employ, the employer may still be able to explain why it did not want to do so, in order to persuade the tribunal to make a lower additional award.

The problem with the additional award is obvious: it is ineffective in persuading employers to comply with re-employment orders. The courts themselves have noted that orders for re-employment are 'wholly unenforceable'.[34] The employer is simply required to pay an additional sum of money and, although conceptually this is punitive, there is no particular element of condemnation or stigma attached.

[28] Unless the employer can establish that compliance was not 'practicable' under s 117(4).

[29] A week's pay is defined in ss 220–229 and is subject to the maximum limit.

[30] *Electronic Data Processing Ltd v Wright* [1986] ICR 76.

[31] Other elements of the award are compensatory: under s 124(4), the statutory maximum may be exceeded in limited circumstances to ensure that the employee receives arrears of pay in full under s 114.

[32] Though the EAT has (rightly) resisted any formal analogy with punitive damages: *Morganite Electrical Carbon v Donne* [1988] ICR 18, 28.

[33] *Mabirizi v National Hospital for Nervous Diseases* [1990] ICR 281, 289.

[34] *O'Laoire v Jackel International Ltd* [1990] ICR 197, 206; and see *R (Mackenzie) v University of Cambridge* [2019] EWCA Civ 1060, [2019] ICR 1477.

It is even possible for the employer to argue for that sum to be reduced if it can produce a reason for choosing not to comply. This is all in marked contrast to what would happen if a re-employment order took the form of an injunction, with the prospect of contempt proceedings in the event of non-compliance.

D. Other Awards in Respect of Non-Compliance with a Recommendation

There are a number of situations in which a tribunal may either make an award, or increase an earlier award, because the employer has not complied with a recommendation it has previously made. The main examples are:

- failure to comply with a recommendation relating to a refusal to hire a person on trade union grounds under section 137 TULRCA[35]
- failure to comply with a recommendation under section 124(2)(c) Equality Act 2010[36]
- failure to comply with recommendations relating to the treatment of a fixed-term,[37] part-time[38] or agency worker[39]

Although tribunals do make recommendations, particularly under the Equality Act 2010, there are few, if any, examples of awards being made to enforce them, and no clear guidance on how they might be quantified. The drafting suggests that any further award would be compensatory, but in practice, recommendations are often quite wide-ranging (requiring the employer to update its policies or provide training, for example) so a very strict focus on losses suffered by the worker would probably result in no award at all. It makes more sense to think of them as a form of punishment. Of course, the lack of evidence of enforcement may be because employers are, by this stage in proceedings, willing to comply, but it seems more likely in practice that claimants do not have the energy or resources to pursue the matter. Again, an injunction would provide a much stronger incentive to comply, but it would also be problematic because of the uncertainties involved in recommendations. It would be necessary for them to be very precisely expressed if contempt proceedings could ensue for non-compliance. Another way of looking at the problem is that recommendations (like equal pay audits, discussed above) cast the tribunal somewhat into the role of a regulator, a role to which it is not well-suited. It does not have the ability to support employers to implement its

[35] TULRCA 1992, s 140.
[36] Equality Act 2010, s 124(7).
[37] Fixed-term Employees (Prevention of Less Favourable Treatment) Regulations 2002 (SI 2002/2034), reg 7.
[38] Part-time Workers (Prevention of Less Favourable Treatment) Regulations 2000 (SI 2000/1551), reg 8.
[39] Agency Workers Regulations 2010 (SI 2010/93), reg 18.

recommendations or to check that they have been complied with. In the absence of a more familiar regulatory structure, it may be difficult to ensure that recommendations are genuinely enforceable, outside of exceptional cases.

E. Conclusion

These different kinds of penalties tell us a lot about how tribunals were envisaged – as a cheap and cheerful alternative to the courts (where the real power lies) with regulatory functions as well as judicial ones. But while that might have been an interesting set of ambitions for the tribunal system, it is hard to conclude that those ambitions have been achieved. Tribunals are increasingly court-like: they deal with complex legal arguments in a relatively formal setting; there is a well-documented advantage to having legal representation; and the role of lay members has declined over time. From this perspective, it is difficult to explain why tribunals do not have at least some of the enforcement powers given to courts, so that full effect can be given to their decisions. Functions of a more regulatory nature would probably be better transferred to existing regulators or to a labour inspectorate.

III. Manner of Breach

I turn, finally, to penalties and punitive awards which are intended to address what might loosely be termed the 'manner' of the employer's breach. The idea here is that there are some situations in which the employer's behaviour is so bad that it is not only insufficiently addressed by a compensatory or vindicatory award, but also warrants judicial condemnation and punishment of some kind. As the discussion will demonstrate, the law is not particularly clear on the type of behaviour that warrants punishment, but one common thread is where the employer has shown contempt for the working person's rights and the law more generally. Indeed, it might be thought that these measures are concerned more with upholding respect for the legal system than with the treatment of the claimant.

The discussion will consider two different approaches to punishing employers, each of which raises slightly different issues. One option is to make an award of punitive or exemplary damages against the employer. These are available at common law in tort claims and, by extension, in statutory employment claims which are regarded as analogous to torts. However, their availability is restricted to particular fact situations, and the courts are reluctant to award them. One of the main reasons given for this is that they give the claimant a 'windfall' over and above any compensatory award. Another option in employment settings is to use the power to order payment of a penalty for 'aggravated breach' under section 12A ETA 1996. This option was introduced as a means for tribunals to punish employers who deliberately or persistently disregarded workers' rights. It avoids the supposed windfall problem because the penalty is paid to the Secretary of State. But it has not been widely used, and it seems unlikely that a little-known civil penalty has much effect on employers against whom it is awarded, or as a deterrent to other employers.

A. Punitive or Exemplary Damages

At common law, 'punitive or exemplary damages are damages whose purpose is to punish the defendant for his or her wrongful conduct'.[40] Since the decision in *Broome v Cassell*, the courts have tended to adopt the term 'exemplary' damages, which is intended to convey the role of awards of this type in expressing the court's disapproval of the defendant's behaviour and seeking to deter others from similar conduct.[41] Others, notably the Law Commission, prefer the term 'punitive'.[42] Nothing turns on the choice of terminology and I use the two labels interchangeably.

Punitive damages are not available in the law of contract as a result of the troublesome decision in *Addis*, a position criticised by Burrows.[43] This has particularly unfortunate implications in employment law, because some breaches of statutory employment rights are treated as analogous to breaches of contract for various purposes, such as the calculation of compensatory awards and the determination of the consequences of illegality. Examples include unfair dismissal, unlawful deductions, NMW infringements, unpaid holiday pay and other Working Time Regulations infringements.[44] Thus, in relation to these types of claim punitive damages are unlikely to be available. As Bogg argues, the division of statutory employment claims into contract-like and tort-like claims has taken place without a great deal of analysis, so it is unfortunate when a range of (possibly unforeseen) consequences flows from this.[45] If punitive damages are to be allowed at all, it would be preferable if their availability turned on the circumstances of the case, rather than on artificial distinctions between different types of claim.

In the law of tort, punitive damages are potentially available in three different situations: where there has been oppressive action by a government servant; where the defendant has calculated that its profit will exceed any damages that are likely to be awarded under normal principles; and where the award of punitive damages is authorised by legislation.[46] Common law tort claims are potentially available

[40] AS Burrows, *Remedies for Torts, Breach of Contract, and Equitable Wrongs* (4th edn, Oxford, OUP 2019), 360.

[41] *Broome v Cassell* [1972] AC 1027, 1073.

[42] Law Commission, *Aggravated, Exemplary and Restitutionary Damages* (No 247, 1997), para 5.39.

[43] *Addis v Gramophone Co Ltd* [1909] AC 488; Burrows, above n 40, 360–61.

[44] A Bogg, '*Okedina v Chikale* and Contract Illegality: New Dawn or False Dawn?' (2020) 49 *Industrial Law Journal* 258.

[45] ibid.

[46] *Rookes v Barnard* [1964] AC 1129.

to working people in cases of negligently-inflicted physical or mental injury, and sometimes poor advice or an inaccurate reference leading to economic loss. Some statutory employment rights are also regarded as analogous to tort claims so, in practice, these are the most likely cases in which an award of punitive damages might be made. The main examples are discrimination, harassment and detriment. Perhaps surprisingly, Parliament has not expressly provided for the availability of exemplary damages in relation to any employment rights. Thus, the claimant must seek such an award on one or other of the first two bases mentioned above.

The first category, 'oppressive, arbitrary or unconstitutional action by servants of the government', is potentially applicable in tort claims against public sector employers.[47] However, it has sometimes been argued that there is a need to show that the public body is performing a public or governmental function in order for the claim to be available.[48] This requirement may be difficult for public sector workers to satisfy where the case concerns the public body's day-to-day activities in its capacity as an employer. The case-law on the point is unclear and conflicting. The EAT in *Virgo Fidelis v Boyle* held that a school, in disciplining an employee, had not been exercising executive power,[49] whereas the Court of Appeal in *Arora* held that councillors interviewing job candidates were so doing.[50] It should be easier to establish a public function where the employer's activities are underpinned by statute, a point illustrated by *Fletcher*, in which the EAT, applying *Arora*, held that the Ministry of Defence was engaged in a public function when operating its statutory complaints procedure for armed forces personnel.[51]

Even if the claimant does succeed in establishing that their public sector employer was exercising state power, the threshold for 'arbitrary, oppressive or unconstitutional' behaviour is very high indeed. Again, this is illustrated by *Fletcher*.[52] The claimant in that case was sexually harassed by a senior officer who then brought disciplinary charges against her on trivial grounds and encouraged others to behave badly towards her. The ET found that the Army had failed to investigate her complaints properly and had tried to use the fact that she had become unable to work through stress as a reason to discharge her. Although the EAT found that the Army's behaviour was 'deplorable', it held that it had not crossed the threshold for exemplary damages. This suggests that it is very difficult to bring a successful claim under this heading.

The second scenario for an award of punitive damages is where the defendant has calculated that the profits it will secure from breach will exceed any damages

[47] ibid 1226 (Lord Devlin).

[48] *AB v South West Water Services Ltd* [1993] QB 507 (overruled on other grounds in *Kuddus v Chief Constable of Leicestershire Constabulary* [2002] 2 AC 122). A similar argument is often made when public sector workers attempt to use judicial review for employment claims: *R v East Berkshire HA, ex parte Walsh* [1984] ICR 743.

[49] *Virgo Fidelis Senior School v Boyle* [2004] ICR 1210.

[50] *City of Bradford Metropolitan Council v Arora* [1991] IRLR 165.

[51] *Ministry of Defence v Fletcher* [2010] IRLR 25 (EAT).

[52] ibid.

awarded against it on ordinary principles. Interestingly, although this scenario is probably not uncommon in practice, it is very rare to find claims under this heading, and certainly not successful ones. One example, but only at ET level, is *Kocur*.[53] In that case, the tribunal had ruled in 2016 that some agency workers at Royal Mail should be given swipe card access to the premises on the same basis as directly-hired workers under regulation 12 Agency Workers Regulations 2010.[54] Royal Mail effectively refused to comply with this aspect of the decision on the ground that it would cost £4,000, with further costs due to high staff turnover, so after a further hearing, the tribunal awarded exemplary damages of £8,000. It is very clear from this case that the tribunal was concerned with the employer's disregard of its legal obligations on the basis that any compensation it would have to pay would be lower than the cost of compliance. The award of exemplary damages sought to disrupt this reasoning. It is noteworthy that in subsequent litigation between the same parties, a tribunal ordered the defendant to pay a penalty under section 12A ETA 1996 for 'aggravated' breach.[55]

Importantly, even if a case falls within one of the two categories for the award of punitive damages, such damages will only be awarded where they are considered necessary to punish the defendant. If the defendant is also the subject of criminal proceedings or if the compensatory award is considered sufficient punishment in itself, no further award will be made.[56] These principles are particularly important in employment cases because, where awards for injury to feelings and aggravated damages may also be made, as is the case in discrimination claims, a court or tribunal may conclude that there is no additional need to punish the defendant through an award of exemplary damages. Although it was held in *Fletcher* that the defendant's conduct had not crossed the threshold for punitive damages, the EAT stated, *obiter*, that the sums already awarded by the tribunal under other heads would have been sufficient in any event 'to mark disapproval of the perpetrator's conduct and to provide a proportionate punitive element'.[57] The same conclusion was reached in the unusual case of *Antuzis*, in which substantial awards of aggravated damages were held to be sufficient.[58] While this may seem to muddle the compensatory purpose of aggravated damages[59] with the punitive purpose of exemplary damages, it reflects the courts' broader concern with ensuring that the overall level of an award is fair and does not involve any double-counting.

[53] *Kocur v Angard Staffing Solutions Ltd and Royal Mail Group Ltd* (Case nos 1805244/2018 and 1805245/2018, 15 November 2017).

[54] SI 2010/93.

[55] This related to a refusal to pay a Christmas bonus even after an earlier tribunal ruling that the claimant agency workers were entitled to it: *Kocur v Angard Staffing Solutions Ltd and Royal Mail Group Ltd* (Case nos 1805244/2018 and 1805245/2018, 29 November 2018), [63]–[65]. Litigation between the parties on other points is ongoing at the time of writing.

[56] See, generally, Burrows, above n 40, ch 20.

[57] *Fletcher*, above n 51, [117].

[58] *Antuzis v DJ Houghton Catching Services Ltd* [2021] EWHC 971 (QB).

[59] *Commissioner of Police of the Metropolis v Shaw* [2012] ICR 464. I analyse the concept of aggravated damages in ch 7 of this volume.

I highlighted in chapter three the importance of a strong deterrent effect in employment settings. Punitive damages are a potentially important weapon in the armoury of courts and tribunals to punish employers for disregarding their legal obligations or treating their workers with contempt, and to deter others in the future. However, there are two difficulties. First, the restriction of this type of award to tort rather than contract claims, and particularly the extension of the tort/contract distinction to statutory employment rights, is confusing and unnecessary. Cases that are suitable for exemplary damages on the facts may be excluded because of the way in which the claim is classified. Second, where punitive damages are available as a matter of principle, such as in discrimination claims, awards for injury to feelings and aggravated damages are also available. This means that punitive damages are unlikely to be awarded because the defendant will already be liable to pay a substantial sum. In effect, punitive damages are available when they are least likely to be needed.

The classic objections to punitive damages – that they give the claimant a windfall or pursue purposes that are irrelevant to private law – carry little weight in employment settings. The courts are careful to ensure that the overall level of an award is fair, so windfalls are unlikely. And the purpose of punishing an employer who behaves oppressively or in self-interested disregard of the law seems generally relevant to the efficacy of the legal system and particularly relevant to an effective system of employment rights. However, in employment cases, there is an added complication in the shape of a penalty regime, to which I will now turn.

B. Penalties for Aggravated Breach

ETA 1996, section 12A, provides a general power for the tribunal to order that the employer be required to pay a penalty to the Secretary of State when it has engaged in an 'aggravated' breach of a working person's rights. This penalty is entirely separate to any remedy awarded to the worker. The provision was introduced by the Enterprise and Regulatory Reform Act 2013 but appears to have had limited impact in practice.

The Explanatory Notes to the 2013 Act explain the purpose of the provision in the following terms:

> Where an employment tribunal finds in favour of a claimant, it has the power to award various remedies. However, it currently has no power to penalise an employer for the actual breach of employment law. In order to encourage employers to take appropriate steps to ensure that they meet their obligations in respect of their employees, and to reduce deliberate and repeated breaches of employment laws, employment tribunals will be given the discretion to impose a financial penalty on any respondent found to have breached the claimant's rights.[60]

[60] Enterprise and Regulatory Reform Act 2013, Explanatory Notes, para 92.

This is quite a muddled statement, since it appears initially to suggest a radical transformation in the enforcement of employment law. Rather than seeing the law largely as a civil matter to be enforced by affected working people against their employers, the first two sentences appear to treat breaches of employment law as a matter of public interest to be penalised by the state. However, this is not the effect of the provision itself – which refers to 'aggravated' breaches – and this is made clearer by the reference in the third sentence to 'deliberate and repeated breaches'. Thus, the provision in fact has a different aim: to punish employers for certain types of especially egregious infringements.

Despite this objective, a striking feature of section 12A is that it does not define the circumstances in which it applies. The tribunal may order a penalty to be paid where 'it is of the opinion that the breach has one or more aggravating features'[61] but the concept of 'aggravating features' is not explained. The Explanatory Notes offer some suggestions:

> A non-exhaustive list of factors which an employment tribunal may consider in deciding whether to impose a financial penalty under this section could include the size of the employer; the duration of the breach of the employment right; or the behaviour of the employer and of the employee …
>
> An employment tribunal may be more likely to find that the employer's behaviour in breaching the law had aggravating features where the action was deliberate or committed with malice, the employer was an organisation with a dedicated human resources team, or where the employer had repeatedly breached the employment right concerned. The employment tribunal may be less likely to find that the employer's behaviour in breaching the law had aggravating features where an employer has been in operation for only a short period of time, is a micro business, has only a limited human resources function, or the breach was a genuine mistake.[62]

The Notes also make clear that the concept of 'aggravating features' is not the same as the aggravated damages regime in equality law.[63]

The general theme here seems to be that a breach is 'aggravated' where the employer knew or was well-placed to know what the law required because of its size and resources (an idea which features in determining whether a dismissal is fair or unfair, for example) and deliberately or repeatedly breached those requirements. The only appellate case to consider the provision, the EAT decision in *First Great Western*, summarised this as 'deliberate, malicious or negligent' but did not consider the definition of 'aggravated' in any serious detail.[64] In the recent ET decision in *Williams*, a penalty was ordered where the employer had unfairly dismissed the employee by making a case against him which the tribunal described as 'manufactured'.[65]

[61] ETA 1996, s 12A(1)(b).
[62] Enterprise and Regulatory Reform Act 2013, Explanatory Notes, paras 100 and 101.
[63] ibid.
[64] *First Great Western Ltd v Waiyego* (UKEAT/0056/18/RN, 6 December 2018), [106]–[113].
[65] *Williams v Stow Residential Ltd, t/a Stow Brothers* (Case no 3203211/2021, 20 January 2023) (ET), [114].

Importantly, the decision to award a penalty is discretionary and tribunals are directed by ETA 1996, section 12A(2) to take into account the employer's ability to pay both at this stage and in deciding what amount to award. There are two different routes to calculating the penalty. Where the tribunal does not make a monetary award against the employer, the penalty may be set at any amount between £100 and £20,000.[66] Where the tribunal *does* make a monetary award, the penalty is 50 per cent of that award but subject to the same minimum and maximum figures. Where there are claims by multiple workers against a single employer, the maximum penalty is set at £20,000 per claim, creating at least a possibility of substantial liability, though where a financial award is made in respect of a claim, the 50 per cent rule is expressed as a maximum rather than as the amount of the penalty. There is an incentive for prompt payment because the employer may discharge its liability in full by paying half the penalty, provided that it pays within 21 days of the order.

It is difficult to obtain reliable statistics on the use of the penalty provision, but there are very few reported cases and the tribunal in *Williams* noted that it was 'rare'.[67] Claimants have no particular reason to seek a penalty, since they do not derive any benefit from it, and indeed it may be unhelpful if there is doubt about the employer's ability to pay any compensatory or vindicatory award made to the claimant. Moreover, awarding a penalty is unfamiliar territory for tribunals, and there may be some anxiety about taking this step given the uncertainty, discussed above, about the definition of an aggravated breach.

From the perspective of the employment-specific considerations discussed in chapter three, the penalty provisions are potentially beneficial. They were clearly intended to have a deterrent effect, and they offer some additional state recognition that certain kinds of breaches are particularly serious infringements of a working person's dignity. Although the financial effect of an unfair dismissal may be similar whether it was due to malice or ignorance, its effect on the working person may be more severe in the former case. The claimant may derive some satisfaction from the tribunal's decision to punish the employer, even if there is no direct financial gain. One possible avenue for reform would be to clarify the meaning of an 'aggravated' breach and place tribunals under a duty to consider whether a penalty is appropriate in any given case,[68] in order to increase usage of the provisions.

Nevertheless, there are two reasons to be cautious about a strengthened penalty regime. First, while the problem of employer disregard of workers' rights is a genuine and serious one, imposing penalties on a subset of employers should only ever be a part of a much broader strategy for tackling the problem. An employer

[66] The maximum was increased from the original £5,000 to £20,000 in 2019: Employment Rights (Miscellaneous Amendments) Regulations 2019 (SI 2019/731).

[67] *Williams*, above n 65, [113].

[68] The Taylor review proposed a more limited duty to consider a penalty where an employer had previously lost a similar case: M Taylor, *Good Work: The Taylor Review of Modern Working Practices* (July 2017), 63. This has not been implemented, probably because it would not be easy to apply in practice.

deciding to engage in a deliberate breach of a worker's rights may take into account the low likelihood that the worker will bring a claim and, depending on the nature of the right, the low level of any likely compensatory or vindicatory award. The prospect of having to pay a penalty, even if it arose more frequently than it does now, might not outweigh these calculations. Improving working people's access to advice and support, and addressing deficiencies in remedies more generally, should also be part of the solution. Second, it is worth considering whether wider availability of punitive damages – which would at least benefit the working person – would be preferable to greater use of penalties. The arguments here are finely balanced. On the one hand, claimants would have more of an incentive to argue for punitive damages than they do for penalties. On the other hand, the courts' concern to ensure that there is no double-counting or provision of a 'windfall' to the claimant is a limiting factor in their use. A separate penalty regime might make it easier to separate questions of appropriate compensation or vindication from questions of punishment. A further alternative – and perhaps a preferable one – would be to increase the availability of awards for injury to feelings and aggravated damages. This option allows courts and tribunals to compensate working people for the hurt caused by the manner of the employer's breach, which may be a more helpful way of upholding their dignity (with some additional deterrent effect) than any measure designed to punish the employer.

IV. Conclusion

Some of the points made in this chapter – the inability of tribunals to enforce their orders in the same way as courts can – are well-known. But by grouping different kinds of penalties and punitive awards together, I have been able to highlight broader issues about poor system design or 'fit', and weak deterrent effects. First, it is not clear that enforcing an obligation simply by means of a penalty or punitive award, with no element of regulatory intervention or persuasion, is always the best way to secure compliance. The penalty or award is liable to become another 'cost of doing business', particularly if the sum involved is insubstantial. Examples include the use of penalties to enforce equal pay audits or punitive awards in respect of tribunal recommendations. A better example of the strategic use of a penalty was the old NMW regime, in which the prospect of having to pay a penalty gave employers an incentive to pay their arrears promptly. Second, there is an unfortunate tendency to come up with a new statutory scheme, typically involving a financial penalty, to deal with problems of non-compliance with, or disrespect for, the system. The penalty scheme for non-payment of tribunal awards and the penalties for 'aggravated breach' are examples of this. The difficulty with these schemes is that they are not well-known and the sums involved are often small, so their capacity to create a deterrent effect is limited. More fundamentally, they are a poor substitute for deeper thinking about why employers do not always take employment law seriously – low levels of trade union presence in workplaces to encourage compliance, for example, or difficulties for individuals in bringing tribunal claims – and for more strategic solutions to these problems. Third, the best way to secure respect for tribunal orders (not recommendations) would be to give them the same status as court orders, backed by contempt powers. This might require some changes to the selection or training of employment judges, or perhaps the use of modified contempt powers involving fines rather than imprisonment – questions beyond the scope of the present enquiry.[69] But it is clear that 'additional awards' are insufficient to promote compliance with re-employment orders. Fourth, given the importance of protecting workers' dignity, it may be appropriate to acknowledge situations in which the employer has behaved particularly badly, for example, by deliberately refusing to comply with its obligations. But this may be more effectively achieved by making awards for injury to feelings and aggravated damages more widely available, than through little-used penalties or punitive damages.

[69] Some of the logistical difficulties are highlighted in Law Commission, *Employment Law Hearing Structures* (No 390, April 2020), ch 8, which ultimately rejected the idea.

6

Replicative Remedies

This chapter considers what Smith labels 'replicative' remedies.[1] These are orders requiring the employer to do something identical to, or very close to, the duty it has infringed. Examples in the employment context include ordering the employer to pay money it owes to the working person, such as unpaid wages, or to complete a contractual disciplinary procedure. In one sense, replicative remedies are uncontroversial: the employer is already subject to the duty in question, and the court or tribunal is not making any new demands. In another sense, though, these remedies may seem odd: if the defendant has already failed to comply with its obligations, what is the point of the court or tribunal making a further order? However, as Smith explains, the fact of a specific order requiring the defendant to comply may concentrate the mind in the way that the claimant's arguments and assertions may not. This is particularly so where strong enforcement mechanisms are attached to the order, such as the possibility of contempt proceedings. In practice, there is a world of difference for the employer between an employee alleging that they are owed money and being in receipt of an order to pay the employee the sum owed.

From the perspective of the employment-specific considerations identified in chapter three, replicative remedies are an attractive option. Many of the duties to be considered in this chapter are procedural in nature – duties to consult or to conduct a disciplinary process, for example – and these play an important role in protecting the dignity of working people. They ensure that collective or individual voices are heard. Damages awards are a poor substitute for not being able to have one's say, and for losing the opportunity to change the employer's mind. Ordering the employer to do what it was supposed to do is also a strong statement in favour of the employment-specific concern with promoting compliance and deterring breaches. It makes it harder for the employer to treat employment obligations as a 'tax' on doing business, that can be disregarded provided that compensation is paid.

However, as the chapter will demonstrate, replicative remedies are restricted in employment law in two main ways. First, where such remedies exist, they are often harder to obtain or more limited than one might expect. For example, the

[1] SA Smith, *Rights, Wrongs and Injustices: the Structure of Remedial Law* (Oxford, OUP, 2019), ch 6.

recovery of money owed is, in many cases, subject to a two-year limit on arrears, rather than the usual six years for contractual and other civil claims. Employees seeking an injunction to force the employer to conduct a disciplinary procedure face additional hurdles, for example, in the requirement to show that mutual trust and confidence continues to exist between them and their employer. This is so even though a proper process ought to be conducted before the employer reaches any conclusion about its level of trust in the employee. Second, there are numerous examples of cases in which a replicative remedy would be a good fit for the situation and would promote the employment-specific goals of dignity and compliance, but is not made available by the relevant legislation. For example, if the employer fails to consult on collective redundancies, a sum of money is payable to the affected employees. This is an obvious example of a case in which an order stopping the redundancies until the consultation is carried out would be a better option for fulfilling the legislative purpose and preventing employers from buying their way out of the obligation.

Both of these weaknesses reflect the 'burdens on business' argument discussed in chapter three. This argument takes slightly different forms depending on the context. In relation to claims for back-pay, there is obviously a worry about 'burdening' the employer with substantial money claims. In relation to orders to continue to employ a person whilst conducting a disciplinary or consultation process, there may be concerns about interfering with managerial prerogative, disrupting relationships in the workplace or slowing down economically-necessary decision-making. While all of these are valid considerations, it may be questioned why the threshold for accepting them is so low, given that the employer is only being ordered to fulfil its duties, and why so little consideration is given to alternative points of view, particularly those of working people who might derive considerable benefit from such orders. For example, a remedy requiring an employer to conduct a collective consultation exercise before making employees redundant would be a strong deterrent to non-compliance if the employer was indeed anxious to implement the redundancies as quickly as possible. These arguments will be explored in more depth later in the chapter.

The discussion will be organised around a loose classification focusing on the context for the order of the court or tribunal.[2] The four categories are payments of money owed, orders during employment, orders potentially connected with the termination of employment, and recommendations. This grouping is not logically watertight, but helps to highlight key features of the situation in which the court or tribunal is being asked to intervene, and thus the kinds of arguments that might arise around the key themes of dignity, compliance and burdens on business. I have deliberately chosen not to split the discussion into remedies available at common law and in statute, because it is often instructive to compare and contrast how common law and statute deal with similar contexts. I have also

[2] The various orders that may be made by the Central Arbitration Committee in the context of eg a recognition claim under Schedule A1 TULRCA 1992 are beyond the scope of this chapter.

avoided classification into procedural and substantive obligations, since the two are often closely connected: for example, an order to follow a procedure might result in a (substantive) decision not to dismiss the employee.

I. Orders to Pay Money Owed

There are several different situations which might give rise to the simple replicative remedy of an order to pay money owed. These include:

- the employer's failure to pay the working person the wages they were due, which can be addressed either through an action for the sum due under the contract[3] or through a statutory claim for unlawful deductions;[4]
- failure to pay the NMW;[5]
- equal pay claims;[6]
- failure to pay (or to pay appropriately) during periods of annual leave; and[7]
- failure to pay during time off (where there is a right to payment), for example, for trade union officials.[8]

From a remedies perspective, orders to pay money owed are relatively straightforward: the quantification of the sum owing is a matter of substantive law (because the remedy replicates the employer's duty), and the court or tribunal simply orders the employer to pay that amount.

However, one area of controversy is the length of time for which arrears of pay can be claimed. In many cases, this is not a problem because the employer's default is a 'one-off', which must be challenged promptly under the three-month time limit for bringing a tribunal claim.[9] But it is not uncommon to find that the employer's default has gone on for a number of years before the working person has realised that what was happening was unlawful or found the means to bring a claim. In these cases, the extent of the arrears that can be claimed is significant.

Under the Limitation Act 1980, there is a six-year limit on contract, tort and statutory claims, with some exceptions.[10] This is relevant to some types of

[3] It is important that the employee does not accept the employer's repudiatory breach for these purposes: *Rigby v Ferodo Ltd* [1988] ICR 2. If the contract is brought to an end by acceptance, a claim lies in damages instead: *Gunton v Richmond-upon-Thames London Borough Council* [1980] ICR 755. On acceptance, see *Geys v Societe Generale* [2012] UKSC 63, [2013] 1 AC 523.

[4] ERA 1996, s 13, with remedies in ss 23–26.

[5] NMWA 1998, s 17, and see s 28. Again, this can be brought in the tribunal as an unlawful deductions claim or in court as a breach of contract claim.

[6] Equality Act 2010, ss 127–135.

[7] Working Time Regulations (SI 1998/1833) (WTR), regs 16 and 30. Note that this right is not contractual: reg 16(4).

[8] TULRCA 1992, ss 168–169 and 172(3).

[9] Eg (in unlawful deductions cases) ERA 1996, s 23(2).

[10] Limitation Act 1980, ss 2, 5 and 9.

employment case, for example, when a working person brings a claim for money owed under their contract.[11] In an equal pay claim, section 132 Equality Act 2010 provides that arrears of pay may be claimed for up to six years, and for longer in cases where the claimant has been unable to bring the claim or the defendant has concealed a material fact.[12] A previous two-year limit on claims was challenged in the *Levez* case, in which it was found to breach the EU principle of 'equivalence' by prescribing a shorter time period for equal pay claims than was the case in national law for other similar claims.[13]

However, a two-year limit does apply for *some* statutory employment claims. For example, a claim for unlawful deductions from wages can be brought in respect of a series of deductions.[14] In such cases, the claim must normally be brought within three months of the last deduction in the series, but the tribunal may not consider any deductions which took place more than two years before the date on which the claim was brought.[15] This change was brought about in 2014 to limit the impact of the decision in the *Bear Scotland* case, which had expanded the definition of 'pay' for the purposes of statutory holiday pay claims.[16] The limitation also applies where a claimant uses the unlawful deductions route to bring a claim for NMW arrears. This can be avoided by bringing a contract claim for NMW arrears instead (since the NMW is a contractual entitlement[17]), where up to six years of arrears are potentially available, but this claim may only be brought in the tribunal where it arises or is outstanding on termination of employment, and is subject to a maximum limit.[18] Otherwise, the claimant must seek redress in the civil courts, which raises issues of accessibility.

The position relating to holiday pay is also unsatisfactory. Under regulation 30(2) Working Time Regulations, a claim relating to holiday pay must be brought within three months, with the effect that the worker must bring a separate claim in respect of each default by their employer.[19] One way to avoid this inconvenience is to bring an unlawful deductions claim in respect of a series of deductions, as described above. In the *Bear Scotland* case, the EAT held that a gap of more than three months between deductions (which is much more likely to arise in relation to holiday pay, given its sporadic nature) would break the 'series',[20] but

[11] Limitation Act 1980, s 5.

[12] As defined in Equality Act 2010, s 135. Different arrangements apply to pension claims.

[13] *Levez v TH Jennings (Harlow Pools) Ltd (No. 2)* [2000] ICR 58.

[14] ERA 1996, s 23(3). I discuss the definition of a 'series' below. There is a 12-month limit on claims under the new tips legislation: Employment (Allocation of Tips) Act 2023, s 7, inserting new s 27K(3) ERA 1996.

[15] ERA 1996, s 23(4A), but note that a number of claims are excluded from this limit under s 23(4B).

[16] *Bear Scotland Ltd v Fulton* [2015] ICR 221, and see Deduction from Wages (Limitation) Regulations 2014 (SI 2014/3322).

[17] Above n 5.

[18] Employment Tribunals Act 1996 (ETA 1996), s 3, and Employment Tribunals Extension of Jurisdiction (England and Wales) Order 1994 (SI 1994/1623).

[19] WTR, reg 30(2).

[20] Above n 16, [73]–[83].

this has recently been overruled by the Supreme Court in the *Agnew* case.[21] It was held that gaps of more than three months did not break the series where all the deductions stemmed from the same kind of 'fault' on the part of the employer. In *Agnew* itself, this was failing to include overtime pay in the holiday pay calculation. However, the two-year time limit on arrears remains applicable. WTR regulation 16(4), as amended in 2014, provides that a claim for holiday pay is not contractual, which prevents claimants from avoiding that particular restriction by bringing a contract claim instead.[22] Where the employment relationship comes to an end, the worker is entitled to a payment in lieu of holiday.[23] In the *Pimlico Plumbers* case, applying the CJEU's decision in *King*,[24] it was held that where the employer had refused to permit the worker to exercise the right to paid leave (either by not permitting it at all or by allowing unpaid leave only) the entitlement could accrue until the termination of the relationship.[25] This means that a worker who is denied paid annual leave over a longer period of time may be able to bring a substantial claim for backdated holiday pay at the end of the employment relationship.

The limitations on employment claims highlighted here are a clear illustration of the concern, discussed in chapter three, to protect employers' economic interests. Once again, this concern is misplaced. Any limitation period is, of course, arbitrary. But setting a relatively long period, such as six years, gives the claimant ample time to discover that they have a cause of action and to bring proceedings, whilst also ensuring that defendants are not subject to claims in relation to events in the distant past, for which evidence may no longer be readily available. In employment cases, as chapter two explained, there are particular challenges for working people in discovering that what has happened to them was a breach of the law, getting access to legal advice and preparing a claim. As a result, a shorter than usual limitation period is particularly hard to justify. Of course, there are cases in which the law is unclear, and substantial claims for back-pay may be brought at the point at which the law is clarified – the gradual development through case-law of rules on which payments and allowances should be included in holiday pay is a good example of this phenomenon[26] – but there is no obvious reason why this loss should fall on claimants (who are denied money they were owed) rather than on employers (who were liable to pay the money in the first place). This is particularly so where employers have tried to minimise their liabilities in situations in which it would have been obvious that their strategy might not succeed if tested in court.

[21] *Chief Constable of Northern Ireland v Agnew* [2023] UKSC 33. *Bear Scotland* was doubted but not overruled in *Smith v Pimlico Plumbers Ltd* [2022] EWCA Civ 70, [2022] ICR 818, [91]–[101].

[22] Amended by Deduction from Wages (Limitation) Regulations 2014 (SI 2014/3322), reg 3.

[23] WTR, reg 14.

[24] Case C-214/16 *King v Sash Window Workshop Ltd*, ECLI:EU:C:2017:914, [2018] 2 CMLR 10.

[25] Above n 21.

[26] For one of many examples see Case C-155/10 *Williams v British Airways Plc*, ECLI:EU:C:2011:588, [2012] 1 CMLR 23.

II. Dealing with Rights-Threats (1): During Employment

I now turn to two types of replicative remedy that might be available during the employment relationship: orders to restrain breaches of contractual or statutory obligations,[27] and orders to reconsider or retake decisions. The former is the classic legal response to what Smith terms a 'rights-threat': an injunction designed to stop the employer from carrying out the threat.[28] The latter is more familiar from public law – where ministers are often required to retake a decision where they have failed to follow a proper process or taken into account irrelevant considerations, for example[29] – but it has relevance in employment cases too, where employers often have similarly complex discretionary decisions to take in accordance with legal standards. An order to retake a decision in the proper way upholds those legal standards whilst leaving the decision in the hands of the appropriate decision-maker.

The law makes both types of remedy available in certain circumstances, but neither is particularly common in practice. As I will explain, a more compliance-orientated system of employment law might make these orders more readily available in a wider variety of situations. However, there are some practical considerations to take into account too. Litigation during the employment relationship is relatively unusual: even if a working person believes that the employer is not complying with the law, they may not wish to sue unless the relationship is ending anyway, fearing that there might be adverse consequences even if they won their case. Moreover, particularly where the aim is to restrain a threatened breach, the claimant must act quickly. This, in turn, requires knowledge of one's legal rights and prompt access to legal advice and to a court or tribunal, advantages many working people may lack.[30]

It is important to note that there is no bright line between some of the orders to be considered here and orders arising in connection with the termination, or potential termination, of employment. For example, I discuss the right to be accompanied at a disciplinary or grievance procedure here, but this could equally form part of a process leading up to dismissal, and be discussed in the next section.[31]

[27] Injunctions can be positive (ordering the employer to do something) or negative (ordering the employer to refrain from doing something). The former type are often thought to be harder to obtain because they may require more supervision on the part of the court. However, the line between the two is not straightforward: an order not to dismiss an employee without following a procedure is, in fact, a combination of negative and positive requirements.

[28] Above n 1.

[29] See, generally, CF Forsyth and J Ghosh, *Wade & Forsyth's Administrative Law* (12th edn, Oxford, OUP, 2023), ch 16.

[30] Eg *Geys v Societe Generale*, above n 3, confirmed that the elective theory of termination applies to contracts of employment, but it is important that the employee does not accept the employer's repudiatory breach if they want to seek an injunction.

[31] Employment Relations Act 1999, s 10.

However, I think it is useful to compare the treatment of cases where termination is a less obvious or immediate issue. This is because a particular set of concerns arises, or is thought to arise, where there is a possibility that the order might keep the working person in their job against the 'wishes' of the employer.

A. Orders to Restrain Breaches of Statutory or Contractual Obligations

Most of the injunction cases are concerned with stopping the employer from breaching the contractual commitments it has made, although occasionally the courts are willing to grant injunctions to prevent breaches of the employer's statutory duties. The latter may sometimes raise a broader policy question as to whether it is legitimate for the courts to use injunctions to supplement the remedies laid down by Parliament (typically a compensatory or vindicatory award) for infringement of the working person's statutory rights.

One group of challenges concerns allegedly unlawful decisions or instructions by the employer. Here, the courts have been willing to grant interim injunctions barring the employer from implementing the decision or instruction pending a trial to determine its lawfulness.[32] For example, in *Powell v Brent LBC*, the claimant successfully applied for a promotion and began work in her new job, but was then told to return to her old job because a grievance from one of the unsuccessful candidates had exposed flaws in the appointment process (largely to do with a failure to keep proper records).[33] She argued that she had been properly appointed to the new post, so the council could not simply withdraw the offer and would instead have to pursue disciplinary or dismissal proceedings. The Court of Appeal granted the injunction on the basis that she had an arguable case, claims by the council that it did not have confidence in her were not substantiated, and damages would not compensate for the disappointment and embarrassment involved in having the promotion withdrawn. Similarly, in *Hughes v Southwark LBC*, the council sought to redeploy the claimant hospital social workers to work in its community teams because of a funding crisis.[34] The judge held that there was a serious issue to be tried as to whether the instruction was lawful, because the claimants had not been consulted or given an opportunity to raise a grievance about it in accordance with contractual procedures, and because the instruction itself was arguably unreasonable in that it would damage the social work provision in the hospital without necessarily resolving the council's wider staffing problems. There were no obstacles to granting the injunction because the council continued to have confidence

[32] The general test is that laid down by the House of Lords in *American Cyanamid Co v Ethicon Ltd* [1975] AC 396. In most cases, the parties resolve their dispute at this point without proceeding to trial.

[33] *Powell v Brent LBC* [1988] ICR 176 (CA).

[34] *Hughes v Southwark LBC* [1988] IRLR 55. See also *Wadcock v Brent LBC* [1990] IRLR 223.

in the claimants' work (indeed, the council's belief in their abilities was part of the reason for wanting to redeploy them) and damages would not have been an adequate remedy because money would not compensate for the distress and loss of job satisfaction that would result from the redeployment.

These cases offer a good illustration of the potential for replicative remedies to promote compliance and to address the non-financial aspects of claimants' employment problems. From a compliance perspective, these injunctions required the employer to observe the contractual commitments it had already made in the context of its ongoing relationship with the employee. In terms of non-financial considerations, it was seen as legitimate for the claimants in *Hughes* to express concern about the impact on their existing work of the council's proposed redeployment,[35] and in *Powell*, the court was acutely aware of the humiliation involved in having a promotion withdrawn and having to return to one's old role.[36] Of course, a key part of the claimant's case to obtain the injunction is to demonstrate that damages would not be an adequate remedy, so it is not surprising to see these kinds of points being made. But the cases show that the courts are, sometimes at least, capable of recognising that having a job is not just about the money it brings in.

An interesting question for present purposes is whether the courts' welcome recognition of working people's non-financial interests is an exception confined to certain types of employment, or whether it is potentially applicable in any work relationship. The case-law so far might be taken to suggest that the courts' willingness to acknowledge factors such as job satisfaction or avoiding embarrassment may be confined to cases involving workers in professional occupations, where reputational issues may be thought to be more acute.[37] This point has not been tested because it is rare for other kinds of workers to bring these claims. This is probably because workers in professional occupations, particularly those in the public sector covered by collective bargaining, are more likely to have detailed contracts setting standards of behaviour for employers – giving something for the courts to enforce – and the practical and financial resources to bring a case to court. My own view, explained in chapter three, is that all work relationships involve a range of social and emotional benefits, so an injunction to restrain a threatened breach of contract by the employer should be available in principle to any working person. A wide variety of contract terms could potentially be enforced via this route.[38]

Turning to statutory rights, the courts have sometimes also been willing to use declarations (though not injunctions) to enforce the WTR.[39] This is more controversial because it involves using common law remedies to bolster a

[35] ibid [12].

[36] Above n 33, [80].

[37] See the discussion in Z Adams, C Barnard, S Deakin and S Fraser Butlin, *Deakin and Morris's Labour Law* (7th edn, Oxford, Hart Publishing, 2021), para 4.61.

[38] Eg the car allowances at issue in *Keir v Hereford and Worcester CC* [1985] IRLR 505.

[39] Above n 19.

statutory scheme. In *Barber*, the claimants were asked by their employer to sign an opt-out when the Regulations came into force because they routinely worked more than 48 hours per week.[40] They refused to sign (in the context of ongoing negotiations with the employer on pay) and sought a declaration that, having already worked in excess of 48 hours per week on average in the reference period, they could refuse to work any more hours until their average fell within the limit. The judge held that regulation 4(1) could be treated as a standalone contractual obligation on the employer not to require its workers to work more than 48 hours per week.[41] Although regulation 4(2) provided for a duty on the employer to take reasonable steps to ensure compliance, which was enforceable via the criminal law, this did not preclude other routes to enforcement of the clear-cut duty in regulation 4(1). However, while the judge was content to confirm the workers' rights by means of a declaration, he refused to grant the injunction because to stop the employer insisting (even in breach of contract) that the workers continued to work would have serious consequences for the employer's ability to carry on its business.[42] A declaration was also granted in the *Fire Brigades' Union* case that a shift system in operation in some fire stations in South Yorkshire was in breach of regulation 10 WTR, providing an entitlement to 11 hours' rest in every 24 hour period.[43] Although there were exceptions to regulation 10, these did not apply in the case because the authority had not sought to provide the workers with the equivalent periods of rest they would require. Under the Regulations, a remedy of individual complaint to the tribunal was provided for breach of regulation 10, but the court held that it could also grant the union (which would not be able to bring a claim in the tribunal) a declaration that the shift system was unlawful.[44] The court was particularly unsympathetic to the authority's position that firefighters at the relevant stations had accepted the unlawful arrangements (in return for a pay rise) and that it was simply too expensive to comply with the law.[45]

These cases are unusual and it is not clear whether they will ever give rise to a significant body of doctrine in practice. Nevertheless, they are important as a matter of principle. The judges in both cases recognised that the workers' rights were under threat from the employer's insistence on long-hours working in breach of the WTR, and that it was appropriate to attempt to bring this threat to an end (albeit that they did not grant an injunction in either case). This has the advantage of recognising the value to workers of compliance with the law – not just compensation after the fact, where this is available – and the possibility of getting

[40] *Barber v RJB Mining (UK) Ltd* [1999] ICR 679.
[41] ibid 690.
[42] ibid 692–93.
[43] *R (Fire Brigades Union) v South Yorkshire Fire and Rescue Authority* [2018] EWHC 1229 (Admin), [2018] IRLR 717.
[44] ibid [132]–[150].
[45] ibid [147].

employers in long-term employment relationships to do what they are supposed to do. The argument that these orders might subvert the statutory scheme seems to be misplaced here, since they do not impose new duties or liabilities, but simply replicate existing ones.[46]

The approach could be extended to other statutory duties where a breach can be anticipated and potentially restrained. For example, there are several statutory provisions requiring the employer to give a working person time off: to attend ante-natal appointments,[47] to carry out public duties,[48] to serve as a trade union representative[49] and so on. As chapter eight explains, the remedy for an infringement of these rights is typically a monetary award, which I classify as 'vindicatory'.[50] It does not compensate the working person for losses suffered, and in many cases there are no such losses, but simply expresses the idea that they have been wronged in not being allowed to take time off when they needed it. While this remedy is better than nothing, it is a long way from encouraging compliance with the law. A much better approach would be to give the working person the opportunity to seek an order restraining the employer from requiring them to work in breach of an applicable time-off right.[51] This would improve the chances of the working person getting the time off when they needed it. It would also improve compliance: the vindicatory awards typically made in this context are so small that they are not normally worth claiming, with the result that the employer can ignore the law with impunity.

B. Orders to Reconsider a Decision

In public law, orders quashing a public body's decision and remitting the case for reconsideration are very common, for example, when the public body has failed to take into account relevant considerations or has failed to follow a proper procedure.[52] This approach enables the public body to rectify the defect in the original decision whilst continuing to exercise the discretion conferred on it, usually by statute. This is particularly important in cases where, even once the defect has been corrected, multiple lawful decisions remain open to the public authority, and it would not be appropriate for the court to usurp the authority's decision-making function. In employment law, remedies of this kind are rare, despite the

[46] Cf cases on the implied term of mutual trust and confidence: *Johnson v Unisys Ltd* [2001] UKHL 13, [2003] 1 AC 518.
[47] ERA 1996, s 55.
[48] ERA 1996, s 50.
[49] TULRCA 1992 s 168.
[50] Where the right is to paid time off and the working person did not receive the pay to which they were entitled, this may also be recovered.
[51] Of course, this would require procedural reforms to be effective, a point to which I return in ch 9 of this volume.
[52] Above n 29.

many decisions employers take every day. It seems likely that this reflects some of the concerns about 'burdens on business' discussed in chapter three. Orders to reconsider would interfere with managerial prerogative by slowing down decision-making and taking up additional management time. It might also be thought that they would be difficult to implement in practice, given that there are long waits for tribunal hearings and that employers cannot be relied upon to comply in the same way that public bodies generally can.

Nevertheless, one example of an obligation to reconsider is found under section 80I ERA 1996, the remedial provision for the right to request flexible working under section 80F. Where the tribunal finds a breach of section 80F, it must make a declaration and may also 'make an order for reconsideration of the application' alongside an award of compensation.[53] While this does not have the equivalent status to an injunction, it does mean that the clock starts ticking again on the timetable for the employer to consider the employee's request.[54] If the employer were to fail to consider the request by the deadline, or refuse it again, these decisions would be open to further challenge by the employee. Moreover, although the right to request flexible working itself has relatively limited remedies, in many cases claimants are also able to bring discrimination or detriment claims alongside an action under section 80F.[55]

Another example may be found in the new legislation on tips.[56] In the event of a successful claim that tips have not been allocated fairly by the employer, the tribunal may make an order requiring the employer to deal with tips in accordance with the principles laid down by the Act.[57] In particular, this order may:

> (a) require the employer to revise an allocation made by the employer under section 27D;
> (b) make a recommendation to the employer regarding that allocation;
> (c) require the employer to make a payment to one or more workers of the employer in accordance with this Part (including a worker who is not the complainant).[58]

This requires the employer to reconsider its principles for allocating tips and, potentially, to pay workers more money. Importantly, where the new allocation would result in some workers receiving less, the legislation prevents the employer from seeking repayment.[59] The recommendation under paragraph (b) of section 27L(2) is stated not to be binding, but any failure to comply may be taken into account in future tribunal proceedings.[60] This gives the tribunal an opportunity

[53] ERA 1996, s 80I(1)(a).
[54] ERA 1996, s 80I(4).
[55] The maximum award is eight weeks' pay (subject to the statutory limit on a week's pay) under reg 6 Flexible Working Regulations 2014 (SI 2014/1398).
[56] Employment (Allocation of Tips) Act 2023, amending ERA 1996.
[57] ERA 1996, s 27L(1)(b)(i).
[58] ibid s 27L(2).
[59] ibid s 27U.
[60] ibid s 27L(3).

to influence the employer's allocation of tips, whilst leaving the decision with the employer.

An example of a situation currently dealt with through a small vindicatory award, but which could be addressed much more effectively through an order to reconsider, is the right to be accompanied at a disciplinary or grievance hearing.[61] This right acknowledges the fact that attending such a hearing is a stressful situation for many working people, who may not be able to present their case effectively under pressure. A monetary award for breach of this right acknowledges that the employer has not complied with the law, but does nothing to address the fact that the working person may not have been able to present their grievance or respond to allegations in the best way possible.[62] Requiring the employer to pause and retake the decision after a fresh hearing with the worker's chosen companion would clearly be a much more appropriate remedy.

C. Conclusion

Where an employer threatens to breach contractual or statutory obligations during an ongoing employment relationship, injunctions offer a way to secure compliance and to protect any interests of the working person (such as reputation or job satisfaction) that could not easily be compensated in monetary terms. Similarly, orders to reconsider a decision can provide the working person with an opportunity to be heard and the chance to get the outcome they were seeking. I have argued here that injunctions should not be seen by the courts as exceptional, either in terms of the type of claimant who can obtain them or the type of obligation they can be used to enforce. I have also suggested that Parliament should make orders to reconsider a decision more widely available as a remedy in appropriate cases.

Of course, there are a number of practical obstacles to implementing these proposals. Contracts of employment drafted without the benefit of collective bargaining may contain few enforceable constraints on employers' behaviour. Claimants may be reluctant to litigate in an ongoing employment relationship, or may lack the knowledge or resources to bring a claim. Severe delays in the employment tribunals mean that orders to reconsider may be granted too late to be of practical benefit. Some of these problems – particularly claimants' own nervousness – would persist even in a perfect environment for enforcement. But others could be fixed if there was greater political commitment to enforcing employment law in some of the ways outlined in chapter two.

[61] Above n 31.

[62] The maximum award is two weeks' pay (subject to the statutory limit on a week's pay) under s 11(3) Employment Relations Act 1999.

III. Dealing with Rights-Threats (2): Termination Situations

In this section, I turn to the use or potential use of replicative remedies in termination situations. As noted above, there is no sharp dividing line between the use of these orders during employment and at the point of termination, but the distinction is useful for explanatory purposes because there is greater political and judicial reluctance to interfere with the employer's discretion to bring the employment relationship to an end. The discussion will consider three bodies of law. First, and most obviously, I will examine the use of injunctions to restrain a threatened termination in breach of the working person's contractual rights. Most commonly, the cases are concerned with the employer's refusal to conduct a contractual disciplinary procedure, or to conduct it properly, but there are some other examples too. I explore the courts' treatment of these injunctions as exceptional, rather than routine, and their struggles with the requirement that mutual trust and confidence should continue to exist in the parties' relationship. Second, I will consider the statutory 'parallel': re-employment orders in unfair dismissal cases. These are rarely used and widely criticised, principally because of their weak enforcement, but the discussion highlights another key problem: that they are not available until after the dismissal has occurred. I suggest ways to make these orders more effective. Third, I examine the law on consultation in collective redundancy cases. This is a good example of a situation in which a replicative remedy – an order halting the redundancies until the employer conducts the consultation exercise in accordance with the law – would be a much more effective remedy than the vindicatory award currently on offer.

A. Injunctions

At common law, injunctions offer a possible route by which working people may restrain employers from purporting to dismiss them in breach of contract. In theory at least, they could help to promote the key employment law goals of compliance – by forcing employers to fulfil their contractual obligations – and dignity – by fulfilling employees' expectations of how they will be treated under their contracts. Despite these potential benefits, the courts have tended to be reluctant to grant injunctions in employment cases. This reflects both general restrictions on the availability of injunctions, and employment-specific considerations. I focus on two main issues: adequacy of damages and mutual trust and confidence.

A core component of the test laid down in *American Cyanamid* for the grant of an interim injunction is whether damages would be an adequate remedy for the person seeking the injunction.[63] If so, there is no case for using an injunction

[63] Above n 32.

to preserve the status quo. This approach reflects the common law's preference for damages over specific performance as a remedy in the law of contract.[64] Commercial parties are expected to accept the money and secure performance by other means, rather than insisting on performance by the counterparty. However, the considerations in employment law are different, as chapter three explained. Damages are not an adequate remedy for the loss of a person's job because they do not take into account the wide range of non-financial benefits associated with having a job – social status, job satisfaction, friendships, career progression and so on – and the non-financial harms associated with losing that job in an unfair or improper way. However, the courts have only accepted this argument in relation to certain types of employment relationship, for example, where the employee's reputation and future job prospects will be irreparably harmed by the dismissal. They have been much less willing to recognise these factors in so-called 'ordinary' employment cases.

There is now a long line of cases relating to professional employment in which injunctions have been granted, which began with the decision in *Irani*.[65] The claimant was an ophthalmologist who had fallen out with the consultant in charge of the department. Although there was no criticism of his work, the employer, an NHS hospital, wanted to dismiss him because of the breakdown in relationships. He was granted an injunction to force the employer to go through the disciplinary process before dismissing him. One of the factors that persuaded the judge to grant the injunction was that the claimant would not be able to secure another job in the NHS if his record showed that he had been summarily dismissed.[66] In *Gryf-Lowczowski*, a more complex case in which the claimant had been ordered to undergo a period of retraining, the judge granted the injunction after noting the following:

> If Mr Gryf-Lowczowski is dismissed, he will be deprived of the disciplinary procedures which would provide him with the opportunity to justify and vindicate himself in that context. What is more, Mr Gryf-Lowczowski would lose the congenial (albeit stressful) employment he has had with the trust and might well find himself unable to find alternative employment at least within the NHS.[67]

The courts' refusal in the *Edwards* case to make substantial awards of damages in respect of breaches of contractual disciplinary procedures has, if anything, reinforced this position,[68] a point noted by the Supreme Court in *Chhabra*.[69]

[64] Though Bogg and Brodie draw attention to the fact that there is a growing trend towards creative use of injunctions in commercial contexts: A Bogg and D Brodie, 'Every Little Helps: Permanent Benefits, Contract Interpretation, and "Fire and Rehire"' (2023) 52 *Industrial Law Journal* 246, 265–69.

[65] *Irani v Southampton and South West Hampshire HA* [1985] ICR 590.

[66] ibid 597.

[67] *Gryf-Lowczowski v Hinchingbrooke Healthcare NHS Trust* [2005] EWHC 2407 (QB), [2006] ICR 425, [76].

[68] *Edwards v Chesterfield Royal Hospital NHS Foundation Trust* [2011] UKSC 58, [2012] 2 AC 22.

[69] *Chhabra v West London Mental Health NHS Trust* [2013] UKSC 80, [2014] ICR 194, [39].

There are a few examples of cases in which an employee who had been threatened with dismissal in breach of contract succeeded in obtaining an injunction outside the context of disciplinary procedures applicable to professionals. One is *Anderson*, a Scottish case in which the employer had agreed with a trade union representing the workforce to apply a 'last in, first out' redundancy selection process, which (prima facie at least) had been incorporated into the employees' terms and conditions.[70] The judge granted an interim interdict on the basis that the claimant was faced with losing his job, whereas the firm had no urgent need to make the redundancies, so the balance of convenience favoured maintaining the status quo until trial. Although the judge did not discuss the adequacy of damages as a remedy, it was clear that he recognised the advantage of potentially retaining one's job over receiving redundancy compensation.[71]

However, the position is not straightforward. In *Alexander v Standard Telephones*, an English case with similar facts to *Anderson*, the judge refused to grant the injunction on the basis that the claimants would be adequately protected by an award of damages, even though he recognised that no award of damages would compensate them 'for the very real distress that they will be caused by reason of their loss of employment'.[72] In *Ashworth v Royal National Theatre*, the claimants were dismissed from their roles in the orchestra for a theatre production because the employer had decided to use recorded music instead, even though the contract stated that their employment could only be terminated if the production closed.[73] The court only acknowledged that they would lose earnings as a result of the employer's breach, and therefore held that damages would be an adequate remedy. Similarly, in *Marsh*, the claimant was dismissed summarily even though he was entitled, under his contract, to three months' notice.[74] Damages for lost earnings were held to be an adequate remedy in these circumstances. This was the case even though a disciplinary process had exonerated the claimant of any wrongdoing, so there was no basis for dismissal without notice.

Although it is difficult to generalise on the basis of a relatively small body of case-law, it seems clear that the courts' willingness to recognise the inadequacy of damages to compensate a person for the loss of their job is largely confined to cases involving professionals whose reputation and future employment prospects will be significantly damaged by a dismissal without due process. Injunctions are much less likely to be available in 'ordinary' employment cases, though some judges have been willing to grant them. A similar pattern was apparent in the cases not relating to termination discussed in the previous section. It appears that two factors are at play here. One is a reluctance to recognise the non-financial aspects of employment relationships (discussed in chapter three) outside the professional context.

[70] *Anderson v Pringle of Scotland Ltd* 1998 SLT 754, [1998] IRLR 64.
[71] ibid 757.
[72] *Alexander v Standard Telephones & Cables Ltd (No 1)*, [1990] ICR 291, 308.
[73] *Ashworth v Royal National Theatre* [2014] EWHC 1176 (QB), [2014] IRLR 526.
[74] *Marsh v National Autistic Society* [1993] ICR 453.

While judges seem to be prepared to uphold dignity in relation to doctors, for example, they are less keen to do so for factory workers. This introduces a class divide into employment law which is harmful and unfair, reflecting judicial biases about the nature of different types of work. All working people derive non-financial benefits from their jobs and the law should recognise this.

Another factor at play in these cases is the 'burdens on business' argument discussed and rejected in chapter three. The courts seem to be reluctant to hold employers to the promises they have made in their contracts with working people. A good example of this is the *Ashworth* case.[75] It would have been a simple matter for the employer to have included a term in that contract allowing it to terminate the musicians' engagement with notice, but it chose not to do so. The court, in effect, allowed it to buy its way out of a bargain it regretted. Similarly, in the *Alexander* case, the employer agreed to a 'last in, first out' redundancy selection procedure, but then decided that it wanted to select for redundancy on a different basis.[76] The court allowed this change of heart on the basis that compensation could be paid instead. Of course, there is a much larger debate here in the substantive law about the relationship between contract clauses limiting the employer's power to dismiss, and the general principle that contracts of employment can be terminated with notice, which the courts have never satisfactorily resolved. It is not surprising that this substantive dilemma also plays out in the law of remedies. However, it is difficult to understand why employers, typically well-advised and with superior bargaining power to that of their workers, should not be held to contractual promises voluntarily undertaken.

This issue arose in particularly sharp form in the *Tesco* case, in which the employer had offered enhanced pay to a group of workers in order to persuade them to move to a new place of work.[77] Strongly-worded commitments were made that this pay would be 'guaranteed for life'. At a later date, the employer decided that it no longer wished to give the employees this enhanced pay and proposed to dismiss and re-hire them on lower wages. The High Court judge granted an injunction to stop the employer from carrying out this proposal in breach of contract.[78] The Court of Appeal adopted a different construction of the promises made by the employer, holding that the promise of pay 'guaranteed for life' did not preclude use of the employer's power to terminate.[79] For present purposes, more significant was the Court of Appeal's conclusion that, even if it had agreed with the judge on the construction of the contract, it would not have been appropriate to grant a permanent injunction restraining the employer from terminating

[75] Above n 73.

[76] Above n 72.

[77] *Union of Shop, Distributive and Allied Workers (USDAW) v Tesco Stores Ltd* [2022] EWCA Civ 978, [2022] ICR 1573. At the time of writing, this decision is being appealed to the Supreme Court.

[78] *Union of Shop, Distributive and Allied Workers v Tesco Stores Ltd* [2022] EWHC 201 (QB), [2022] ICR 722.

[79] Above n 77, [32]–[51].

contracts of employment.[80] As Bogg and Brodie have pointed out, the Court of Appeal's reasoning on this point is limited and unpersuasive, appearing to place weight on the fact that there was no precedent for the injunction being sought and that other cases had dealt with public rather than private sector employers.[81] And since the injunction would only have prevented termination in order to remove the employees' enhanced pay (as promised to them by the employer), it is hard to see how it would have been an undue fetter on the employer's freedom of action in other respects. For example, it would not have precluded a fair dismissal of any of the employees for misconduct or incapability.

Another element in the test for the grant of an injunction is the requirement that there be 'mutual trust and confidence' between the parties. This is an employment-specific requirement, reflecting the 'personal' nature of the employment relationship. It is regarded as unduly onerous to force the parties to remain in a relationship in which mutual trust and confidence no longer exists.[82] As commentators have pointed out, this argument loses a lot of its force in workplaces where the employer is a large firm or public body rather than an individual human being, though even in larger settings, it is important that the employer has some faith in the worker's ability to carry out their job satisfactorily.[83] In *Irani*, discussed above, a factor pointing in favour of the grant of the injunction was that the hospital did not have any criticism of the claimant's professional practice, even though it no longer wanted to employ him because of the breakdown in relationship with his superior.[84] The claimant also agreed not to attend work while the disciplinary process took place.[85]

However, the facts of *Irani* are unusual. In most cases, the claimant is seeking an injunction to force the employer to conduct disciplinary proceedings, or to conduct them properly, when an allegation has been made about the claimant's behaviour or professional competence. In these cases, the employer *ex hypothesi* has concerns about the claimant's performance at work. Brodie points out that if mutual trust and confidence is treated as a subjective requirement, the employer can simply assert that it does not have confidence in the employee, based on the allegations.[86] This would allow the employer to bypass the contractual requirement to conduct disciplinary proceedings and to undermine the protection supposedly being afforded to the employee. Unfortunately, there are examples of cases in which this approach has been adopted. One such is *Lakshmi*, in which the claimant doctor was accused of signing cremation forms without seeing the deceased's

[80] ibid [55]–[56].

[81] Above n 64.

[82] An obligation to maintain mutual trust and confidence is an implied term of the contract of employment. For detailed discussion, see MR Freedland, *The Personal Employment Contract* (Oxford, OUP, 2005), ch 3.

[83] For an excellent critique of traditional arguments against granting injunctions see D Brodie, 'Specific Performance and Employment Contracts' (1998) 27 *Industrial Law Journal* 37.

[84] Above n 65, 603.

[85] See also *Robb v Hammersmith and Fulham LBC* [1991] ICR 514.

[86] Brodie, above n 83, 40.

body on multiple occasions.[87] Her employer, a hospital, refused to adjourn a disciplinary hearing for a short period of time while the police conducted further enquiries and the Crown Prosecution Service decided whether to prosecute. She had been advised by her lawyer to offer no comment while the police investigation was ongoing.[88] The judge held that an injunction could not be granted because the relationship between the parties had broken down, even though the claimant had not had an opportunity to explain her conduct because of the employer's refusal to delay the disciplinary process.[89]

In other cases, the courts have been more willing to accept that the disciplinary process should play a part in determining whether or not the employer has grounds for its lack of trust and confidence in the employee. For example, in *Barros D'Sa*, the employer received an investigator's report into allegations of misconduct which did not recommend dismissal, but it decided to dismiss anyway on the basis of its own view that its relationship with the employee had broken down.[90] This argument was rejected on the basis that it would wholly undermine the safeguards intended to be put in place by the disciplinary process. The Court of Appeal upheld the judge's order prohibiting the employer from considering any matters during the disciplinary process other than the investigator's report. Although *Barros D'Sa* was a procedural decision about the evidence to be considered at a disciplinary hearing, it also reveals a more robust approach to trust and confidence: the judges were not impressed by the employer's claim that it no longer had (subjective) trust and confidence in the employee when this was not supported by the investigator's (objective) report.[91]

Perhaps the strongest decision on this point is that in *Jones*.[92] The claimant in that case, a college lecturer, had been cleared of an allegation of gross misconduct at a disciplinary hearing, but the college governors did not want her to return to her old job because they believed that a breakdown in relationships would occur. They conducted a further disciplinary process, which the claimant refused to attend, and persuaded the local council (technically her employer) to dismiss her. The judge granted a permanent injunction prohibiting the council from acting on its dismissal letter, and an interim injunction 'restraining the defendant council from dismissing her unless proper grounds exist and after carrying out a proper procedure in accordance with her contract of employment'.[93]

This objective approach is to be welcomed. The employer should not simply be able to assert that it no longer trusts the employee, and particularly not where its

[87] *Lakshmi v Mid Cheshire Hospitals NHS Trust* [2008] EWHC 878 (QB), [2008] IRLR 956.
[88] The judge criticised this legal advice (ibid [34]) but recognised that it would have been difficult for the claimant to disregard her own lawyer's opinion.
[89] Above n 87, [51].
[90] *Barros D'Sa v University Hospital Coventry and Warwickshire NHS Trust* [2001] EWCA Civ 983, [2001] IRLR 691.
[91] ibid [28]–[29], [35].
[92] *Jones v Gwent CC* [1992] IRLR 521.
[93] ibid [55].

own procedures have exonerated the employee, or where it has failed to conduct its own procedures in a proper way.[94] Moreover, as noted above, the 'interference' with the employer's managerial prerogative in these instances is much less severe than is sometimes alleged. Where disciplinary proceedings are pending, the employee may be suspended from work or given restricted duties. And a requirement to conduct a disciplinary procedure does not prevent the employer from dismissing the employee if proper grounds exist and that procedure is duly followed.[95] Nor would it preclude termination on other grounds, such as redundancy.

Injunctions are a potentially powerful weapon to force employers to comply with the contractual commitments they have made. This is particularly so where the working person is threatened with a dismissal in breach of contract because, as I argued in chapter three, financial compensation cannot truly make up for the loss of various non-financial benefits of keeping one's job. These benefits apply not just to professionals but to all kinds of workers. However, the courts have placed a number of barriers in the way of the widespread use of injunctions in this context, by adopting the position that damages are an adequate remedy for some people, and by failing to take a uniformly objective approach to the requirement of mutual trust and confidence. The creation of these barriers seems to be motivated by a fear of interfering with managerial prerogative or creating burdens on business, even though what the courts are being called upon to do is to enforce promises that the employer itself has voluntarily made.

B. Statutory Re-Employment Orders

Since 1976, re-employment (either reinstatement in the original job, or re-engagement in an equivalent position) has supposedly been the primary remedy for unfair dismissal.[96] Under what is now section 112(2) ERA 1996, the tribunal is supposed to 'explain to the claimant what orders can be made' and offer them the option of saying whether they want a re-employment order. Compensation is awarded under section 112(4) only if the claimant does not request re-employment. However, it is well-known that, despite this change, re-employment is rarely requested by claimants and even more rarely ordered, despite its potential to protect claimants' dignity by ensuring that they get their jobs back and are not expected to make do with a (limited) compensation award. It is estimated that reinstatement and re-engagement are ordered

[94] Brodie, above n 83.

[95] In theory, the employer could bypass these requirements by dismissing with notice, but to allow this would undermine contractual disciplinary procedures completely: Adams et al, above n 37, para 4.60.

[96] P Davies and M Freedland, *Labour Legislation and Public Policy: A Contemporary History* (Oxford, OUP, 1993), 380.

in about one per cent of cases.[97] The remedies perspective, and particularly the juxtaposition with injunctions, helps to explain why re-employment orders are fundamentally flawed. I advance two arguments here. First, the test for making an order tips the balance in the employer's favour, by giving greater weight to the allegedly burdensome nature of the order than to the dignity-upholding benefits to the employee. Second, re-employment orders are not true replicative remedies, in the sense that they do not harness the power of the legal system to prevent a rights-threat. This is because they are not available until *after* the dismissal has taken place, and they are not backed by the contempt powers of the courts.

The decisions as to whether to make a re-employment order, and whether that order should be for reinstatement or re-engagement, are both for the tribunal to make, taking into account the preference of the employee and the employer's views on practicability.[98] According to *Coleman v Magnet Joinery*, 'practicable' means not merely 'possible' but 'capable of being carried into effect with success'.[99] It is a question of fact for the tribunal, so an appeal is available only in limited circumstances.[100] A clear example of impracticability is provided by *Kelly*, in which the claimant's old job did not exist after a re-organisation, and the only equivalent job required the ability to speak Mandarin, which the claimant could not do.[101] It will be argued here that the courts have taken a generous approach to practicability, heavily influenced by the common law concept of mutual trust and confidence.

One problem is that, in arguing that re-employment is not practicable, employers are allowed to rely on allegations against an employee, for example, that they are incompetent or have been guilty of wrongdoing, provided that their belief in those allegations is genuine and rational.[102] This is so even if the dismissal has been found to be procedurally unfair. For example, in *Wood Group*, the employer believed based on witness statements that the dismissed employee had been dealing drugs on work premises and had committed various time-keeping offences.[103] The tribunal held that it had not provided the employee with any details of the allegations against him, so that he had not had a proper opportunity to explain or defend himself, thus rendering the dismissal unfair on procedural grounds. However, the employer was still allowed to rely on its belief that the employee was guilty of misconduct in order to argue against a remedy of re-employment, even

[97] Adams et al, above n 37, para 4.142. For discussion, see L Dickens, M Jones, B Weekes and M Hart, *Dismissed: A Study of Unfair Dismissal and the Industrial Tribunal System* (Oxford, Blackwell, 1985), K Williams, 'Unfair Dismissal: Myths and Statistics' (1983) 12 *Industrial Law Journal* 157.

[98] ERA 1996, s 116.

[99] *Coleman v Magnet Joinery Ltd* [1975] ICR 46, 52.

[100] Eg *Clancy v Cannock Chase Technical College* [2001] IRLR 331, [15].

[101] *Kelly v PGA European Tour* [2021] EWCA Civ 559, [2021] ICR 1124, esp [42]–[51], [67].

[102] *United Lincolnshire Hospitals NHS Foundation Trust v Farren* [2017] ICR 513, [25].

[103] *Wood Group Heavy Industrial Turbines Ltd v Crossan* [1998] IRLR 680, on which see D Lewis, 'Re-Employment as a Remedy for Unfair Dismissal: How can the Culture be Changed?' (1999) 28 *Industrial Law Journal* 183.

though – in the absence of effective investigation – it could not be said to have had any objective basis for its belief. The threshold of 'genuine and rational' belief sets a low and largely subjective bar.

Another problem is that employers are allowed to invoke the absence of mutual trust and confidence in the employment relationship as a reason for claiming that re-employment is not 'practicable'. There is a risk that mutual trust and confidence is a more demanding standard than that originally envisaged by the statutory language. Arguably, the term 'practicable' sets a relatively low threshold of what is workable for the parties, whereas mutual trust and confidence implies a trouble-free relationship of the kind that is unlikely to exist after a dismissal situation has arisen. Moreover, mutual trust and confidence is another criterion that the courts have tended to apply subjectively rather than objectively in this context.[104] Some judges have shown awareness of the risks here. In a short concurring judgment in *Kelly*, Underhill LJ expressed concern about importing common law notions of mutual trust and confidence into the statutory enquiry:

> In particular, I am wary of tribunals becoming too focused on the language of 'trust and confidence', which may carry unhelpful echoes from its use in other contexts. In this context it simply connotes the common sense observation that it may not be practicable for a dismissed employee to return to work for an employer which does not have confidence in him or her, whether because of their previous conduct or because of the view that it has formed about their ability to do the job to the required standard. Of course any such lack of confidence must have a reasonable basis.[105]

While this is an important warning, it simply reinforces the low threshold set out in *Wood Group*, above, and does not refer to the more objective approach now being taken in some injunction cases discussed above.

More broadly, the difficulty here is that the test of 'practicability' as applied by the courts focuses largely on whether re-employment would work *for the employer*, partly through the way in which the requirement has been construed and partly because of the importation of common law ideas. What is not much discussed is the corresponding benefit *to the employee* of being able to retain a job from which they have been unfairly dismissed or to secure an equivalent job with the same employer. These are significant benefits in terms of vindicating the employee's claim that the dismissal was unfair and avoiding the host of non-financial losses that would otherwise ensue. Nothing in the statutory language directs tribunals to weigh these benefits against the concerns raised by employers. As a result, the balance is permanently skewed against the employee.

A further problem with re-employment orders is that, when compared with injunctions, they are not true replicative remedies. The sanctions for non-compliance are weak, and they do not operate in a preventative manner. This is a stark illustration of the way in which employees' rights are treated as less worthy

[104] ibid.
[105] *Kelly v PGA European Tour* [2021] EWCA Civ 559, [2021] ICR 1124, [69].

of protection by the legal system, even though more effective remedies can readily be imagined.

As Davies and Freedland explain, when the then industrial tribunals were created, there was an unwillingness to give them the same status or powers as courts.[106] Thus, they do not have the power to find the employer to be in contempt for breach of a re-employment order.[107] Instead, partial compliance with a re-employment order results in an award of compensation for any losses suffered as a result of the employer's non-compliance.[108] Total non-compliance results in an award of compensation for unfair dismissal along normal lines, plus an additional award of between 26 and 52 weeks' pay.[109] Moreover, it is possible for the employer even to avoid paying the additional award if it can demonstrate that it was not 'practicable' to comply with the re-employment order.[110] This seems particularly generous since the employer's views on practicability are taken into account when the tribunal decides to make the order, and there is no wording to (for example) confine the employer's input to matters arising after the tribunal's initial decision. Indeed, it is generally accepted that the tribunal's initial assessment of practicability should be regarded as 'provisional', with a final decision only made in the event of non-compliance.[111] This weakens the order even further.

As section III.A above demonstrated, injunctions can be used at common law to stop the employer from dismissing the employee in breach of contract. For these purposes, it is crucial that the employee does not accept the employer's repudiatory breach and acts quickly to secure the court order.[112] While this can cause problems for employees who are not aware of their rights, it does mean that the court intervenes at the optimal moment, before the employment relationship has ended. Re-employment orders try to achieve a similar effect, but they work very differently. Under section 114(1), an order for reinstatement is defined as 'an order that the employer shall treat the complainant in all respects as if he had not been dismissed'. The significant difficulty is that the order can be made only once the claimant's unfair dismissal case has been heard. This could mean a wait of months or years, during which time the claimant is not at the workplace. In many cases, the claimant will secure another job during that time, or decide that

[106] Above n 96, 210. The Law Commission recommended maintaining this position, largely because the High Court is better equipped to deal with injunction applications, particularly in urgent cases: Law Commission, Employment Law Hearing Structures (Law Com No 390, HC 308, 2020).

[107] An attempt in *R (Mackenzie) v University of Cambridge* [2019] EWCA Civ 1060, [2019] ICR 1477 to obtain an injunction to force the employer to re-engage the employee was unsuccessful, with the Court of Appeal holding that the statute provided a comprehensive remedial regime that should not be disrupted by the common law: [22].

[108] ERA 1996, s 117(2).

[109] ERA 1996, s 117(3).

[110] ERA 1996, s 117(4). The Court of Appeal in *Mackenzie* (above n 107) found that this meant that the right to be re-employed was not absolute: [20].

[111] *Port of London Authority v Payne* [1994] ICR 555, 569, approved by *McBride v Scottish Police Authority* [2016] UKSC 27, [2016] ICR 788, [37].

[112] *Geys v Societe Generale*, above n 3.

the prospect of going back to their old workplace is simply too daunting. Research by Dickens found that some claimants who initially wanted re-employment were deterred by the employer's hostile conduct during the litigation.[113]

One possible option to address this problem is the provision of interim relief. At present, this is only available in a small group of cases listed in section 128 where the reason for dismissal is related to whistleblowing, trade union activities or serving as a worker representative.[114] An application for interim relief must be made within seven days and heard promptly by the tribunal.[115] If the tribunal finds that one of the listed reasons is 'likely' to be found to be the reason for dismissal, it must ask the employer whether it is willing to reinstate or re-engage the employee.[116] If the employer fails to attend or refuses to re-employ the dismissed employee, the tribunal must make an order to continue the employee's contract of employment.[117] This order applies for the purposes of pay, other benefits and continuity of employment. If an order is made but the employer does not comply, the tribunal must order the continuation of the contract instead, and the payment of compensation to the employee.[118] In theory at least, interim relief should help by maintaining the employment relationship until the time of trial, making it more likely that the employee can keep their job over the longer term. However, there are a number of flaws in the scheme as it stands. First, the true focus is on keeping the contract alive (which has various financial benefits for the employee) and not on keeping the employee in their job. This is demonstrated by the fact that the employer can simply refuse to take the employee back either by not turning up to the hearing or by stating that it is 'unwilling' to do so. There is no opportunity for the tribunal to scrutinise the employer's decision. Second, in the unlikely event that an order is made, the consequences of non-compliance are purely financial and, again, there is nothing approximating to the contempt powers of the courts. As a result, it seems implausible that the interim relief regime does anything to increase the chances of re-employment being ordered, and being successful, at trial.

Although interim relief is ineffective as it stands, there is another potential use for it in an enhanced remedial regime under the statute. As things stand, there is no unfair dismissal equivalent of the injunction to force an employer to go through a disciplinary procedure. If the employer fails to follow a fair process when dismissing an employee, compensation (which may be increased by up to 25 per cent where the employer has unreasonably failed to follow the ACAS Code[119])

[113] See L Dickens, 'Unfair Dismissal Applications and the Industrial Tribunal System' (1978) 9 *Industrial Relations Journal* 4.

[114] An attempt to use human rights law to argue that interim relief should be available in discrimination cases was unsuccessful in *Steer v Stormsure Ltd* [2021] EWCA Civ 887, [2021] ICR 1671.

[115] ERA 1996, s 128(2) and (3).

[116] ERA 1996, s 129.

[117] ERA 1996, s 129(9).

[118] ERA 1996, s 132.

[119] TULRCA 1992, s 207A. ACAS Code of Practice on Disciplinary and Grievance Procedures (2015): https://www.acas.org.uk/acas-code-of-practice-on-disciplinary-and-grievance-procedures.

is the only remedy. As chapter seven will demonstrate, compensation may be much reduced, even to zero, where the tribunal finds that the employee would or might have been dismissed in any event: in other words, where the dismissal was procedurally but not substantively unfair.[120] This is problematic in two respects. First, where a fair process has not been followed, the employee loses the benefit of the procedure, such as the opportunity to persuade the employer not to dismiss them. Second, the employer may calculate that it need not comply with procedural requirements because the consequences of breach are purely financial, and the sums involved may in practice be quite limited because of the way in which compensation is calculated. An effective regime of interim relief could be used by employees to stop their dismissal from taking effect until the employer had complied with the procedural requirements of the ACAS Code.

Much of the academic debate has focused on the low levels of usage of re-employment orders, and on whether this flows from the poor design of the system (particularly the lack of contempt powers and the ability of employers to 'buy their way out') or from the understandable reluctance of many employees to return to a workplace from which they have been unfairly dismissed.[121] The remedies perspective draws out some useful additional points. First, replicative remedies can offer strong protection of the claimant's dignity by preventing the various non-financial losses associated with dismissal which are unlikely to be remedied in any other way, but this benefit needs to be factored in when deciding whether to award such remedies. The common law approach focuses on the needs and interests of both parties, whereas the 'practicability' test skews the balance in favour of the employer. Second, a replicative remedy in the true sense is available to restrain the defendant when it threatens to infringe the claimant's rights. Re-employment orders, operating after the event, are unlikely ever to be as effective as prevention. Of course, staying on at work when the employer has made an attempt at dismissal will not be an appealing prospect for some people and perhaps for a majority, but it is clearly a better option than returning to work at a later date. Modest reforms would include redrafting the test for granting a re-employment order and making interim relief available in all cases. But the only reform likely to have a truly beneficial impact would be to give tribunals the power to grant injunctions, or to enable employees to seek injunctions in court, to restrain a threatened unfair dismissal.[122]

C. Failure to Consult on Collective Redundancies

Before concluding, I want to explore one example of a right which could be much more effectively protected by means of a replicative remedy: the right to

[120] *Polkey v AE Dayton Services Ltd* [1988] AC 344.

[121] Eg references at n 97, above.

[122] Note that this is more radical than the strategy attempted in *Mackenzie*, above n 107, to get an injunction to enforce a re-employment order.

be consulted in the event of collective redundancies. This example is particularly striking because of the P&O Ferries case, in which the firm made 786 workers redundant with immediate effect in March 2022, and replaced them with agency workers.[123] According to a TUC report, the firm chose not to consult because it believed that no union would be willing to accept the proposed changes, though the law on consultation does not in fact require the parties to reach agreement on the proposals.[124]

Under the current law, the remedy for a failure to consult on collective redundancies is a so-called 'protective award' of up to 90 days' pay for each affected employee.[125] I argue in chapter eight that this is an example of a vindicatory award. It is not compensatory, because there is no requirement to prove loss in order to obtain the award, nor does it necessarily correspond to the time it would have taken to conduct the consultation exercise. Although the courts have sometimes said that it is punitive, it is simply an example of non-compliance with the law and there is no requirement to show that there has been particularly bad employer behaviour warranting punishment.[126] Although the vindicatory award is no doubt welcome for employees who are potentially facing redundancy, it does very little to protect the right to be consulted. First, as the P&O example illustrates, some employers seem to be content to ignore the requirement to consult and to simply add the protective award to the redundancy payment they will have to make to their employees. This fails to serve the compliance goal. Second, in the absence of any consultation, there is no opportunity for affected employees and their representatives to contribute their ideas on ways of avoiding redundancies, reducing their number or mitigating their effects.[127] The value of the right lies in employees having their voices heard and having the opportunity to change the employer's mind even if, in many cases, this does not prove possible in practice. A vindicatory award does not protect the dignity value of being able to participate in the decision-making process.

A replicative alternative would be an injunction prohibiting the employer from implementing the redundancies until it had completed the consultation process. This would benefit the employees financially – because they would continue to be paid during that time – but, most importantly, it would fulfil the purpose of the right to be consulted. One obvious objection is that this would slow down the decision-making process for management, perhaps in the midst of an economic crisis for the firm, but this is more of an objection to the right than to the remedy. If employers were aware that non-compliance would be met with a strong legal

[123] See eg BBC News, 'Outrage and no ferries after mass P&O sackings' (18 March 2022).

[124] TUC, *P&O Ferries Mass Sackings – One Year On* (17 March 2023). https://www.tuc.org.uk/sites/default/files/2023-03/P%26O%20Ferries%201%20year%20anniversary%20Final%20Draft%20130323%20%281%29.pdf. See TULRCA 1992, s 188(2).

[125] TULRCA 1992, s 189.

[126] *Susie Radin Ltd v GMB* [2004] EWCA Civ 180, [2004] ICR 893, [45] (Peter Gibson LJ), and see discussion in ch 8 of this volume.

[127] TULRCA 1992, s 188(2).

response, they would have a much greater incentive to comply. And the right itself admits of exceptions in genuine emergency situations.[128]

D. Conclusion

When an employee is threatened with a dismissal in breach of legal requirements, the seemingly obvious thing for the law to do would be to restrain the employer from carrying out its threat. The employer would only be able to proceed with the dismissal if it followed a proper process and had good grounds for its decision. But, as this section has shown, this is not the norm. Most employees are expected to make do with a financial remedy, even though this will do little to ensure compliance with the law or to protect the various non-financial interests at stake when a person loses their job. Although injunctions can sometimes be granted at common law to restrain dismissals in breach of contract, they are not easy to obtain and the process is stacked in the employer's favour. In statute, the re-employment orders differ from injunctions in ways that render them largely ineffectual, and in many other situations – notably collective redundancies – nothing resembling a replicative remedy is made available.

It is true that deciding to terminate an employment relationship is a core element of an employer's prerogative, but it is also one of the worst things that can happen to an employee. The idea that employees should be content with a money payment and should simply look for another job is highly unfair where they should not have been dismissed in the first place. The fact that this is tolerated and even expected is one of the starkest illustrations of the low value given to working people and their rights in the legal system as a whole.

IV. Recommendations

Some statutes make provision for a tribunal to make a recommendation if the claim is successful.[129] Although recommendations are not strictly replicative in nature – much depends on the exact content of the recommendation made by the tribunal – they do share important characteristics with replicative remedies, so it is appropriate to examine them here.

The best-known example is the Equality Act 2010, section 124, which gives the tribunal a discretion to make an 'appropriate recommendation'. This is defined in section 124(3) as follows:

[128] TULRCA 1992, s 189(6), on which see *Clarks of Hove Ltd v Bakers' Union* [1978] ICR 1076.

[129] There are also powers under s 42 Health and Safety at Work etc. Act 1974 and reg 29E WTR for a court to make an order upon the defendant's conviction requiring them to remedy the cause of the breach, but they are rarely used in practice.

> An appropriate recommendation is a recommendation that within a specified period the respondent takes specified steps for the purpose of obviating or reducing the adverse effect on the complainant of any matter to which the proceedings relate.[130]

Similar provisions are found in relation to *refusal of employment* on trade union grounds,[131] and in the various regulations on 'atypical' forms of work.[132] Although these are all anti-discrimination provisions, there is no particular logic to the presence or absence of a power to make recommendations. For example, the power is not available in cases of *detriment or dismissal* on trade union grounds.

The original version of section 124 provided that the recommendation could relate to the complainant or to 'any other person'.[133] This approach potentially carved out a broader role for the tribunal in encouraging the employer to make changes to its policies and practices in respect of its whole workforce, not just the complainant, but the 2015 amendment to that section shifted the focus onto the complainant and made the recommendation more analogous to a replicative remedy.[134] In practice, tribunals have continued to adopt a creative approach to this provision, making a mix of recommendations relating to both the claimant and the wider organisation. For example, in *Giwa-Amu*, the employment tribunal recommended that the employer should provide a standard reference letter and a letter of apology explaining the reason for the claimant's departure that she could show to future employers.[135] Senior leaders in the organisation should meet the claimant to discuss what had happened and what lessons could be learned, and should apologise to her. In addition to these claimant-focused recommendations, the tribunal also recommended that the employer approach the Equality and Human Rights Commission to review its diversity awareness training and implement improved training. While this might be a broad interpretation of the statute as now drafted, it is often the case that victims of discrimination want some reassurance that the wrong they have suffered will not happen to anyone else, so it is arguable that this type of 'preventative' recommendation can still be justified even under the narrower statutory formulation.

Under section 124(7), if the employer fails to comply with the recommendation 'without reasonable excuse', the tribunal may increase any award of compensation already made, or make such an order if it has not already done so. The recommendation itself typically requires the employer to write to the tribunal by a specified

[130] The power should not be used to recommend payments to the claimant, since these are properly dealt with through the compensatory award: *Prestcold Ltd v Irvine* [1981] ICR 777 (CA).

[131] See TULRCA 1992, s 140; Employment Relations Act 1999 (Blacklists) Regulations 2010 (SI 2010/493), reg 8.

[132] Agency Workers Regulations 2010 (SI 2010/93), reg 18; Fixed-term Employees (Prevention of Less Favourable Treatment) Regulations 2002 (SI 2002/2034), reg 7; Part-time Workers (Prevention of Less Favourable Treatment) Regulations 2000 (SI 2000/1551), reg 8.

[133] As enacted in 2010.

[134] Words repealed by Deregulation Act 2015, s 2.

[135] *Giwa-Amu v Department for Work and Pensions* (Case No 1600465/2017, February 2020) (ET), [81].

date setting out the steps it has taken in order to comply. However, in the *Hill* case, an interesting possibility emerged.[136] There, the successful claimant in a disability discrimination case sought reassurance that she would not have to work with two individuals who had been responsible for the discriminatory treatment. The EAT accepted the proposition that its recommendation could take the form of a requirement on the employer to give an undertaking that the claimant would not have to work with the named individuals. If the employer failed to give the undertaking, the tribunal would be able to 'enforce' it under section 124(7), but if the employer breached the undertaking, that would be a contractual matter enforceable through other routes, such as a constructive dismissal claim. This has the potential to give recommendations additional bite.

Recommendations are a forgotten bywater of employment law, but they could be made to serve an important purpose in encouraging compliance, one of the key objectives identified in chapter three. They could be used across all kinds of case to encourage employers to behave better in relation to the claimant – particularly important in ongoing relationships – and to improve compliance with legal requirements for the rest of the employer's workforce. There is no obvious reason for confining them to certain types of case or for limiting their focus to the claimant. Of course, there is a limit to the extent to which tribunals can supervise compliance with recommendations, so the approach may be somewhat formal – focused more on employers' stated commitments than on their actions – but recommendations could still play a useful role.[137]

V. Conclusion

It is important to acknowledge that there are a number of practical obstacles to making greater use of replicative remedies in employment law. Even if all enforcement difficulties could be overcome, some working people would not want to try to use the law to force an employer to reconsider a decision or to keep them in a job. They might be afraid of the awkwardness of returning to the workplace, or the prospect of being bullied or simply forced out at a later date. Of course, the law might offer further protection, for example, against constructive dismissal, but many people would prefer not to enter into a long-running dispute with their employer. These issues would be easier to address if there was more widespread collective representation at work, since trade unions could perform a useful role in

[136] *Lloyds Bank Plc v Hill* [2020] IRLR 652, [20]–[29].

[137] Future-regarding commitments may play an important role in other kinds of regulatory regimes, as the example of the Fair Work Ombudsman in Australia suggests: see eg T Hardy and J Howe, 'Too Soft or Too Severe? Enforceable Undertakings and the Regulatory Dilemma facing the Fair Work Ombudsman' (2013) 41 *Federal Law Review* 1, and Hardy and Howe, 'Creating Ripples, Making Waves?: Assessing the General Deterrence Effects of Enforcement Activities of the Fair Work Ombudsman' (2017) 39 *Sydney Law Review* 471.

supporting individuals who choose to challenge their employer's decisions and to return to the workplace afterwards. This would require a range of reforms beyond the scope of this book.

Another problem is that the effective use of replicative remedies requires that the working person has prompt access to legal advice and to a court or tribunal with the appropriate powers. For example, an employee threatened with dismissal in breach of a contractual disciplinary process must not act in any way that might signal acceptance of the employer's repudiatory breach, and obviously needs to get to court quickly to obtain an interim injunction. The current system is beset with backlogs and delays and, as discussed in chapter two, there is very little advice readily available to working people. Implementing a more strongly replicative remedial regime would require significant investment both in the legal system and in the provision of advisory services.

Nevertheless, it is important not to let these (admittedly real) practical concerns distract from the importance of replicative remedies. As chapter three explained, an effective remedial regime for employment law would promote compliance wherever possible and would seek to uphold the dignity of working people, with a particular focus on the non-financial benefits of a job. Replicative remedies have an important role to play in achieving both of these goals. On the compliance front, the point of a replicative remedy is to force the employer to do what it was supposed to have done in the first place, with sanctions for non-compliance. On the dignity front, replicative remedies give the working person a variety of dignity-affirming opportunities: to be heard or to have the chance to change the employer's mind, or to keep their job, or to avoid having to comply with unlawful instructions or requirements. Of course, replicative remedies are not appropriate in every situation: they operate principally to restrain rights-threats, so they are of limited value once the threat has been carried out. Compensation may be the only practical alternative in these circumstances.

But what this chapter has sought to demonstrate is that, even where replicative remedies are available or would be of value, they are either provided grudgingly, ineffectually or not at all. Considerable weight is given to the interests of employers: in limiting the payment of money owed, for example, or in the use of tests such as 'trust and confidence' or 'practicability'. Both the courts and the legislature, in different contexts, are reluctant to weigh these interests carefully against the rights of working people. Replicative remedies do nothing more than to require employers to comply with their statutory obligations or their contractual promises, and should not be particularly controversial. The only reason that they might be seen as controversial is that they threaten to redress the balance in favour of employees.

7

Compensation

This chapter considers compensation as a remedy. The aim of compensation is to put things right for the claimant who has suffered loss as a result of the employer's breach.[1] There are complex rules for calculating loss, with variations depending on whether the claim is contractual, tortious or statutory. My aim is not to provide an overview of these detailed rules, but to focus instead on two of the three issues identified in chapter three: whether the law on compensation reflects the employment-specific considerations of dignity and deterrence, and whether it gives appropriate priority to the most important employment rights.

As the discussion will demonstrate, the law is reasonably effective at identifying the different types of economic loss a person is likely to suffer when they are refused a job or promotion, or dismissed, and compensating accordingly. But, as chapter three explained, an important feature of employment cases is that work is not just a commercial transaction: because the worker is inseparable from their labour, employer breaches can also cause a variety of dignitary harms. While compensation for financial losses can, in itself, help to assuage harm to dignity, the law on compensation is less good at explicitly recognising affronts to dignity as a basis for compensation. The most obvious route to doing this is to make an award for injury to feelings. This is established practice in discrimination claims (and some trade union claims) but is forbidden in other contexts, notably dismissal (whether unfair or wrongful). This also reflects the strong priority given to equality over other employment priorities, such as security. I critique the law's position on injury to feelings awards in this chapter. Another dignity-related issue is that some of the standard rules on the calculation of loss – how future losses are to be determined, whether the working person is to blame for some of their own losses, whether they have taken steps to mitigate their loss – can inadvertently have the effect of disadvantaging working people. There are several examples of situations in which seemingly neutral, technical rules operate to reduce compensation in unreasonable or unfair ways.

Another employment-specific concern identified in chapter three was deterrence. I argued that, although it is important not to exaggerate the law's deterrent effect, employers do often take decisions with legal advice and calculate the

[1] SA Smith, *Rights, Wrongs and Injustices: The Structure of Remedial Law* (Oxford, OUP, 2019), ch 7.

costs and benefits of different courses of action. From this perspective, the level of compensation an employer might have to pay is a relevant consideration. Of course, it is important not to exaggerate this argument: the purpose of compensation is to provide redress for the claimant's losses, not to change the thinking of a particular employer or employers in general. However, measures which reduce the level of compensation payable may (as well as disadvantaging affected working people) reduce the deterrent effect of the law. I suggest that rules on mitigation and contributory fault, whilst legitimately concerned with the correct identification of the claimant's losses, may sometimes inadvertently have that effect. But the most glaring example is the 'cap' on compensatory awards for unfair dismissal, which means that an employer which has caused substantial losses may not have to compensate the claimant in full. This reflects the argument that employers' interests (or those of the wider economy) should be taken into account in the law on remedies, an argument I challenged in chapter three.

Chapter three also identified important questions of fit between rights and their corresponding remedies. It is worth noting that there are two big questions about fit in relation to compensation, but they are the business of other chapters of the book. First, I argued in chapter six that the law tends to treat compensation as the 'go to' remedy, even though it does not do a good job of upholding working people's rights. Instead of providing a sum of money when employers fail to follow proper procedures, for example, it would be preferable to force employers to re-take their decisions after complying with the law's requirements. Second, the law often provides what is described as a compensatory award as a remedy, particularly for statutory rights, even when there is little chance that the claimant has suffered any financial loss as a result of the employer's breach. Often, awards are made in these situations without proof of loss because to do otherwise would be to deny the claimant any remedy at all. I argue in chapter eight that it is appropriate to develop a category of 'vindicatory awards', the aim of which is to recognise the infringement of the claimant's rights rather than to compensate them for their losses. On this view, many supposed awards of compensation are, in fact, wrongly classified.

The structure of the chapter is as follows. I begin in section I by looking at how courts and tribunals calculate the claimant's economic losses, focusing in particular on how the law deals with lost future earnings in wrongful and unfair dismissal and discrimination claims. I also consider the doctrines of mitigation and contributory fault. While the legal rules here all reflect the logic of compensation, I highlight some of the ways in which they can operate unfairly. In the second section of the chapter, I explain the complex legal position on the availability of awards for injury to feelings. I argue that reform in this area would enhance the law's capacity properly to reflect harms to working people's dignity caused by breaches of their employment rights. I conclude in section III with a critical discussion of the maximum limit, or cap, on compensation in unfair dismissal cases.

I. Calculating Loss

In simple terms, the aim of compensation is to put right the claimant's loss.[2] At common law, this could be expressed in more precise terms as to put the claimant in the position they would have been in if the defendant had not committed the tort in question, or had complied with its contractual obligations. These approaches give different 'measures' of damages – which may generate different amounts of money where the same facts give rise to a claim in both tort and contract – but the overarching principle is the same.[3] Statutory employment rights typically draw heavily on common law approaches to identifying and calculating loss. In some cases, most notably discrimination claims, courts and tribunals are simply directed to award damages as if the wrong were a tort.[4] In other cases, the statute invokes common law principles on specific points, such as mitigation.[5] Even where legislation appears to set out its own, novel approach to compensation, courts and tribunals have tended to rely on familiar common law principles to structure their discretion.[6]

One of the commonest claims for compensation in an employment context is, of course, in respect of an unfair dismissal. The compensatory award for an unfair dismissal, according to section 123(1) ERA 1996,

> shall be such amount as the tribunal considers just and equitable in all the circumstances having regard to the loss sustained by the complainant in consequence of the dismissal in so far as that loss is attributable to action taken by the employer.

Similar wording is used in relation to other statutory employment rights, such as the remedy for detrimental treatment under section 49(2) ERA 1996. Compensation is principally a matter for the tribunal.[7] It is difficult to overturn an award on appeal unless the tribunal has failed to provide reasons for its decision, or has provided reasons which do not correspond to the sum awarded. Although the reference to 'just and equitable' might have been thought to give tribunals a broad discretion to make an appropriate award, the higher courts have, in practice, insisted on a more structured approach, in which tribunals must calculate compensation under various different 'heads', following established principles.[8]

In an unfair dismissal claim, the principal 'heads' identified in the *Norton Tool Co* case are loss of earnings between the dismissal and the hearing, future

[2] AS Burrows, *Remedies for Torts, Breach of Contract, and Equitable Wrongs* (Oxford, OUP, 2019), ch 3.

[3] ibid 38.

[4] Equality Act 2010, s 124 and s 119(2).

[5] Eg ERA 1996, s 123(4).

[6] *Norton Tool Co Ltd v Tewson* [1972] ICR 501.

[7] *Fougère v Phoenix Motor Co Ltd* [1976] ICR 495.

[8] *Norton Tool Co*, above n 6, and for a powerful critique, see H Collins, 'The Just and Equitable Compensatory Award' (1991) 20 *Industrial Law Journal* 201.

loss of earnings, expenses flowing from the dismissal, loss of statutory rights and pension loss.[9] Although discrimination claims are to be assessed based on tort principles, compensation for a discriminatory dismissal is assessed along similar lines.[10] It is harder to generalise about other types of claim, such as detriment, given the variety of different fact scenarios which might occur, but again, similarities often emerge. For example, if the detriment which the employee has suffered consists in wrongfully denying them a promotion, a substantial part of the claim would be for lost earnings calculated by reference to the difference between what the claimant was earning and what they would have earned had they been promoted.

Awards of compensation may also be adjusted for various different reasons. Reductions may be made for the employee's contributory fault in relation to the dismissal or detriment they have suffered,[11] or in respect of a failure to mitigate their losses once the breach has occurred.[12] A failure to comply with the ACAS Code of Practice in relation to a disciplinary dismissal may lead to an increase of up to 25 per cent where it is attributable to the employer and a reduction of up to 25 per cent where it is attributable to the employee.[13]

In calculating compensation, tribunals have to make a series of delicate and speculative judgements. For example, they need to decide what would have happened to the employment relationship had the dismissal not occurred and, in many cases, what the dismissed employee's prospects of obtaining another job might be. They also need to evaluate the employee's behaviour to determine whether it contributed to the dismissal, and to assess whether steps taken by the employee to secure fresh employment were reasonable. Nowadays, particularly outside the discrimination context, these decisions are often taken by Employment Judges sitting alone, without the employment experience of lay members to guide them on issues such as reasonable behaviour in the workplace or the state of the local labour market.[14] In the next three subsections, I focus on areas where a particular risk of unfairness arises: the employment relationship counterfactual at common law (section I.A) and in respect of statutory rights (section I.B) (what would have happened had the employee not been dismissed in a particular way at a particular time), mitigation and contributory fault (section I.C). I do not suggest that these are inappropriate issues for tribunals to consider in themselves – they all form part of the logic of compensation in working out which losses can properly be laid at the employer's door – but they all have potential to work against the interests of employees in certain circumstances.

[9] ibid.

[10] The main differences are that an award for injury to feelings is possible in a discrimination claim (Equality Act 2010, s 119(4)) and there is no upper limit on the award that can be made (cf ERA 1996, s 124).

[11] ERA 1996, s 123(6).

[12] Above n 5.

[13] TULRCA 1992, s 207A(2) and (3).

[14] See ch 2 of this volume.

A. Counterfactuals at Common Law

As Barmes explains, at common law, the courts adopt an assumption of 'minimum performance': that the employer (or, indeed, any other contracting party) will do the minimum necessary to fulfil its legal obligations.[15] This means that, in a 'standard' wrongful dismissal case in which the employee is dismissed without the contractual notice to which they were entitled, the courts assume that, had the wrongful dismissal not occurred, a lawful dismissal would have occurred in which the employee was given due notice.[16] Thus, all the employee can usually expect – and can therefore obtain in contract damages – is payment for the notice period itself.[17] No consideration is given to the possibility that the employee might in practice have expected to continue working for the employer for a much longer period of time, something which is taken into account in (statutory) unfair dismissal law, discussed below.

Another factor not taken into account at common law is the impact of the dismissal on the employee's future employment prospects.[18] This type of claim is sometimes referred to using the term 'stigma damages', though this is unhelpful in failing to distinguish damages for harm to reputation (which seem likely in practice to be similar to damages for injury to feelings, discussed further below) from compensation for lost future earnings due to the stigma of having been dismissed.[19] I will avoid the term 'stigma damages' and focus on lost future earnings here. The decision in *Addis* has long been taken as authority for the proposition that the employer is not liable for the effect of the dismissal on the employee's future earning potential, even though this statement only appeared in one of the opinions and may not represent the *ratio* of the case.[20] One possible explanation for this aspect of the ruling is linked to the notice rule itself: if the law does not control the reason for dismissal, no adverse inferences can be drawn from the fact that an employee has been dismissed. Of course, this apparently straightforward legal position bears no resemblance to the practical reality of losing one's job.

[15] L Barmes, 'The Contract of Employment and the Remedial Dimension' in M Freedland (et al) (eds), *The Contract of Employment* (Oxford, OUP, 2016), 167, at 184.

[16] Minimum notice periods are set out in ERA 1996, s 86.

[17] This may be extended where the claimant was contractually entitled to a disciplinary procedure prior to termination, to reflect the additional time this would have taken to conduct: *Gunton v Richmond-upon-Thames LBC* [1980] ICR 755, though this case was doubted by some of the judges in *Edwards v Chesterfield Royal Hospital NHS Foundation Trust; Botham v Ministry of Defence* [2011] UKSC 58, [2012] ICR 201.

[18] For analysis of the issues considered in this section, see H Collins, 'Compensation for Dismissal: In Search of Principle' (2012) 41 *Industrial Law Journal* 208.

[19] Damages of the latter type are recoverable in unfair dismissal and discrimination claims as part of the assessment of future loss: *Abbey National plc v Chagger* [2010] ICR 397.

[20] *Addis v Gramophone Co Ltd* [1909] AC 488. See *Johnson v Unisys Ltd* [2001] UKHL 13, [2001] ICR 480, [3]–[4] (Lord Steyn), for discussion.

In *Johnson*, a creative attempt was made to get around the rule in *Addis* by invoking the implied term of mutual trust and confidence.[21] It was argued that the employer could be liable for lost future earnings (and injury to feelings) where the manner in which it had dismissed the employee had infringed the implied term of mutual trust and confidence. In a much-criticised decision, the House of Lords rejected this claim on two linked grounds. First, the judges expressed concern about the extent of the common law development they were being asked to undertake: to extend a term concerned with the maintenance of the parties' ongoing relationship to the termination of that relationship and, in doing so, to limit (express[22]) provisions allowing termination with notice.[23] Second, given that the common law development could not be regarded as incremental, they declined to undertake it on the basis that Parliament had already occupied the field through the law on unfair dismissal.[24] Any limitations on the remedies there provided – the claimant in *Johnson* had already received the maximum award but remained undercompensated for his extensive losses – were for Parliament to address. The decision has been the subject of an extensive critical literature which cannot be addressed here.[25] But from the perspective of remedies, the key point emerges from Lord Steyn's dissent. He noted that, even if a claim could have been brought based on the implied term, it would have been difficult to distinguish losses flowing from the manner of dismissal (recoverable) from losses flowing from the dismissal itself (not recoverable).[26] This suggests that the real problem here is *Addis*, and that the most effective solution would be either to overrule that decision, or to address the deficiencies in the statute law of unfair dismissal.

Some employees have a disciplinary process laid out in their contract of employment. Even if this sits alongside a provision allowing dismissal with notice, it might be expected that the contract would be construed so that the two provisions would work together. The employer would be entitled to terminate with notice except where the disciplinary process applied, in which case the employer would be obliged to follow the procedure first. This might result in no dismissal at all, a dismissal with notice, or an immediate dismissal for gross misconduct. A failure to follow the disciplinary process might give rise to a variety of claims for economic loss:[27] lost earnings for the time it would have taken to go through

[21] ibid. The argument was based on the use of the implied term in *Mahmud v Bank of Credit and Commerce International SA* [1997] ICR 606.

[22] There was a four-week notice provision in Mr Johnson's contract.

[23] *Johnson*, above n 20, eg [47] (Lord Hoffmann).

[24] ibid [58].

[25] Eg L Barmes, 'Common Law Implied Terms and Behavioural Standards at Work' (2007) 36 *Industrial Law Journal* 35; D Brodie, 'Legal Coherence and the Employment Revolution' (2001) 117 *Law Quarterly Review* 604; 'Mutual Trust and Confidence: Catalysts, Constraints and Commonality' (2008) 37 *Industrial Law Journal* 329; J Fudge, 'The Spectre of *Addis* in Contracts of Employment in Canada and the UK' (2007) 36 *Industrial Law Journal* 51.

[26] Above n 20, [29]. This problem also exists where *Eastwood v Magnox Electric Plc* [2004] UKHL 35, [2005] 1 AC 503, applies.

[27] And injury to feelings, discussed in the next section.

the procedure, loss of a chance of not being dismissed, and lost future earnings where the employee, dismissed after a flawed process, found it hard to get another job. The first of these possibilities was accepted in the *Gunton* case, in which the employee successfully claimed damages for the notice period plus some additional weeks to cover the disciplinary process.[28] The chance of not being dismissed has never been acknowledged by the courts as a compensable head of loss in wrongful dismissal,[29] even though it is recognised in contract law more generally.[30]

Considerable controversy surrounds the third option: the claim for future loss of earnings where the flawed disciplinary process negatively affects the employee's ability to get another job. This was the case in the joined *Edwards* and *Botham* cases, in which the employees alleged that their dismissals in breach of disciplinary procedures had made it difficult for them to get other work, since they both worked in positions of trust in highly-regulated sectors.[31] The Supreme Court held that these claims were precluded by *Johnson*, even though there was no need to engage in any judicial creativity because the standards of behaviour to be observed by the employer had been agreed by the parties and set out in the contract.[32] *Johnson* was treated as authority for the proposition that Parliament had occupied the field even though, as explained above, the reasoning in *Johnson*, though flawed, was more subtle than that and also reflected uncertainty surrounding the extension of the implied term which was not relevant in *Edwards*. Three of the judges in *Edwards* held that contractual disciplinary procedures did not have the usual effect one would expect of contract terms because they were included to satisfy the requirements of the unfair dismissal legislation, a view that does violence to the law of contract and has little basis in fact.[33] As Collins says, there can be little doubt that the Supreme Court in *Edwards* decided, as a matter of policy, that it wanted to maintain the orthodox position that damages for wrongful dismissal are for wages during the notice period only.[34]

Different majorities also held that, in the case of *Botham*, the damage to his future employment prospects had been caused by the dismissal, not the procedure, and in *Edwards*, that it was not possible to distinguish the damage caused by the flawed procedure from that caused by the dismissal per se.[35] This meant that, even if the contractual terms had been allowed to operate normally, the claims would

[28] Above n 17.

[29] *Janciuk v Winerite Ltd* [1998] IRLR 63. The employee may be able to get an injunction to force the employer to complete the procedure, which may give them some chance of keeping their job: see ch 6 of this volume.

[30] *Chaplin v Hicks* [1911] 2 KB 786.

[31] Above n 17. For critique, see eg L Barmes, 'Judicial Influence and *Edwards v Chesterfield Royal Hospital NHS Foundation Trust* and *Botham v Ministry of Defence*' (2013) 42 *Industrial Law Journal* 192; Collins, above n 18.

[32] *Johnson*, above n 20.

[33] Lords Dyson, Walker and Mance. See A Bogg, 'Express Disciplinary Procedures in the Contract of Employment: Parliamentary Intention and the Supreme Court' (2015) 131 *Law Quarterly Review* 15.

[34] Collins, above n 18, 227.

[35] Baroness Hale dissented on this point in *Botham*, and Baroness Hale and Lords Kerr and Wilson dissented on this point in *Edwards*.

have failed on causation. This reasoning can also be questioned, since the impact on the claimants' job prospects flowed specifically from the fact that they had been dismissed for misconduct, not just from the fact of dismissal. Clearly, their arguments were that a properly-conducted disciplinary process would not have led to a dismissal on this ground.

From a remedies perspective, two points may be made to conclude this discussion. First, although it is anomalous that contractual disciplinary procedures may be enforced by injunction (as discussed in chapter six) but do not give rise to substantial damages claims, this is probably the best way of protecting the interests of working people. Where the claimant has a chance of being exonerated and remaining in their job, it is likely to be better for them to have the opportunity to present their case than to have a sum of money after the event (even if the law recognised loss of a chance as a valid head of claim in this context). Second, it is worth remembering the obvious point that unfair dismissal law was enacted to overcome the limitations of the common law in setting standards about dismissal and compensating unfairly dismissed employees. Litigants have only returned to the common law because unfair dismissal is now failing in its task, due to the cap on the damages which can be recovered. I critique the cap in section III of this chapter. Removing the cap would be a far simpler solution to the problem of under-compensation than developing the common law, though of course that requires parliamentary, rather than judicial, intervention.

B. Counterfactuals in Unfair or Discriminatory Dismissals

As Langstaff P explained in *Contract Bottling Ltd v Cave*, a dismissal case, the starting-point for the assessment of future loss of earnings is that the employee suffers the loss of the exact income they were receiving from the job they no longer have for an indefinite period.[36] However, in practice, awards are never made for an indefinite period because of the assumption that the dismissed employee will, eventually, find another job.[37] This requires the tribunal to consider when that new job would likely be obtained and whether it would be better, worse or equally well-paid, an issue I consider further below. The second assumption – that, absent the dismissal, the employee would otherwise have continued in the same job paid at the same rate – is also readily displaced, usually by one of two possibilities: that the employee would have stopped working due to factors such as ill-health or retirement, or that the employer would have dismissed the employee fairly. My focus in this section is on tribunals' approach to the second assumption.

In an unfair dismissal case, the assumption that the employer would have terminated the relationship fairly is less 'automatic' in its operation than it is at

[36] *Contract Bottling Ltd v Cave* [2015] ICR 146, [13].
[37] Or retire in the case of career-long loss.

common law, not least because the requirements of a fair dismissal under the statute are much more complex than just giving a period of notice. However, tribunals do consider how long the employment relationship would have lasted had the unfair dismissal not taken place. To take a simple example, an employee might be unfairly dismissed by a firm which is about to go out of business.[38] In that situation, it is open to the tribunal to find that the employee has suffered little or no loss of future earnings from the unfair dismissal, because their employment would have been terminated anyway when the firm ceased to trade. But the most well-known example of this approach is the making of *Polkey* reductions.[39] In the *Polkey* case the House of Lords overruled previous case-law, notably the decision in *British Labour Pump Co*,[40] which had held that a dismissal would be fair where the employer's failure to follow a fair procedure had made no difference to the outcome.[41] This represented an important advance in the protection of employees, in that it recognised the importance of procedural as well as substantive considerations in determining the fairness of a dismissal. However, the House of Lords also recognised that the 'no difference' rule would play a role when it came to questions of remedy. Compensation would be reduced, potentially to zero, if the tribunal found that the employee would have been fairly dismissed in any event.[42]

Some examples may help to illustrate the different ways in which *Polkey* reductions are applied in practice. In *Perkin*, the claimant's dismissal was found to have been procedurally unfair because the person who had chaired the disciplinary panel had made it clear in previous correspondence that she wanted the claimant to be dismissed.[43] However, the Court of Appeal upheld a 100 per cent *Polkey* reduction on the basis of the claimant's hostile and unreasonable behaviour during the disciplinary process (in circumstances in which he was unaware of the panel's bias). It is more common to find a percentage reduction where there is a chance that the claimant would have been fairly dismissed at some point, but the circumstances are less clear-cut. For example, in *Hamer*, the claimant was dismissed for disclosing confidential payroll information, but the tribunal found the dismissal to be unfair because the claimant was seeking to make a protected disclosure of what she believed to be a breach of the employer's legal obligations in respect of sick pay.[44] The employer made other allegations about the claimant's conduct, including other non-protected disclosures of confidential information and rudeness to superiors. The employment tribunal (ET) applied a 100 per cent *Polkey* reduction to the claimant's compensation on the basis that she would have

[38] *James Cook & Co (Wivenhoe) Ltd v Tipper* [1990] ICR 716.

[39] *Polkey v AE Dayton Services Ltd* [1988] AC 344.

[40] *British Labour Pump Co Ltd v Byrne* [1979] ICR 347.

[41] Under *Polkey*, it is still possible for a dismissal to be fair if the employer reasonably concludes that the procedure would be 'utterly useless': above n 39, 345 (Lord Mackay).

[42] The judges noted that re-employment would be a possibility, though this is unlikely in practice: ibid 365 (Lord Bridge).

[43] *Perkin v St George's Healthcare NHS Trust* [2005] EWCA Civ 1174, [2006] ICR 617.

[44] *Hamer v Kaltz Ltd* (UKEAT/0502/13, 4 August 2014).

been dismissed anyway on the same day, had the employer relied on these other reasons for dismissal. However, the Employment Appeal Tribunal (EAT) overturned this and applied a 40 per cent deduction, on the basis that there would have been disciplinary proceedings and the claimant might well have been dismissed, but the matter was not certain because the employer had not acted on the other allegations at an earlier stage and appeared to have confidence in the claimant's ability to do her job. A final written warning was a more likely outcome. A third option is to make an award in respect of future loss of earnings, but to limit it as to time. This is common in unfair redundancy cases, where the employer has failed to conduct a proper consultation exercise. The tribunal may choose to make an award in respect of what the claimant would have earned during the time it would have taken to carry out a proper consultation exercise.[45] This may be combined with the second option where the tribunal determines that there was a chance that the claimant would not have been made redundant or would have been offered alternative employment.[46]

Thus, although *Polkey* emphasises the importance of procedural protections as a matter of substantive law, this strong position is undermined when it comes to remedies.[47] In practice, the employer may disregard its procedural obligations without incurring substantial liability where it is able to make a strong argument that the dismissal would have taken place in any event. However, this problem can only be solved either by using remedies which do not focus on compensation, or by broadening the definition of loss to include non-economic considerations, both possibilities I discuss elsewhere. But within the logic of compensation – working out what loss the employee has suffered – it is hard to argue against the application of *Polkey* as a matter of principle. Nevertheless, I want to highlight two major concerns about the use of *Polkey* in practice: the tendency to make employer-friendly assumptions in some of the more speculative cases in which it is unclear what would have happened absent the dismissal; and the tendency to make potentially unfair judgements about how employees would have behaved.

More speculative applications of *Polkey* tend to arise where the dismissal is substantively unfair, as well as or rather than procedurally unfair. The task of imagining what would have happened had a fair procedure been followed (had there been an unbiased tribunal in the *Perkin* case, for example[48]) is not particularly difficult, though even here it is important not to be too quick to assume that the claimant could not have said something to change the outcome.[49] But determining the counterfactual in a case of substantive unfairness is much more challenging.

[45] Rather like *Gunton* at common law, above n 17.

[46] Eg (on different facts) *Venkatesan v Surabi Ltd* (UKEAT/0193/14/DM, 15 October 2014).

[47] See J McMullen, 'The Resurgence of Proceduralism in Unfair Dismissal Law – The End of the *British Labour Pump* Principle' (1988) 51 *Modern Law Review* 651.

[48] Above n 43.

[49] 'the path of the law is strewn with examples of open and shut cases which, somehow, were not; of unanswerable charges which, in the event, were completely answered; of inexplicable conduct which was fully explained': *John v Rees* [1970] Ch 345, 402 (Megarry J).

This was recognised by the EAT in the *Kirkwood* case.[50] There, the employer was found to have acted unfairly in selecting the claimant for redundancy based on a pool consisting only of the one other employee on his shift. Since the firm was conducting a wider reorganisation, the tribunal found that the redundancy pool should have been broader. The EAT rejected an argument that the tribunal should have applied *Polkey*, holding that it was inappropriate to consider whether the employee would still have been made redundant on the basis of a different selection process. As the EAT memorably put it:

> To adopt an example familiar in the field of administrative law, if an employer selects men for redundancy on the grounds of the colour of their hair, he can scarcely maintain thereafter that no compensation should be payable because a different basis of selection might have led to the choice of the same employees for dismissal.[51]

However, this was disapproved by the Court of Appeal in *O'Dea*, in which it was held that *Polkey* could and should be applied in cases of substantive as well as procedural unfairness, not least because of the practical difficulty of drawing a clear distinction between different types of case.[52]

The modern approach is captured by the *Gover* case.[53] There, the tribunal found that the claimants had been unfairly dismissed when they resigned in response to the employer's proposal to halve their commission payments without any proper consultation or discussion. However, it then went on to consider the counterfactual: that the employer would have proposed cuts to the employees' payment terms that did not amount to a repudiatory breach of contract, but which they would not have been prepared to accept. Thus, their employment would have come to an end fairly in any event, quite soon after the date of dismissal. The only compensation payable was for the time it would have taken to conduct a fair consultation process, assessed at four months. The Court of Appeal approved this approach. Guidance subsequently provided by Elias P in *Software 2000 v Andrews* indicates that a tribunal should make every effort to work out what would have happened even if some speculation is involved:

> It must recognise that it should have regard to any material and reliable evidence which might assist it in fixing just compensation, even if there are limits to the extent to which it can confidently predict what might have been; and it must appreciate that a degree of uncertainty is an inevitable feature of the exercise.[54]

The difficulty is that the speculative exercise rarely seems to involve factors favouring the employee, such as the possibility that they might have said something during a hearing to save their job, or that they might have willingly accepted worse terms and conditions to avoid redundancy. Instead, the exercise seems to be one in

[50] *Steel Stockholders (Birmingham) Ltd v Kirkwood* [1993] IRLR 515.
[51] ibid [7].
[52] *O'Dea v ISC Chemicals Ltd* [1996] ICR 222.
[53] *Gover v Propertycare Ltd* [2006] EWCA Civ 286, [2006] ICR 1073.
[54] *Software 2000 Ltd v Andrews* [2007] ICR 825, [54].

which the tribunal is encouraged to imagine a world in which the employer finds a fair way to dismiss the employee, even though the one certainty in all of these cases is that the employer has already dismissed the employee unfairly.[55]

A second, linked concern is that the *Polkey* exercise sometimes involves making judgements about how the employee would have conducted themselves, in ways which can seem unfair. A leading example is the *O'Donoghue* case, which is also noteworthy for its application of *Polkey* reasoning in the context of a discrimination claim.[56] The claimant in that case successfully argued that a decision not to appoint her into a new job during an internal reorganisation was tainted by sex discrimination. The employer subsequently dismissed her and, at a further hearing, the tribunal found that the dismissal was unfair because it amounted to victimisation based on her previous claim. However, the tribunal assessed her compensation based on a finding that she would have been dismissed fairly within six months in any event, given her 'extremely poor' working relationships with colleagues.[57] This was despite arguments advanced on behalf of the claimant that she had not previously been the subject of disciplinary proceedings and that it was not plausible to assume that the employer would have been able to complete a fair process so rapidly. The Court of Appeal did emphasise that the application of *Polkey* in this context required clear evidence and would be unusual.[58] Nevertheless, there are obvious dangers in concluding that poor working relationships would have led to dismissal in a context in which the claimant has already been a victim of both discrimination and victimisation. It seems unlikely that a person in such a situation would be well-placed to form positive relationships at work, given the stressful circumstances, and there is a real risk that a person who is simply trying to assert their rights may be regarded as 'difficult' by the employer or by colleagues.

Assumptions about employees' likely future behaviour apply not only in *Polkey* situations, but more generally in determining how long an employment relationship would have lasted absent the unfair dismissal which is the subject of the claim. This provides a further opportunity for tribunals to speculate about the possibility that the employee would have retired or resigned in a way that operates to reduce the compensation payable by the employer.

Although few employees are awarded damages until retirement age, a person's intended retirement date can be important, particularly for older workers who may be retiring in the near future. Now that there is no standard retirement age, this is a matter for the tribunal to decide. In *Essex County Council v Jarrett*, the claimant was seeking lost future earnings up to the age of 70, on the basis that she enjoyed her job and wanted to continue working until then.[59] The EAT held that

[55] See eg *Walker v Dysch Rosen Shoes Ltd* (EAT/341/90, 28 February 1991), in which there does not appear to have been any intention to dismiss fairly.

[56] *O'Donoghue v Redcar and Cleveland BC* [2001] EWCA Civ 701, [2001] IRLR 615.

[57] ibid [56].

[58] See also *Thornett v Scope* [2006] EWCA Civ 1600, [2007] ICR 236.

[59] *Essex County Council v Jarrett* (UKEAT/0087/15/MC, 1 May 2015).

the defendant was entitled to ask her about the pension entitlements she enjoyed from other sources, on the basis that she might not in fact continue working until the stated age if she had other income. Of course, there is a risk that working people might argue that they intended to work beyond the 'expected' retirement age in order to inflate their damages claims when, in reality, they had no plan to do so. But the EAT's approach entrenches the stereotype of retirement at 60 or 65, despite the law on age discrimination, and makes it more difficult for working people who do not want to follow the herd to prove their cases.

Where retirement is not an issue, tribunals may still decide that a working person might not have continued in their job for much longer beyond the date of the unfair or discriminatory dismissal for other reasons. A recent example is *Health and Safety Executive v Jowett*, in which HSE was allowed to adduce evidence that, when the claimant had worked for it some years previously, he had not stayed very long.[60] This was considered to have some probative value in relation to his likely future conduct, with the potential to limit his damages for lost future earnings. Of course, the exact value of the evidence was for the tribunal to determine, and it was open to it to conclude, as the claimant contended, that the two periods of employment were quite distinct. In *Shittu*, the claimant was found to have been constructively dismissed, because the employer had not dealt with his grievance properly.[61] But the EAT upheld a reduction in his compensation to nil, on the basis that he would have resigned on the same date because he was very unhappy at work and had exhausted his sick pay entitlement. While the logic of compensation requires that a claimant who was planning to leave anyway should not be given a large sum in respect of future earnings, it is important not to assume too readily that employees will resign their jobs. Many people will tolerate an unhappy situation at work because they need the money, and cannot afford to resign unless they can secure alternative employment.

Perhaps the most worrying example is the *Vento* case.[62] Although this case is best known for its guidance on injury to feelings, the argument about lost future earnings is also significant. The claimant was dismissed at age 30 from the police on grounds that were found to be discriminatory. She argued that, had she not been dismissed, she would have passed her probation and continued to work until the standard retirement age for police officers of 55. However, the employer sought to adduce statistical evidence that female officers rarely remained in the force for the length of time this would entail. The tribunal assessed her chances of doing so at 75 per cent, due to her determination to pursue this career. This was ultimately upheld by the Court of Appeal, because of the high perversity threshold for overturning a tribunal on this point, but it was clear that the judges felt that the tribunal's assessment had been overly generous. While it is important for tribunals

[60] *Health and Safety Executive v Jowett* [2022] EAT 151.
[61] *Shittu v South London & Maudsley NHS Foundation Trust* [2022] EAT 18.
[62] *Vento v Chief Constable of West Yorkshire Police* [2002] EWCA Civ 1871, [2003] ICR 318.

to be realistic, there was a sense in which the employer was seeking to benefit from its own wrongdoing here: some of the reasons why female police officers did not serve for very long might have included the discriminatory treatment they encountered and the difficulty of securing adequate childcare given the hours they were expected to work.

The task of awarding compensation requires the tribunal to make a realistic assessment of the employee's losses flowing from the unfair dismissal or other unlawful act of the employer. In most cases, career-long loss of earnings until retirement would not be realistic, because it is reasonable to suppose that either the employer or the employee would have brought the relationship to an end long before that.[63] This is particularly so where the employer is already 'armed' with a fair reason for dismissal. However, courts and tribunals do seem too ready to assume, in the employer's favour, that procedures make little difference to outcomes, that dismissals found to be unfair on one ground could readily be implemented fairly on another, or that unhappy employees are likely to resign. Even in the absence of radical reform to the compensatory principle, some changes could be made to make the process of assessment fairer to employees. First, the making of a 100 per cent reduction should be regarded as exceptional, even in a procedural unfairness case. A nil award should only be made where there is no doubt as to what the outcome would have been in the absence of any unfairness. The *Perkin* case illustrates the point nicely: although the claimant's behaviour during the disciplinary procedure had strongly influenced the outcome, it seems unjust to deny any possibility that an unbiased tribunal might have approached the case differently.[64] Second, tribunals should decline to make a reduction, or at least limit any reduction, where the counterfactual presented by the employer is too speculative. This can sometimes be the case in redundancy selection cases where it is found that either the scoring method was unfair, or the pool was wrongly constituted. Redundancy selection is a complex process, and it is difficult for tribunals to say with any certainty what would have happened had the dismissed employee's performance been assessed differently or compared with a different group of colleagues. Third, when the reduction is expressed in terms of time, tribunals should be realistic in their assessment of how long it would have taken the employer to carry out a fair dismissal, or how long it would have taken an unhappy employee to resign, given the need in most cases to find another job to go to. For example, in *O'Donoghue*, it seemed improbable to suggest that a claimant who had already been successful in discrimination and victimisation claims could have been dismissed fairly within six months, given the complexity of the case and the high degree of care the employer would need to have taken to establish fair grounds for termination.[65]

[63] Though there are exceptions in both unfair dismissal and discrimination cases, where it is clear that the claimant is highly unlikely to work again: *Abbey National plc v Chagger* [2010] ICR 397; *Wardle v Crédit Agricole Corporate and Investment Bank* [2011] ICR 1290.

[64] Above n 43.

[65] Above n 56.

Reforms along these lines would improve the capacity of compensatory awards to contribute towards the employment-specific goals of deterring breaches and upholding employees' dignity.

C. Job Prospects and Mitigation

The discussion so far has focused on the counterfactual – working out what would have happened to the employee's original job had they not been dismissed. The other crucial element in calculating an employee's future losses is their prospect of getting another job. Sometimes, this is straightforward because the employee has already got another job between the time of dismissal and the hearing of the claim. In these cases, the tribunal can take into account their earnings in the new job when calculating their losses. Where the new job pays as well as or better than the old job, losses (if any) will be confined to the period during which the employee was looking for the new job.[66] Where the new job pays less well, compensation may be awarded for the difference in pay, taking into account how long it might take the employee to get back to their original level of earnings. The tribunal's task is more challenging where the employee has not yet found a new job: in these cases, their role is to work out when, if ever, the employee is likely to find work and how much it is likely to pay.

In most cases, the rules on mitigation also apply. Mitigation is a common law concept applicable in contract and tort,[67] but is also expressly applicable to a number of statutory employment rights, including unfair dismissal and discrimination claims.[68] The employer may ask the court or tribunal to make a reduction in the claimant's compensation where they have failed to take reasonable steps to limit their losses, or incurred unreasonable expenditure in response to the losses. In dismissal cases, where this issue arises most frequently, mitigation is usually concerned with what efforts the claimant has made to find another job, and with decisions made by the claimant in relation to any job offers they have received.

Both the general rules on assessing future losses and the specific doctrine of mitigation reflect the logic of compensation. If the effect of the dismissal is that the employee ends up with a better-paid job, there is little or no loss to be attributed to the employer, even though it acted unfairly. If the employee could have got another job but made no effort to do so, it is unfair to require the employer to compensate the employee for losses which could readily have been avoided. Of course, this means that the employer may 'get away with' an unfair or discriminatory

[66] See *Ging v Ellward Lancs Ltd* [1991] ICR 222 (decided 1977); *Whelan v Richardson* [1998] ICR 318.

[67] See, generally, Burrows, above n 2, ch 7; MG Bridge, 'Mitigation of Damages in Contract and the Meaning of Avoidable Loss' (1989) 105 *Law Quarterly Review* 398.

[68] ERA 1996, s 123(4) (unfair dismissal – compensatory award); *Ministry of Defence v Hunt* [1996] ICR 554 (providing guidance in discrimination claims).

dismissal in some circumstances, but this reflects the fact that compensation is about remedying losses, not punishing wrongdoing or some other objective. As noted in section I.B, the only way to avoid these scenarios is to adopt some other remedy or basis of assessment for a financial award.

A risk with the assessment of future loss in general, and mitigation in particular, is that attention may be diverted from the losses caused by the employer and turned instead onto the subsequent conduct of the claimant. This was addressed by the EAT in the *Cooper Contracting* case, in which guidance was laid down on how mitigation should be applied in the unfair dismissal context.[69] It was emphasised that the burden of proof was on the employer to show that the employee had acted unreasonably, and that the claimant was 'not to be put on trial as if the losses were his fault when the central cause is the act of the wrongdoer'.[70] Importantly, it is not enough for the employer to show that there were steps the employee could have taken to mitigate their losses that they did not take: the failure to take steps must be *unreasonable*. Mitigation is tailored to the circumstances of the individual employee and the local labour market, so factors such as the availability of similar jobs and the employee's state of health are relevant. For example, if the circumstances surrounding the dismissal have left the employee in a state of distress, it would not be reasonable to expect them to begin looking for a new job straight away.[71] Nor is the employee expected to settle for a lower-paying job at the outset of their job search.[72]

Nevertheless, one area of particular difficulty is the treatment of re-employment offers.[73] The leading authority on this issue is *Wilding*.[74] In that case, the claimant was found to have been discriminated against on grounds of his disability and unfairly dismissed by his employer. Before the remedies hearing, the employer offered the employee a part-time role which would have accommodated his disability and allowed him to continue working in a highly specialist field. However, the claimant refused the offer on the basis that he did not believe it to be genuine, given the way in which the employer had conducted itself both before and during the proceedings. In particular, the employer had made the offer at the same time as it was seeking to appeal the tribunal's decision on the unfairness of the dismissal. The tribunal held that his refusal was unreasonable and this was upheld, albeit somewhat reluctantly, by the Court of Appeal. Of course, each case turns on its own facts, and it is not always the case that an employee is expected to return to the workplace in unpleasant circumstances. For example, in *Symonds*, the claimant was offered her old job back after a constructive dismissal in which the employer

[69] *Cooper Contracting Ltd v Lindsey* (UKEAT/0184/15/JOJ, 22 October 2015) [2016] ICR D3.

[70] ibid [16]. See also *Edward v Tavistock and Portman NHS Foundation Trust* [2023] EAT 33, [2023] IRLR 463.

[71] Eg *Beijing Ton Ren Tang (UK) Ltd v Wang* (UKEAT/0024/09/DA, 14 October 2009).

[72] Eg *Orthet Ltd v Vince-Cain* [2005] ICR 374.

[73] This is built into the statute where the tribunal orders re-employment: ERA 1996, s 117(8).

[74] *Wilding v British Telecommunications Plc* [2002] EWCA Civ 349, [2002] ICR 1079.

had refused to deal with her grievances.[75] The EAT upheld the tribunal's decision that she had not unreasonably failed to mitigate her losses by turning down the job offer.

The legal threshold for a failure to mitigate is, admittedly, relatively generous to the employee: it must be demonstrated that the employee's actions or decisions were 'unreasonable' and the burden of proof is on the employer. Nevertheless, there is a worrying contrast between the treatment of employees who refuse to go back, and employers who refuse to take an employee back. As chapter six explained, the employer can avoid an order to reinstate or re-engage an employee in the law of unfair dismissal by arguing that it would not be 'practicable' to carry it out. This can include assertions that the employer no longer has confidence in the employee. Thus, it seems particularly harsh for an employee's damages to be reduced where they refuse a re-employment offer under circumstances in which they no longer have confidence in their employer. The failure to uphold the employee's dignity here is painfully obvious.

D. Conduct

In some types of employment claim, there is a power or even a duty on the tribunal to make a reduction in compensation where it is found that the claimant's conduct contributed to the wrongful act about which they are complaining. This is a familiar principle from tort law: for example, a pedestrian hit by a negligent driver may have their compensation reduced to reflect the fact that they did not take sufficient care in crossing the road and thus were partly responsible for their own injuries. Claims subject to a contributory fault principle include:

- unfair dismissal (where it may be used to reduce both the basic and compensatory awards), including dismissals relating to trade union membership or activities;[76]
- detriment claims under ERA 1996 and trade union legislation;[77]
- claims under the part-time, fixed-term and agency work legislation;[78]
- certain refusals of employment on trade union grounds.[79]

There are some related provisions to be aware of too. Compensation for a wide variety of employment wrongs may be reduced by up to 25 per cent where the employee has unreasonably failed to follow the ACAS Code of Practice on

[75] *Symonds (t/a Symonds Solicitors) v Redmond-Ord* (UKEAT/0145/13/BA 22 October 2013) [2014] ICR D6.

[76] ERA 1996, s 122(2) (basic award), s 123(6) (compensatory award).

[77] ERA 1996, s 49(5); TULRCA 1992, s 149(6).

[78] Eg Part-time Workers (Prevention of Less Favourable Treatment) Regulations 2000 (SI 2000/1551), reg 8(13).

[79] Employment Relations Act 1999 (Blacklists) Regulations 2010 (SI 2010/493), reg 8(5).

disciplinary and grievance procedures.[80] There is also a possible 25 per cent reduction in whistleblowing claims where it is found that the claimant's disclosure was not made in good faith.[81]

There are two significant examples of situations in which contributory fault does not apply. One is wrongful dismissal. This is for the obvious reason that wrongful dismissal is not generally concerned with fault. While the employer may be able to dispense with the notice period where the claimant has committed a repudiatory breach ('gross misconduct', in the traditional language), the employee's degree of fault outside that scenario does not affect their entitlement to notice and their compensation when due notice is not given. The other is equality law. This is a tricky area in which the law is not entirely clear. Equality claims are treated as statutory torts, and damages reductions for contributory fault are generally available in the law of tort as a result of the Law Reform (Contributory Negligence) Act 1945, though the Equality Act 2010 itself makes no provision either way.[82] However, the courts have been understandably reluctant to state that the conduct of the working person contributed to an act of discrimination against them.[83] While there is no clear authority on the point from the higher courts, it is generally thought to be the case that contributory fault reductions are applicable in discrimination cases only in the most exceptional of situations.

A typical formulation of a contributory fault provision is as follows:

> Where the tribunal finds that the act, or failure to act, to which the complaint relates was to any extent caused or contributed to by action of the complainant, it shall reduce the amount of the compensation by such proportion as it considers just and equitable having regard to that finding.[84]

This gives the tribunal no discretion about making a reduction once it has made a finding of contributory fault, though it does give considerable scope to determine the *amount* of the reduction using the familiar 'just and equitable' formulation. The tribunal's decision on this point is unlikely to be overturned on appeal. While this type of provision applies to the compensatory award for unfair dismissal, it is worth noting that the provision relating to the basic award for unfair dismissal is different:

> Where the tribunal considers that any conduct of the complainant before the dismissal (or, where the dismissal was with notice, before the notice was given) was such that it would be just and equitable to reduce or further reduce the amount of the basic award to any extent, the tribunal shall reduce or further reduce that amount accordingly.[85]

[80] TULRCA 1992, s 207A(3).
[81] ERA 1996, s 49(6A).
[82] Equality Act 2010, s 124 and s 119(2).
[83] *First Great Western Ltd v Waiyego* (UKEAT/0056/18/RN, 6 December 2018).
[84] Part-time Workers (Prevention of Less Favourable Treatment) Regulations 2000 (SI 2000/1551), reg 8(13).
[85] ERA 1996, s 122(2).

The conduct in this instance is not strictly 'contributory', in the sense that it does not have to be part of the cause of the dismissal, and the tribunal has a broad discretion as to whether to make any reduction at all.[86] It is perfectly possible for the basic and compensatory awards to be reduced by different amounts, or for there to be a reduction in the compensatory award only.

One difficulty with contributory fault provisions is that – rather like *Polkey* reductions – they have a tendency to undermine the law's protection of fair procedures in dismissal settings.[87] Although the two types of reduction are conceptually distinct, they can often arise in the same case, particularly in misconduct dismissals. For example, a tribunal might make a *Polkey* reduction (on the basis that the claimant would still have been dismissed had a fair procedure been followed) as well as a finding that the claimant's conduct contributed to their dismissal. Tribunals are required to consider whether the award remains 'just and equitable' once both types of reduction have been applied, suggesting that it may not be appropriate to apply the 'normal' levels of reduction for both at the same time.[88] Nevertheless, whether contributory fault arises on its own or in connection with *Polkey*, a potential difficulty is that any compensation in respect of elements of the dismissal which were unfair will be much reduced in practice. A memorable example is *Steen*, in which the claimant was dismissed for criticising the managing director in a phone call to the chairman.[89] The disciplinary hearing was conducted by the chairman's wife, even though the claimant and the chairman disagreed as to what had been said on the call. The tribunal's reduction of both the basic and contributory awards to zero on the grounds of contributory conduct was remitted by the EAT to a fresh tribunal on the grounds that the tribunal had failed properly to explain its reasoning. Nevertheless, the EAT found that such a finding was possible, albeit likely to be unusual in practice. This can mean that no award (or perhaps a very reduced award) may be made even in the face of glaring procedural errors.

Another area of concern is the inclusion of contributory fault in the trade union discrimination context. The risk here is that working people's trade union rights may be undermined if they can be held to have contributed to their own detrimental treatment or dismissal on trade union grounds. The law does offer some specific protection in this context by excluding certain types of conduct from consideration. For example, defying an employer's requirement not to join a union or take part in its activities cannot be treated as contributory conduct by virtue of section 155 TULRCA. However, there is House of Lords authority for the proposition that in a section 238 case of selective dismissals or re-engagements after industrial action, it is permissible to take into account an individual's

[86] *Optikinetics Ltd v Whooley* [1999] ICR 984.
[87] *Polkey*, above n 39.
[88] *Rao v Civil Aviation Authority* [1994] ICR 495.
[89] *Steen v ASP Packaging Ltd* [2014] ICR 56.

conduct where it goes beyond 'mere' participation in the industrial action.[90] This is highly problematic because of the risk that individuals who have been heavily involved in organising or supporting the action – and who are thus most in need of the law's protection – may find that their compensation is reduced because their conduct is found to have been contributory.[91] It may also be questioned whether it is appropriate to allow reductions for contributory conduct in cases of detriment or automatically unfair dismissal where protected characteristics are engaged, such as the assertion of some of the rights to take family leave.[92] This may undermine the generally satisfactory position under the Equality Act 2010 that a person cannot normally be found to have contributed to discrimination against them.

A final set of concerns relating to contributory fault is that the rules may create a situation in which ordinary working people are penalised for natural human behaviour under conditions of stress, particularly where they do not have ready access to legal advice to explain to them the importance of behaving in particular ways.[93] For example, an individual who feels that the employer is treating them unfairly may choose not to raise a grievance or participate in a disciplinary process, because they do not believe that there is anything to be gained by doing so. An individual who is under strain during such a process may respond in rude or aggressive ways to questioning, not because they are generally rude or aggressive but because the situation is challenging for them. The EAT has urged caution, stating that a reduction would not be appropriate in 'simple' cases involving 'some matter of personality or disposition or unhelpfulness on the part of the employee in dealing with the disciplinary process in which he or she has become involved'.[94] But the line is difficult to draw. For example, in *Nelson v Clapham*, the claimant was dismissed when the employer found a printout of an email in which she had threatened to make disparaging comments about the employer in the local community, from which much of its business was derived.[95] The dismissal was found to be procedurally unfair because she had had insufficient notice of the charges against her and because the panel hearing the case was biased. However, the EAT upheld a reduction in her compensation of 80 per cent because she had accused the employer of stealing the printout from her bag (when in fact she had left it lying around) and because she had not done anything to explain the contents of the email during the hearing. While there is no denying that baseless accusations against the employer are unlikely to help the employee's cause, failing to explain something during a disciplinary hearing, particularly where there was insufficient notice of the charges, could have an innocent explanation, such as

[90] *Tracey v Crosville Wales Ltd* [1997] ICR 862, though the exception did not apply in the case itself.
[91] Eg in the reinstatement context: *Crowther v British Railways Board* (EAT/762/95, 12 June 1996).
[92] Eg ERA 1996, s 99.
[93] *Nelson v British Broadcasting Corporation (No. 2)* [1980] ICR 110.
[94] *Bell v The Governing Body of Grampian Primary School* (UKEAT/0142/07/CEA, 24 August 2007), [40].
[95] *Nelson v Clapham (t/a Claphams Solicitors)* (UKEATS/0037/11, 24 January 2012).

panic, embarrassment or nerves. Particular care should be taken when applying reductions in these scenarios.

Rules on contributory fault, like rules on mitigation, are a core part of determining the extent of the employer's liability to pay compensation. However, they do need to be applied with care, particularly in the fraught or emotional situations which are likely to arise when the employment relationship is coming to an end.

E. Conclusion

This section has considered some of the main elements in the calculation of compensation, focusing in particular on unfair dismissal and discrimination cases, where there are the largest bodies of case-law. Two important points have emerged from the detailed discussion. First, because compensation is focused on identifying and rectifying (primarily economic) losses, there will be many cases in which no compensation is payable, because the employer's breach of the claimant's rights, however egregious, has not caused any loss recognised by the law. Examples include procedurally unfair dismissals where it can be demonstrated that the employer had a fair reason for dismissal and would have dismissed the employee anyway, and cases in which it can be established that the employee did get or could have got an equally well-paid job soon after termination. This suggests that a remedial regime based solely on compensation, or at least compensation for economic losses, may not be sufficient either to deter employers from infringing their employees' rights, or to uphold the dignity of those employees. I explore the possibility of broadening the law's understanding of loss in section II below, and the use of other forms of redress in chapter six, on replicative remedies.

Second, there are a number of doctrines in operation in this area which require tribunals or courts to make predictions about the future or judgements about the parties' conduct, and there can be a tendency for these predictions or judgements to play out in ways which favour employers. For example, tribunals can seem ready to predict that the employer would have dismissed the employee fairly within a short period of time, or would have selected them fairly for redundancy even in a different pool. And the conduct of claimants can be judged quite harshly: for example, where they refuse to go back to the old employer or get frustrated and lash out in a disciplinary setting. Courts and tribunals should take greater care when applying the rules on compensation to ensure that they do not reduce the deterrent effect of awards on employers or infringe the dignity of employees. Although the desire to compensate on a principled basis is understandable and, in many ways, commendable, it is important not to lose sight of the ultimate objective in most cases of ensuring that compensatory awards are 'just and equitable' for the employee whose rights have been infringed.

II. Injury to Feelings

The preceding discussion highlighted two issues with compensation. The first is that there are many cases in which a claimant may succeed, but receive a nil award of compensation, because the employer's wrong has not caused them any economic loss as recognised by the law. The commonest example is where the employer had a fair reason for dismissal, or grounds for making the person redundant, but failed to follow a proper procedure or to consult appropriately. The second issue, which emerges only indirectly, is that compensation, being focused on the claimant's loss, is not concerned with the employer's behaviour. Deliberate or egregious breaches are treated in the same way as accidental ones, even though they may have a very different effect on the claimant. One possible solution to both of these problems would be to make an award for 'injury to feelings'. This could compensate claimants for the harm to their dignity, even when there is no economic loss, and could be adjusted to reflect the employer's breach and its impact on the claimant.

The law on damages for injury to feelings is in a state of confusion. These awards are available in some statutory claims, most notably under the Equality Act 2010, but not in others, such as unfair dismissal. And since they are not generally available in the law of contract, they are not available in wrongful dismissal claims. In this section, I will examine some of the theoretical issues surrounding these awards, before considering the statutory provisions and case-law in greater detail.

A. Theory

I will make two arguments in this section: that awards for injury to feelings should be regarded as compensating working people for harm to their dignity resulting from the loss of their job or other problems at work, and that they should be available in principle in all employment cases, both at common law and in statute.

Before developing these arguments, it is important to clarify the terminology in use in this area. Some employment law statutes, such as the Equality Act 2010, make express reference to damages for 'injury to feelings'.[96] This indicates that the focus should be on how the defendant's actions, such as the manner in which it committed the relevant wrong or its subsequent conduct of the litigation, have made the claimant feel. However, if this suggests a purely subjective assessment of the claimant's reaction, it is somewhat misleading. While the courts *do* consider how the particular claimant has been affected, they have been keen (for reasons explored further below) to approach awards for injury to feelings in a more objective manner.[97] This tends to involve classifying cases as more or less serious depending not on the claimant's reaction but on the defendant's conduct.

[96] Equality Act 2010, s 119(4).
[97] *Vento*, above n 62.

The underlying assumption is that the worse the defendant's conduct, the more likely it is that the 'reasonable' employee would experience distress as a result.

At common law, there is a related concept of 'aggravated damages'.[98] As Tilbury explains, this label emerged in *Rookes v Barnard* in 1964,[99] when the House of Lords was attempting to bring order to the law on a different topic: punitive damages.[100] Aggravated damages may be awarded on any of three different bases: the 'high-handed, malicious, insulting or oppressive' way in which the wrong was committed, the defendant's malicious motive, or the defendant's subsequent conduct, such as refusing to apologise.[101] Despite the focus on the defendant's behaviour, the House of Lords insisted that aggravated damages were compensatory rather than punitive, and should bear some relationship to the claimant's loss. This suggests that they may be similar to injury to feelings awards, particularly given the objective element in the assessment of such awards.[102] This position was supported by the Law Commission in an important report on the topic.[103] It preferred the label 'damages for mental distress', and considered that these damages sought to capture the idea that claimants should be compensated for feelings of upset and outrage at the defendant's conduct which did not meet the high threshold for compensation for psychiatric injury.

Confusingly, though, the case-law on discrimination (and on whistleblowing, which has adopted a similar approach) indicates that an award may be available for both injury to feelings and aggravated damages in the same case.[104] This arises because the Equality Act 2010 expressly makes available an award for injury to feelings, whilst also directing courts and tribunals to compensate claimants using tort principles, where there is the possibility of an award for aggravated damages.[105] Some judges have cast doubt on the wisdom of this, and nowadays some effort is usually made to consider both sums together and to ensure that the award, taken as a whole, is not excessive.[106]

My own view is that aggravated damages at common law *do* cover similar ground to injury to feelings awards under the relevant statute, but injury to feelings is a broader and more flexible concept and should not become restricted by reference to common law ideas. It can accommodate both the claimant's subjective feelings (for example, where the claimant is especially sensitive) and the objective harm to any reasonable claimant that would be caused by the employer's especially

[98] For discussion, see J Murphy, 'The Nature and Domain of Aggravated Damages' (2010) 69 *Cambridge Law Journal* 353; M Tilbury, 'Aggravated Damages' (2018) 71 *Current Legal Problems* 215.

[99] *Rookes v Barnard* [1964] AC 1129.

[100] Above n 98.

[101] *Alexander v Home Office* [1988] ICR 685, 692.

[102] A view taken by Burrows, above n 2, 287–88.

[103] Law Commission, *Aggravated, Exemplary and Restitutionary Damages* (LC No 247, December 1997).

[104] Eg *HM Prison Service v Johnson* [1997] ICR 275.

[105] Equality Act 2010, s 119(2) and (4).

[106] *Commissioner of Police of the Metropolis v Shaw* [2012] ICR 464, [25]–[28].

bad behaviour. Although the 'categories' of aggravated damages are helpful illustrations of the kinds of problem that can arise, there is no need to constrain statutory awards to those three situations. On this view, there is no need to make an additional award for aggravated damages where one is available because the same losses should already have been dealt with by an increase to the award for injury to feelings.

Having established this point, it is still important to think more carefully about the purpose being served by an award for injury to feelings. In employment settings, the answer is obvious: to address the dignity-related considerations discussed in chapter three.[107] Since the employment relationship is more than just a commercial transaction, it is not sufficient simply to compensate working people for their financial losses when they lose their job or when something else goes wrong at work. It is important also to compensate them for their less tangible losses: loss of status in the community or social opportunities connected with work, or a sense of having been betrayed by a previously trusted employer, for example. Of course, on some levels, a sum of money does nothing to assuage hurt or rebuild relationships, but it is the only option open to the law and may enable the claimant to do something to improve some aspect of their life in a way that counterbalances the harm they have suffered.

In an important analysis of the common law position, the Law Commission argued for damages for mental distress to be generally available as a matter of principle.[108] This would have required legislative change to make them available in the two main areas in which they are denied at present – breach of contract (minus some exceptions, to be discussed further below) and negligence claims. The Law Commission appeared to accept that – in these broader circumstances – mental distress damages could continue to be awarded on the principles already laid down by the common law in other cases, namely where the defendant's bad conduct or motive (including conduct subsequent to the wrong itself) caused the claimant mental distress. However, the government rejected the Law Commission's report and no legislation on the topic has ever been introduced.

An obvious objection to the Law Commission's position is that it would be odd for commercial parties engaged in normal market behaviour (such as an 'efficient' breach of contract) to argue that their feelings had been injured by the other side's conduct. But this objection provides precisely the reason why, even if awards for mental distress or injury to feelings are not made generally available, they should always be a possibility in employment law. Work relationships are not ordinary commercial transactions. The working person's labour cannot be separated from the working person: in the ILO's famous slogan, 'labour is not a commodity'.[109] From this perspective, it is vital that there is always a remedy available to reflect

[107] This is the view taken by Murphy, above n 98, on aggravated damages at common law.
[108] Above n 103.
[109] International Labour Organization, Declaration of Philadelphia (1944), Preamble: http://www.ilo.ch/dyn/normlex/en/f?p=1000:62:0::NO:62:P62_LIST_ENTRIE_ID:2453907:NO#declaration.

any loss of dignity brought about by the employer's behaviour, whether any other award in the case is compensatory or vindicatory in nature, or even an action for money owed. This would not necessarily mean that an award for an infringement to dignity should be made in every case: to do so might risk devaluing the award. Instead, courts and tribunals would need to assess the seriousness of the infringement, viewed objectively, as well as the claimant's reaction, and make no award or a lower or higher award accordingly.

Elsewhere in this book, I argue that employment law makes regular use of a concept of vindicatory damages (and should do so more explicitly), in which a monetary award is made as a public acknowledgement of the infringement of the claimant's rights, usually in circumstances in which compensation is not available because no economic loss has been caused.[110] It is therefore worth considering whether vindicatory awards do or could occupy the same conceptual space as awards for injury to feelings. This issue is particularly acute given that both types of award focus on the seriousness of the employer's breach. The one differentiating factor is that awards for injury to feelings also have a subjective element reflecting the *particular* claimant's reaction to the employer's wrongdoing. The arguments are finely balanced, and it is certainly possible that, in designing a rational system of remedies from scratch, one would not expect to include both types of award. However, two arguments may be made in favour of retaining both in different contexts. First, it may be easier for courts and tribunals in generally compensatory contexts, such as unfair dismissal, to add a (compensatory) award for injury to feelings, rather than to switch to a novel basis of assessment for part of the award. Second, it may be appropriate in some cases to couple a vindicatory award with an award for injury to feelings, where the subjective impact on the claimant has been particularly severe.

In discussions of aggravated damages at common law, it is sometimes argued that (despite the best efforts of the House of Lords in *Rookes*) they cannot be distinguished from punitive damages. Authors in this tradition, such as Cane, point to the fact that the courts' primary focus when identifying 'aggravating factors' and thus determining how much to award is on the defendant's conduct rather than on the claimant's feelings.[111] Where punitive damages are available, they are similarly linked to an assessment of the defendant's motives. However, Beever rightly points out in response to these claims that the courts have very little to guide them other than the defendant's behaviour if they want to take a more objective approach to the assessment of damages in this area.[112] Since aggravated damages cannot depend *solely* on the claimant's subjective reaction, the defendant's conduct is used as a starting-point for determining how serious the infringement of the claimant's

[110] See ch 8 of this volume.

[111] P Cane, *The Anatomy of Tort Law* (Oxford, Hart Publishing, 1997), 114.

[112] A Beever, The Structure of Aggravated and Exemplary Damages' (2003) 23 *Oxford Journal of Legal Studies* 87, 92–93. Note that Beever draws a sharp distinction between injury to feelings and harm to dignity, whereas I regard the two as closely linked.

dignity was. This does not inevitably mean that the defendant is being punished for its bad motives. Moreover, the availability of punitive damages is quite limited in practice.[113]

Having argued that awards for injury to feelings should be properly understood as awards for infringement of dignity (viewed objectively) and made available as a matter of principle in all employment cases, and differentiated them from other types of award, I now turn to consider the approach currently taken, first in statute and then at common law, and the reforms that would be required to bring the law into line with my preferred approach.

B. Statutory Employment Rights

I will begin with the best-known example, discrimination under the Equality Act 2010, before considering other express statutory provisions and the situations in which the possibility of making an award for injury to feelings has been implied by the courts.

The power to make an award in respect of injury to feelings is set out in section 119(4) Equality Act 2010. The award may be made whether or not the tribunal awards compensation on any other ground, indicating that injury to feelings is a separate head of loss. Although the tribunal has a discretion rather than a duty to make an award for injury to feelings, in the discrimination context it is unusual for no award to be made given the nature of the wrong: 'We do not say that in every case a tribunal is bound to award compensation for damage to injured feelings, but we would find it surprising if in most cases such an award … is not made.'[114] The broad principles are that the award should be genuinely compensatory rather than punitive, not so low that it diminishes respect for the law, and not so high that it amounts to a windfall for the claimant.[115] The appellate courts will only intervene in relation to quantum if a tribunal has made a 'wholly erroneous estimate of the loss suffered'.[116]

The task of tribunals in fixing an amount for the award has been simplified since the introduction in the *Vento* case of three 'bands' for injury to feelings.[117] The highest of the three bands, originally £15,000–25,000, is for 'the most serious cases, such as where there has been a lengthy campaign of discriminatory harassment on the ground of sex or race'.[118] The lowest band is for less serious cases, for example, where the discrimination is an 'isolated or one-off occurrence'.[119]

[113] See ch 5 of this volume.
[114] *Ministry of Defence v Sullivan* [1994] ICR 193, 199.
[115] *HM Prison Service v Johnson*, above n 104, 283.
[116] *Vento*, above n 62, [51].
[117] ibid.
[118] ibid [65].
[119] ibid.

Tribunals have flexibility within each of the three bands, but there is a minimum award (originally set at £500) so as to ensure proper respect for injury to feelings where it is found to have occurred. A tribunal's decision is unlikely to be overturned on appeal unless it has placed the case into the wrong band. Of course, the *Vento* case was decided in 2002, so the figures suggested at that time no longer have the same real-terms value. After various attempts to update them through the case-law, since 2017 Presidential Guidance has been used to set new limits.[120] At the time of writing, the most recent figures for claims presented on or after 6 April 2023 are:

- lower band £1,100 to £11,200
- middle band £11,200 to £33,700
- upper band £33,700 to £56,200[121]

The limit of £56,200 is not absolute and may be exceeded in an exceptional case.[122] Finally, it is important to note that although the bands focus on the seriousness of the case and thus its *likely* impact on the claimant, a higher award may be made where the claimant is particularly vulnerable in some way and has thus suffered more as a result of the discrimination than might be expected. This illustrates the compensatory basis of the award and is a reflection of the broader tort law principle that the defendant must take the claimant as they are.

Broadly speaking, damages for injury to feelings are available in two other categories of case. In both, the *Vento* bands are also applicable. The first relates to discrimination on trade union grounds. Where a person is refused employment or the services of an employment agency on trade union grounds, section 140(2) TULRCA 1992 expressly provides that an award for injury to feelings may be made. The same applies to refusal of employment because of a prohibited list under the relevant Regulations.[123] The detriment provisions in TULRCA do not deal with injury to feelings, but the courts have held that such awards can be made. In *Brassington v Cauldron Wholesale*,[124] the wording of section 149(2) was held to be broad enough to cover non-pecuniary losses, and subsequent decisions have upheld awards for injury to feelings.[125] However, the Court of Appeal cast doubt

[120] Presidential Guidance, 'Employment Tribunal Awards for Injury to Feelings and Psychiatric Injury Following *De Souza v Vinci Construction (UK) Ltd* [2017] EWCA Civ 879' (September 2017): https://www.judiciary.uk/wp-content/uploads/2013/08/Vento-bands-presidential-guidance-5-September-2017.pdf.

[121] Presidential Guidance, 'Employment Tribunal Awards for Injury to Feelings and Psychiatric Injury Following *De Souza v Vinci Construction (UK) Ltd* [2017] EWCA Civ 879 (Sixth Addendum to Presidential Guidance Originally Issued on 5 September 2017)' (March 2023): https://www.judiciary.uk/wp-content/uploads/2023/03/Vento-bands-presidential-guidance-April-2023-addendum.pdf.

[122] Eg the ET decision in *Tirkey v Chandhok* (ET/3400174/2013, 4 December 2015), [34].

[123] Employment Relations Act 1999 (Blacklists) Regulations 2010 (SI 2010/493), reg 8(2).

[124] *Brassington v Cauldron Wholesale Ltd* [1978] ICR 405.

[125] *Cleveland Ambulance Trust NHS v Blane* [1997] ICR 851; *Adams v London Borough of Hackney* [2003] IRLR 402.

on *Brassington* in its decision in *Santos Gomes*, a working time case.[126] It noted that the statutory wording at issue in *Brassington* had more in common with that in unfair dismissal cases,[127] so that the EAT's construction was doubtful in the light of *Dunnachie*, discussed below.[128] However, the Court of Appeal chose not to overrule *Brassington* because it was not necessary to do so for its decision in the case, and was a precedent of many years' standing. Tellingly, the judges also noted that claimants in trade union detriment cases might not have experienced any financial loss, so would only be able to obtain an award of any kind if they could claim for injury to feelings. Of course, awards in respect of injury to feelings are not available in dismissal cases in the trade union context because they are not available in dismissal cases more generally.

The second broad group of cases in which awards for injury to feelings may be made are those in which the employer has subjected the claimant to a detriment for asserting rights. The best-known example is whistleblowing under section 47B ERA 1996, as a result of the decision in *Virgo Fidelis Senior School v Boyle*.[129] The EAT held that whistleblowing detriment claims were sufficiently analogous to discrimination claims for the same approach to apply. Other detriment claims have attracted similar treatment. So, for example, a claimant who was subjected to detriment for asserting rights under the Working Time Regulations 1998[130] was found to be able to claim for injury to feelings in *South Yorkshire Fire and Rescue Service v Mansell*.[131] Importantly, this applies even where the underlying claim does not give rise to the possibility of an award for injury to feelings. For example, the Regulations on part-time, fixed-term and agency work expressly exclude awards for injury to feelings in respect of breach of the core rights they contain, but where the claimant is able to bring a detriment claim, they will be able to seek compensation on this ground.[132]

As I will explain below, injury to feelings is not available as a claim in unfair dismissal law, but in the whistleblowing context, the courts have been generous in drawing the line between detriment and dismissal claims. In *Melia*, the claimant brought a grievance against his manager (the protected disclosure) and was then subjected to various forms of harm until he felt compelled to resign and claim constructive dismissal.[133] He brought claims for detriment and dismissal. The ET and EAT held that the cut-off point for the detriment claim was when the employer's behaviour leading to the constructive dismissal began, whereas the Court of Appeal held that it was the date of resignation. This meant

[126] *Santos Gomes v Higher Level Care Ltd* [2018] EWCA Civ 418, [2018] ICR 1571.
[127] ibid [61]–[69].
[128] *Dunnachie v Kingston upon Hull City Council* [2004] UKHL 36, [2005] 1 AC 226.
[129] *Virgo Fidelis Senior School v Boyle* [2004] ICR 1210.
[130] SI 1998/1833.
[131] *South Yorkshire Fire and Rescue Service v Mansell* (UKEAT/0151/17/DM, 30 January 2018).
[132] Eg Part-time Workers (Prevention of Less Favourable Treatment) Regulations 2000 (SI 2000/1551), reg 8(11).
[133] *Melia v Magna Kansei Ltd* [2006] ICR 410.

that the claimant could seek damages for injury to feelings covering a much longer period of time. Only the dismissal itself and subsequent events did not attract that type of award. Presumably, the same approach could also be used in contexts other than whistleblowing where the claimant has a case for both detriment and dismissal.

However, in other contexts, Parliament has either expressly provided that injury to feelings cannot be a head of damage, or it has remained silent on the subject and the courts have not been willing to make the implication. It is sometimes suggested that an award for injury to feelings is not available where the claim is more analogous to a contractual claim than a claim in tort.[134] So, for example, although discrimination claims under the Equality Act 2010 are a core example of where an injury to feelings award is available, such awards are not made in equal pay claims, which have a contractual underpinning.[135] In *Santos Gomes*, the Court of Appeal refused to permit an award for injury to feelings for a claimant who had been denied rest breaks under the Working Time Regulations 1998, preferring instead to award a sum equivalent to the claimant's pay for the untaken breaks.[136]

Most notoriously, awards for injury to feelings are not available in unfair dismissal cases. This stems from the old decision in the *Norton Tool Co* case.[137] Although Sir John Donaldson expressly noted that the unfair dismissal jurisdiction was statutory and was not to be interpreted using common law concepts, he held that 'loss' in the statute, in what he termed its 'natural meaning', referred only to financial loss and could not be construed to include injury to feelings. Expressions such as 'just and equitable' were not intended to give tribunals a broad discretion over damages awards.[138] In the *Johnson* case, Lord Hoffmann questioned this interpretation,[139] but in the subsequent case of *Dunnachie*, in which the point was again tested in the light of Lord Hoffmann's remarks, the decision in *Norton Tool* was upheld.[140] Lord Steyn rejected both an argument that 'loss' could be construed more broadly, noting the difference between 'loss' and 'injury' and the possibility of Parliament having provided expressly for injury to feelings, and an argument that 'just and equitable' could be used to extend compensation beyond financial loss. This position ignores the importance of job security as one of the central values of employment law, and the multitude of non-economic harms which may arise when a person loses their job, issues discussed more fully in chapter three.

Although there are some grey areas, it is now reasonably well-established that discrimination and detriment claims may give rise to an award for injury to

[134] *Santos Gomes*, above n 126.
[135] *Newcastle upon Tyne City Council v Allan* [2005] ICR 1170.
[136] Above n 126.
[137] *Norton*, above n 6.
[138] For critique, see Collins, above n 8.
[139] *Johnson*, above n 20.
[140] *Dunnachie*, above n 128.

feelings, whereas unfair dismissal and other claims with a similar statutory formula for compensation do not. There now seems to be little chance that the courts will reverse the position in *Dunnachie*, so statutory reform would be required to ensure that an award for injury to feelings was potentially available in every employment case, to compensate working people for intangible harms to their dignity. Importantly, this would not mean that an award would always be made: the practice of almost always making an award in discrimination claims could be extended to other important rights, such as trade union discrimination claims, but need not be applied across the board. The *Vento* bands could continue to be used to guide tribunals as to the appropriate level of award and facilitate some consistency across different cases.[141]

C. Employment Rights at Common Law

At common law, the general rule is that damages for injury to feelings cannot be recovered in a contract claim. This proposition stems from the decision in *Addis v Gramophone Co Ltd*, discussed in section I.B for its (supposed) ruling on economic losses flowing from dismissal.[142] There are exceptions, but they are limited. For example, damages for mental distress are available in cases where the purpose of the contract was to enhance the claimant's wellbeing, such as by providing a holiday.[143] Of course, there is some justification for the view that, in a commercial contract, the parties should not be able to claim that their feelings have been hurt by the other side's 'ordinary' market behaviour. However, the same cannot be said of employment cases, a point acknowledged by Lord Cooke (dissenting) in *Johnson v Gore Wood & Co*:

> In severely confining damages for wrongful dismissal, your Lordships' House of those days appears to have seen the relationship of employer and employee as no more than an ordinary commercial one. This is a world away from the concept now …[144]

Lord Cooke's point is a good one: that attitudes towards employment relationships have changed a great deal since the early twentieth century when *Addis* was decided, and there is now much greater recognition of the need to protect the dignity of working people. From this perspective, the overruling of *Addis* in employment cases is long overdue.

However, if wrongful dismissal claims remain confined to the situation in which the employee is dismissed without notice, it seems unlikely that there will be much mileage for injury to feelings claims in practice. This possibility would add more value if, for example, the courts chose to give contractual effect to disciplinary

[141] *Vento*, above n 62.
[142] *Addis*, above n 20.
[143] *Jarvis v Swans Tours Ltd* [1973] QB 233; *Jackson v Horizon Holidays Ltd* [1975] 1 WLR 1468.
[144] *Johnson v Gore Wood & Co* [2002] 2 AC 1, 50.

procedures (overruling *Edwards*) where the employer's conduct during the process might well give rise to a plausible claim for injury to feelings.[145]

D. Conclusion

In conclusion, it is important to note the limitations of this proposal. While awards for injury to feelings would enhance the capacity of compensation to uphold working people's dignity and to deter employers from breaches – particularly ones which cause little or no economic loss – they would not solve the broader problems with compensation as a remedy. As chapter six explained, particularly for employers' procedural obligations, replicative remedies – forcing the employer to go through the procedure in question – are often preferable to financial awards after the event. They get closer to fulfilling the purpose of the original right by giving working people a chance to have their say. And as the next chapter will demonstrate, it is preferable to move away from compensation altogether where claimants are unlikely to suffer any economic loss when particular rights are infringed. An alternative basis for awards, such as vindication, makes the judges' task much easier to explain and justify.[146] Injury to feelings awards can help to fill a gap when compensation is a generally good basis for a remedy in most cases, and can provide an element of differentiation between breaches at different levels of seriousness.

III. Maximum Limits

I turn now to one of the most controversial features of unfair dismissal law: the statutory maximum limit on the compensatory award in section 124 ERA 1996. I explain how the limit works, and identify other areas of employment law in which similar limits apply, before considering whether such limits can be justified. It is worth stating at the outset that the effect of a maximum limit is that a claimant who has proved to the satisfaction of the tribunal that they have suffered loss in accordance with the applicable rules will not be fully compensated in respect of that loss if the sum involved exceeds the maximum. In that respect, it is very different to placing a maximum limit on a vindicatory award, where the sums of money involved are already somewhat arbitrary.[147] In practice, few awards get close to the maximum limit, but it still raises important issues of principle.[148]

[145] *Edwards*, above n 17.

[146] And could still be combined with a compensatory award for injury to feelings in an appropriate case.

[147] See ch 8 of this volume.

[148] K Williams, 'Unfair Dismissal: Myths and Statistics' (1983) 12 *Industrial Law Journal* 157, found that in the period up to 1981, the maximum had never been awarded. Given that the cap is now linked to earnings, its impact is harder to assess. ET statistics for 2022–23 indicate that the mean award for

Compensation for unfair dismissal has always been the subject of a statutory limit. In the Industrial Relations Act 1971, there was no concept of a basic award and compensation was to be determined by the tribunal using the 'just and equitable' formulation still found in the present law. Under section 118(1), compensation was limited to the lesser of two years' pay or £4,160 (which represented two years' pay at the average rate for the time). In 1975, the two-year limit was removed, but the numerical expression of the maximum remained.[149] However, the overall level of compensation available increased because of the creation of a basic award to sit alongside the compensatory award. Commenting at the time, Baker suggested that this was a response to the well-known decision in *Norton Tool Co*, which confined employees to claims for financial loss only and denied any recovery for loss of the job itself or injury to feelings.[150] The *Fairness at Work* White Paper in 1998 proposed the abolition of the maximum,[151] but in the end the government did not proceed with that plan, opting instead to make a substantial increase in the maximum limit (to £50,000) and to index-link it.[152] Although this was a disappointment to some commentators, it was still an important development in practice because the maximum had lost significant value in real terms: although the Secretary of State had *power* to increase the limit, there was no *duty* to do so and the power had not been used.[153]

The Coalition government (2010–15) developed a highly critical narrative about employment rights, suggesting that many claims before employment tribunals were speculative or even vexatious.[154] This led to a further change in the upper limit on unfair dismissal compensation, which remains in force today: the claimant may recover up to one year's gross pay or the statutory maximum (at the time of writing £105,707), whichever is the lower.[155] Thus, for most employees, a year's pay will be the effective maximum in their case, since average earnings are nowhere near the maximum.

Before considering the impact of the maximum, it is worth noting the other, less well-known, contexts in which limits apply.[156] The unfair dismissal maximum limit itself is extended to two other situations. The first is where a worker (rather than an employee) is given a statutory right to claim compensation for

unfair dismissal is £12,000 and the maximum received by any claimant was £184,000 (presumably where the cap did not apply): Ministry of Justice, *Tribunal Statistics Quarterly: April to June 2023* (September 2023), section 7. The average wage in the UK in 2022 was just over £33,000. https://www.statista.com/statistics/1002964/average-full-time-annual-earnings-in-the-uk/.

[149] Employment Protection Act 1975, ss 73–76. The limit was £5,200.

[150] CD Baker, 'Employment Protection: Individual Rights' (1976) 2 *Industrial Law Journal* 65, 72.

[151] Department for Trade and Industry, *Fairness at Work* (Cm 3968, May 1998).

[152] Employment Relations Act 1999, s 34.

[153] ERA 1996, s 124(2) (repealed).

[154] B Hepple, 'Back to the Future: Employment Law under the Coalition Government' (2013) 42 *Industrial Law Journal* 203.

[155] ERA 1996, s 124 (September 2023).

[156] There is also a cap of £5,000 on the compensation payable to the claimant under the Employment (Allocation of Tips) Act 2023, s 7, inserting new s 27M ERA 1996.

detriment in the form of termination of the worker's contract.[157] In these cases, the maximum applies as if they were an employee. Thus, if the detriment is for seeking to enforce rights under the Working Time Regulations 1998, the limit applies, but not if the detriment is in relation to health and safety or whistleblowing, where the compensation awarded to an employee would not be subject to a limit either (discussed below). The second extension of the unfair dismissal limit is where a person is unlawfully refused employment on trade union grounds under section 137 or 138 TULRCA 1992.[158] Presumably, in both of these cases, the thinking is that like cases should be treated alike: the 'dismissed' worker should not be treated better than a dismissed employee, and the person refused a job should not be treated better than a dismissed person.

Under the Employment Relations Act 1999 (Blacklists) Regulations 2010, the compensation in a case of refusal to hire under regulation 5 or 6, or detriment (other than dismissal of an employee) under regulation 9, is capped at £65,300.[159] The dismissal of an employee under the Regulations is dealt with in section 104F ERA 1996 and is subject to the usual unfair dismissal limit. The decision to set a separate figure for the use of a prohibited list adds needless complication to the law. It is also poorly designed, since it is not index-linked and will therefore lose value over time. Bizarrely, lower-paid workers may be better off under this approach because there is no reference to a year's pay, whereas higher-paid workers are worse off because the limit itself is lower than that used in the unfair dismissal formulation.

The position is further complicated by the fact that the unfair dismissal limit does not apply in certain types of case. There does not appear to have been any real attempt to work out and implement a clear rationale for when claimants should be allowed to recover in full. The most well-known exception is where the dismissal is discriminatory under the Equality Act 2010. The cap was removed in sex discrimination cases in response to a ruling by the European Court of Justice that the UK was failing to provide an effective remedy for discriminatory dismissals, and the same approach was subsequently applied to other protected characteristics.[160] The maximum also does not apply in whistleblowing cases (which are often treated analogously to discrimination cases) or to health and safety cases.[161] This makes the situation in relation to trade union dismissals (and refusals to hire) and blacklisting cases very difficult to defend, since the employer's action in these cases is both discriminatory (on trade union grounds) and a breach of the claimant's Article 11 right to freedom of association. Claimants in these cases should be protected at least as well as victims of other forms of discrimination.

[157] ERA 1996, s 49.
[158] TULRCA 1992, s 140(4).
[159] SI 2010/493, regs 8 and 11.
[160] Case C-271/91 *Marshall v Southampton and South West Hampshire AHA (No 2)* [1993] ECR I-4367.
[161] ERA 1996, ss 100 and 103A.

Of course, there would be no need to craft a coherent list of exceptions to maximum limits if no such limits applied. Various arguments have been suggested over the years to explain the presence of the maximum limits. In a note on *O'Laoire v Jackel*, Collins identified three potential purposes, none of which he found particularly persuasive.[162] First, the cap avoids the need for employers to take out excessive insurance cover against unfair dismissal liability. Second, it enables employers to calculate the relative costs and benefits of dismissing someone. Third, it preserves managerial prerogative by keeping awards at an affordable level for employers. In effect, all three arguments boil down to the proposition that the cap creates certainty for employers and their insurers about the 'worst case scenario' they will face if the employee brings a successful claim. In addition, it might also be argued that the cap promotes settlement: because both employees and employers know the maximum award, it may be easier to negotiate and agree on a figure.

However, all these propositions can be questioned. Compensatory awards for unfair dismissal are based on a careful calculation of the employee's losses, as discussed above. For the most part, these are closely linked to the employee's earnings so, as Collins points out, the figures involved are already known to the employer and the employee.[163] With the aid of some advice, employers, employees and insurers could calculate the likely award to a high degree of accuracy even in the absence of a cap. It is possible that the removal of the cap might make tribunals more generous – there is some sense that tribunals do not award career-long loss of future earnings in unfair dismissal cases because the cap renders such awards pointless in most cases – but the jurisdiction is now well-established and it seems unlikely that the removal of the cap alone would fundamentally change tribunals' approach to their task.

A slightly different view, which is sometimes advanced in the context of debates on unfair and wrongful dismissal, is that unfair dismissal was intended to provide 'cheap and cheerful' justice to lower-paid employees, who were less well-served by the common law. However, this claim is also underwhelming since the basis for assessment of compensation is different at common law. Even if a well-paid employee has a long notice period and gets a large sum in contract damages via the common law, this will not compensate them for any *future* loss of earnings caused by the dismissal and the difficulty of finding another equally good job, at least under the current law.

I suggest that the most likely explanation for the cap is twofold. First, the unfair dismissal jurisdiction is unpopular with employers because it constrains what they regard as a fundamental component of managerial prerogative. The cap makes this more palatable. Second, the cap serves wider economic purposes, in that it encourages dismissed employees to get back into the economy by looking

[162] *O'Laoire v Jackel International Ltd (No 2)* [1991] ICR 718. H Collins, 'Reinstatement and Upper Limits of Compensation' (1990) 19 *Industrial Law Journal* 193.

[163] ibid.

for another job. However, neither of these explanations is satisfactory. The first simply involves saying that employers do not like paying damages so they should not have to pay more than a certain amount, an argument that would be unlikely to be accepted in any other context. The second explanation seems to hark back to the concern some judges have expressed in termination cases that dismissed employees might 'sit in the sun' rather than making productive use of their time.[164] However, it seems unlikely in practice that many employees would eschew the chance of finding another job, giving them the opportunity to earn more money and exercise their skills, and even if they did, it is not clear why the law should adopt a moralising tone on the matter. In short, the cap on damages in unfair dismissal and elsewhere is a central example of the way in which employment rights are treated as less important or valuable than other kinds of rights in the legal system as a whole, because of an inherent pro-business or anti-employee bias.

IV. Conclusion

Having spent much of this chapter criticising the law on compensation, it is important to emphasise in conclusion that compensation plays a useful and important role as a remedy in employment law. Many breaches of employment rights cause significant loss to working people, usually in the form of lost earnings, and it is entirely appropriate that employers should be required to put the situation right. One of the major difficulties with compensation is that the law does not always ensure that working people are *fully* compensated. The most obvious example of this is the cap on unfair dismissal compensation. Although this does not affect all claimants, it is wrong as a matter of principle that employees should not be able to recover proven losses because of an artificial limit. There is no clearer illustration of the low value placed on the rights of working people than this rule.

But there are more subtle problems too, as section I explained. Even seemingly dry and technical rules on the correct identification of losses can serve to limit employees' recovery in ways which are sometimes unrealistic or unfair. For example, courts and tribunals seem very ready to assume that employers could have dismissed a person fairly anyway, and would have done so quickly, or that an unhappy employee will resign. And employees may be unfairly judged for refusing an offer of re-employment, or for lashing out in the heat of the moment during disciplinary proceedings. These various rules limit employers' liability, with consequent impact on the capacity of compensatory awards to serve the purposes of employment law: to deter employers from breaching employment rights, and to recognise and protect employees' dignity.

[164] *Denmark Productions Ltd v Boscobel Productions Ltd* [1969] 1 QB 699, 726 (Salmon LJ).

Finally, in section II, I made a case for allowing awards for injury to feelings to be available in principle in all employment cases, given the particular importance of dignity in this setting. Although I accept the need to prioritise as between different employment rights, the current position prioritises freedom from discrimination (claims under the Equality Act 2010) over other equally important rights, such as job security and freedom of association. Courts and tribunals could continue to differentiate between cases by declining to make an award where there was no real harm to dignity, and by using the *Vento* bands, which would also help to ensure consistency and moderation in the use of these awards.

8

Vindicatory Awards

Vindicatory awards are intended neither to compensate the claimant for losses suffered, nor to punish the employer for particularly egregious breaches, but simply to acknowledge that the claimant's rights have been infringed. Awards of this type are relatively unusual at common law, at least on a traditional analysis.[1] However, they are encountered with greater regularity in employment law, where there are many statutory employment rights which have a monetary award as their principal or sole remedy, even though breach does not give rise to any obvious loss as normally understood and there is typically no need to prove loss in order to bring a claim. Although these awards are often explained by the courts as intended to punish the employer, it will be argued in this chapter that vindication rather than punishment offers the most convincing explanation of their purpose.

It is important to be clear at the outset that vindication is not pursued solely through the making of vindicatory awards, as chapter three explained. The very act of the court or tribunal making an order of any kind against the defendant can be seen as the state vindicating the claimant's rights. This chapter is concerned with monetary awards that cannot be explained as primarily compensatory in nature, or as orders to pay money owed.

Vindicatory awards give rise to a number of questions. One is whether the vindicatory award is the right choice of remedy in all the circumstances. Are there losses that should be compensated? Is the defendant's conduct so egregious that a punitive approach is warranted, either through civil penalties or, perhaps, even through the criminal law? Or could a replicative remedy be created that would do a better job of putting things right for the claimant than the award of a sum of money?

Where the vindicatory award is the best or only choice, a further question arises as to how to quantify the award. This presents particular challenges for those steeped in the common law tradition because there is no loss on which to base the award, and judges sometimes express concern about the claimant receiving a 'bonus' or windfall.[2] However, the windfall problem assumes that compensation is the only legitimate basis for awards, so it falls away once it is recognised that some awards may be solely vindicatory. Setting figures for vindicatory awards is bound

[1] Though see R Stevens, *Torts and Rights* (Oxford, OUP, 2007).

[2] For example, *Hasler v Tourell Precision Engineers Ltd* (Case No 11431/83, 21 June 1983) (IT), [5].

to be somewhat subjective, but this process can be interrogated in various ways. For example, do infringements of workers' fundamental human rights attract higher vindicatory awards than infringements of lesser rights or interests? How do the sums of money involved compare with compensatory awards? Are the awards for breaches of lesser rights or interests sufficient to prompt working people to bring claims, or do they consign some rights or interests to the 'dustbin'?[3] These difficulties have, in many cases, prompted Parliament to set a sum or a formula for vindicatory awards rather than leaving them to the discretion of the tribunal, and this decision is also worthy of analysis.

I. Theoretical Framework

In this section, I define what I mean by a vindicatory award and explain how this differs from some of the uses of the term found in the academic literature and in certain types of tort case. I also offer some thoughts on the factors that should influence the choice of this type of award over other remedial options. It is important to note at the outset that these factors are rarely discussed because, although vindicatory awards are not uncommon in employment law, they are not usually explicitly identified as such in the judgments of tribunals and courts, let alone justified. Finally, I consider how vindicatory awards should be calculated, given that familiar measures of loss are, *ex hypothesi*, inappropriate in this context.

A. Definition

A vindicatory award is one designed not to compensate the claimant or punish the defendant, but to acknowledge that the claimant's rights have been infringed. The measure of damages is not related to the claimant's losses or the defendant's bad motives, but to the seriousness of the infringement.

I will demonstrate in this chapter that vindicatory awards are quite common in relation to statutory employment rights, even though they are almost never acknowledged as such in practice. They fall into two groups. First, there are situations in which the statute does not require proof of loss in order for the claimant to receive an award, for example, where a fixed sum is laid down in statute.[4] These examples are prima facie vindicatory, though it is still necessary to consider whether the purpose of the fixed sum might be to offer compensation for losses that might exist in practice but be difficult for tribunals to calculate.[5] Second, there

[3] G Meeran, 'The Employment Tribunals', in L Dickens and A Neal (eds), *The Changing Institutional Face of British Industrial Relations* (Alphen aan den Rijn, Kluwer Law International, 2006), 131.

[4] For example, s 145E(3) TULRCA 1992 (inducements to give up collective bargaining).

[5] An example of this is the basic award in unfair dismissal cases (ERA 1996, s 119), which compensates for loss of redundancy rights.

are a number of examples of statutory employment rights where the drafters have used terms like 'compensation' in setting out the remedy, but in practice it is very difficult to identify any economic loss likely to be suffered by the claimant as a result of the infringement of the right, other than in exceptional cases.[6] It seems unlikely that the intention was to provide an award that would rarely be available, so tribunals often make some kind of award in these cases without proof of loss, though they typically struggle to explain what they are doing and why.[7] Vindication offers a much clearer account.

Some judges have noticed that they may be called upon to make financial awards which are not truly compensatory in nature, and they have tended to resort to the vocabulary of 'punishment' to describe the purpose of these awards. For example, it has been held that the award payable when an employer fails to consult on collective redundancies should be regarded as a 'sanction' against the employer.[8] However, as I explained in chapters four and five, it is not helpful to over-use the concept of punishment. To do so risks devaluing its impact in genuinely serious cases. It also creates the possibility that the courts may treat accidental or unintentional breaches of employment rights as somehow trivial or irrelevant, despite their potentially serious impact on the claimant. While some statutory provisions *do* include a reference to the employer's behaviour, it is generally not the only factor in determining quantum, and thinking about these awards as vindicatory encourages tribunals to maintain an appropriate focus on valuing the claimant's rights.

Of course, one possible response to the idea that it is difficult to identify losses flowing from the breach of certain employment rights is to point to the narrow way in which the law identifies loss. By thinking more creatively about loss, it might be possible to treat awards as compensatory in a wider variety of cases.[9] By way of illustration, vindicatory awards (in my scheme) are often found in cases where the employer has infringed the worker's procedural rights, such as the right to be accompanied at a disciplinary or grievance hearing.[10] At common law, awards are sometimes made for 'loss of a chance', though this is less frequently recognised in employment law.[11] It could be argued that the employer's breach of the right to be accompanied results in a lost opportunity to change the employer's mind. However, this would often be highly speculative, and would not apply in cases in which it could be convincingly argued that the outcome would have been the same.[12] The idea that the award vindicates the right to be accompanied

[6] For example, TULRCA 1992, s 172(2) (refusal to permit trade union officials or members to take time off).

[7] *Skiggs v South West Trains Ltd* [2005] IRLR 459 (EAT).

[8] *Susie Radin Ltd v GMB* [2004] EWCA Civ 180, [2004] ICR 893, [45] (Peter Gibson LJ).

[9] This is an ongoing discussion among private law theorists too. See eg S Steel, 'Damages Without Loss' (2023) 139 LQR 219.

[10] Under Employment Relations Act 1999, s 10.

[11] A Burrows, *Remedies for Torts, Breach of Contract, and Equitable Wrongs* (4th edn, Oxford, OUP, 2019), ch 5.

[12] Cf *Polkey v AE Dayton Services Ltd* [1988] AC 344.

(regardless of the impact on the employer's decision) is much less convoluted and more persuasive.

Another way to expand the definition of compensable loss is, of course, to allow awards to be made for injury to feelings in a wider range of employment cases, an argument I made in chapter seven. If this change were to be made, an award for injury to feelings would always be available even when the claimant had not suffered any other compensable loss, such as financial loss. However, there are two reasons for thinking that awards for injury to feelings cannot entirely solve the problem. First, although courts and tribunals have been concerned to inject an objective element into awards for injury to feelings, they combine objective and subjective elements.[13] Claimants may be tempted to exaggerate the impact on them personally in order to receive a higher award. And although these awards are intended to address harms to dignity, some claimants may not find it particularly attractive that all they can get is an award for injury to feelings. Vindication is a more empowering concept for the affected worker. Second, awards for injury to feelings can be used to differentiate between breaches according to their impact on the working person.[14] Thus, there is no reason why they could not be used in combination with a vindicatory award in appropriate cases. For example, in some of the trade union discrimination cases to be discussed later in the chapter, a vindicatory award could be used to recognise the infringement of the claimant's rights, and an award for injury to feelings could be added where the impact on the claimant in question was particularly severe.

B. When Should a Vindicatory Award be Used?

It may seem odd to ask when a vindicatory award should be used, since I have already defined this type of award as a default option for cases in which there is not likely to be any economic loss to compensate, and where the high threshold for a punitive approach has not been met. Nevertheless, there are two important normative questions to address: why make a financial award at all, and why not use a replicative remedy instead?

One obvious way in which the law can vindicate the claimant's rights is through a declaration. In cases involving statutory employment rights, it is very common to find that the tribunal 'shall' make a declaration if the claimant succeeds.[15] However, there are some good pragmatic reasons for concluding that confining the claimant to obtaining a declaration is unlikely to be an effective way of upholding employment rights. Few people would go to the trouble of litigating simply to prove a point by obtaining a declaration, and few employers would take

[13] *Vento v Chief Constable of West Yorkshire Police* [2002] EWCA Civ 1871, [2003] ICR 318.

[14] ibid.

[15] For example, ERA 1996, s 49(1) (right not to be subjected to a detriment).

a declaration seriously. Supplementing the declaration with a financial award may help to promote these goals, if the award is high enough.

However, a monetary award may not be the best option in all circumstances. While claimants may welcome a financial award, in cases where they have suffered no loss, the award is not providing them with much-needed redress. There may be some good arguments for giving greater consideration to replicative remedies in some of the cases currently dealt with through vindicatory awards. For example, an employer's failure to consult on collective redundancies currently results in a financial award which is vindicatory by my account.[16] This contrasts with the (current) position in public law settings, where a failure to consult may lead to an order quashing the public authority's decision and requiring it to conduct a proper process before taking the decision again.[17] This is a much stronger 'echo' of the right to be consulted and the decision not to use an analogous approach in employment cases requires careful interrogation.[18]

C. Vindicatory Awards at Common Law

Having explained my approach to vindication, it is important to note how this differs from an emerging discussion in both the case-law and the academic literature about the possibility of awards of vindicatory damages being made at common law.

An express use of the term 'vindicatory damages' may be found in the Privy Council's decision in the *Ramanoop* case, in which the claimant had been mistreated by a police officer in breach of his rights under the constitution of Trinidad and Tobago.[19] The Privy Council held that:

> An additional award, not necessarily of substantial size, may be needed to reflect the sense of public outrage, emphasise the importance of the constitutional right and the gravity of the breach, and deter further breaches.[20]

While this definition shares a significant similarity with my definition of vindicatory damages – the idea of emphasising the importance of the right infringed – it also has some significant differences. It is clearly designed to be additional to a compensatory award and to reflect the particular circumstances of bad behaviour by state agents leading to a breach of constitutional rights. In any event, vindicatory damages in the *Ramanoop* sense do not form part of English law. A majority in the Supreme Court in *Lumba* (in which the applicants had been unlawfully detained) rejected a claim for vindicatory damages, describing the concept as an

[16] TULRCA 1992, s 189, which uses the term 'protective award'.

[17] CPR Part 54, rule 19(2).

[18] J Gardner, 'What is Tort Law For? Part 1: the Place of Corrective Justice' (2011) 30 *Law & Philosophy* 1, 33.

[19] *Attorney General of Trinidad and Tobago v Ramanoop* [2005] UKPC 15, [2006] 1 AC 328.

[20] ibid [19].

'unruly horse' and holding that it was too unpredictable to be incorporated into English law.[21] The decision was clearly influenced by the existing possibility of obtaining punitive or exemplary damages for 'oppressive, arbitrary or unconstitutional action by the servants of the government'.[22] There is clearly an overlap between this idea and *Ramanoop* damages, even though the Privy Council in *Ramanoop* rejected the notion that vindicatory damages were punitive in nature.[23]

Leaving aside express uses of the term 'vindicatory damages', some scholars have argued that it is possible to discern examples of vindication at work in the common law. Sometimes courts make substantial awards even though the claimant has not suffered any significant loss, and although the judges usually describe what they are doing using conventional compensatory language, vindication offers a more persuasive account.

Pearce and Halson identify a number of possible examples of vindicatory damages in property and contract.[24] In *Attorney-General v Blake*, the defendant intelligence officer published sensitive information in his memoirs in breach of the Official Secrets Act and his duty of confidentiality to his employer.[25] The government had not suffered any recognisable loss but Blake was ordered to hand over the profits he had made from sales of the book. Although it is sometimes argued that the award in *Blake* was restitutionary, it was held that he was not a fiduciary, and thus it is not clear on what basis it might be argued that the government had an interest in the money he had made.[26] The award of an account of profits can be seen as vindicating the government's interest in compliance with the confidentiality clause. A similar analysis works for the well-known *Ruxley* case, in which the builder of a swimming pool built a perfectly useable pool but not to the depth specified in the contract.[27] The House of Lords ruled out awarding the 'cost of cure' because this would have been disproportionate. This also meant that he had not suffered any loss of amenity. There was no basis for a restitutionary award because the builder had not profited by the defective performance. But the award did recognise that the claimant did not receive the contracted-for performance: it vindicated his contractual rights.

In tort, Varuhas makes a persuasive case for vindicatory damages in relation to the various torts actionable in themselves without proof of loss, like trespass, false imprisonment or defamation.[28] Varuhas suggests that what the courts are in fact

[21] *R (Lumba) v Secretary of State for the Home Department* [2011] UKSC 12, [2012] 1 AC 245, [101] (Lord Dyson).

[22] *Rookes v Barnard* [1964] AC 1129.

[23] Above n 19.

[24] D Pearce and R Halson, 'Damages for Breach of Contract: Compensation, Restitution and Vindication' (2008) 28 *Oxford Journal of Legal Studies* 73.

[25] *Attorney General v Blake* [2001] 1 AC 268 (HL).

[26] Pearce and Halson, above n 24, 90.

[27] *Ruxley Electronics and Construction Ltd v Forsyth* [1996] AC 344 (HL), and see Pearce and Halson, above n 24, 94–95.

[28] JNE Varuhas, 'The Concept of "Vindication" in the Law of Torts: Rights, Interests and Damages' (2014) 34 *Oxford Journal of Legal Studies* 253.

doing in these cases is awarding 'normative damages' to acknowledge or vindicate the wrong done to the claimant's interests.[29] For example, damages are available for battery even if the claimant has incurred no medical expenses and has not experienced any pain or suffering, whereas this would not be the case in a negligence claim.

Thus, the idea of vindicatory damages in the sense in which I am using the term is not unknown to the common law, even though the judges themselves tend to stick to traditional compensatory language, and when they do use the term 'vindication', they have a different idea in mind altogether. However, I will not be placing undue emphasis on the common law material since it is important to understand statutory employment rights on their own terms, and not solely through a common law lens.[30]

A final point to note is that while – like the authors just cited – I am interested in identifying and correctly classifying examples of vindicatory awards, I would not seek to reconceptualise *all* awards in the employment context as vindicatory in nature. Stevens has offered a radical reconceptualisation of the law of torts with vindication at its heart.[31] On his view, it is necessary first to identify a right of the claimant that has been infringed, such as the right to liberty or bodily integrity, and then to award damages for the infringement of that right. These damages are regarded as 'substitutive' for the right or as 'valuing' the right: reflecting the price the claimant would have paid not to have their right infringed. According to Stevens, the existence of substitutive damages as a concept is usually 'obscured' by the fact that the value of the right is often the same as the loss suffered by the claimant.[32] This approach has proved too radical for many commentators, dispensing as it does with the familiar compensatory basis for awards for the whole of the law of torts (not just in exceptional cases) and in requiring the identification of a right infringed rather than a wrong done in every case.[33] From an employment perspective, the approach would not be helpful because it would not provide any more clarity than does the current law, in which almost all awards are described as compensatory, with occasional ideas about punishment. What is urgently needed is a richer, more sophisticated vocabulary, not the replacement of one blunt conceptual tool with another.

D. Quantification

I noted above that correctly classifying an award as vindicatory is helpful from the perspective of quantum. Treating the award as compensatory can result in judges

[29] ibid 275–89. It is worth noting that Varuhas (ibid 258–59) prefers to speak in terms of valuing 'interests' rather than 'rights'.

[30] S Anderman, 'The Interpretation of Protective Employment Statutes and Contracts of Employment' (2000) 29 *Industrial Law Journal* 223.

[31] Stevens, above n 1, especially ch 4.

[32] Stevens, above n 1, 61.

[33] For example, Varuhas, above n 28, 273–75.

making very low awards because they cannot identify any loss, even though it is not likely to be present, and treating the award as punitive risks a very low award where the employer's breach was accidental. However, this does not mean that it is easy to quantify a vindicatory award, so it is necessary to consider what principles are appropriate and whether awards should be at the judges' discretion or fixed by Parliament.

It seems essential that vindicatory damages should be a non-trivial sum. Pearce and Halson argue that an award of nominal damages could, in principle at least, serve a vindicatory function, as a public acknowledgment on the part of the court that the defendant has infringed the claimant's rights.[34] However, as they explain, this approach may not work particularly well in practice because it feels like a hollow victory for the claimant and may be too easily confused with cases in which the court makes a 'derisory' award implying criticism of the claimant's conduct. Of course, it is also the case that most claimants will not pursue litigation at all if they anticipate a trivial award, thereby rendering some rights effectively unenforceable.

It might nevertheless be argued that vindicatory damages should be set at generally lower levels than compensatory damages, given that no loss has been suffered. But this is simply the 'windfall' argument in a slightly different guise. Although it is clearly difficult to rank rights infringements against losses, a breach of a working person's fundamental rights should attract a substantial award. I explore this point further below (in section II.C) in relation to freedom of association cases.

As Stevens explains, there is no 'naturally correct quantification' for awards of damages that are vindicatory or, as he puts it, 'substitutive' for the right infringed, in the absence of any loss.[35] As with loss of amenity damages in the law of tort, all the law can do is to set a tariff which is applied consistently and gives higher awards for infringements of more important rights. The selection of the points at the top and bottom of the scale is bound to be somewhat arbitrary. The relative ranking of rights may be easier to explain and justify but even this is not straightforward.

A second important question about vindicatory awards is who should determine the level at which they are set, Parliament or the tribunals? The subjectivity of these awards may argue in favour of Parliament fixing the appropriate levels. Simply prescribing a sum or a formula for calculation in a statute ensures consistency as between different tribunals and avoids any risk of unduly high or low awards. Low awards seem to be a particular risk, given the compensation mindset of many judges steeped in the common law tradition. Statutory sums can be, and often are, regularly adjusted for inflation.[36] Of course, there are routes by which the judges themselves can develop guidance on levels of award, as the *Vento* bands for injury to feelings, which are occasionally adjusted through Presidential Guidance,

[34] Pearce and Halson, above n 24, 75–77.
[35] Stevens, above n 1, 78.
[36] Employment Relations Act 1999, s 34.

demonstrate.[37] But this process is, arguably, less accountable than Parliament setting a figure when a right is enacted.

Setting a precise sum in statute does not allow for any variation in awards to accommodate different types of case. However, it is perfectly possible to set a formula instead – an award of 'up to' two weeks' pay, for example – so that tribunals can vary the amounts they award.[38] One difficulty tribunals have faced with this approach is working out appropriate principles for variation. Unfortunately, because tribunals (and courts) are unfamiliar with the concept of a vindicatory award, they are often tempted to invoke other ideas, such as suggesting that the claimant should receive a lower award because they did not suffer any economic loss, or suggesting that the maximum should be awarded to punish the employer for a deliberate breach. In the vindicatory context, since the purpose is to vindicate the claimant's rights, the seriousness of the breach itself should be the main criterion for variation.

II. Vindication under the Current Law

This section pursues two objectives. First, it seeks to map out the use of vindicatory awards in the current law. This is a complex and potentially contested exercise, given the need to consider a combination of the way in which statutes are drafted, the language judges use when explaining the awards they are making, and the likely practical consequences for the claimant of any particular breach. Second, this section considers the two important evaluative questions identified in the previous section: is a monetary award the most appropriate remedy and, if so, is the amount likely to be awarded justifiable?

I have chosen to organise the material under five headings: (A) rights to time off work, (B) rights to be consulted, (C) freedom of association cases, (D) 'procedural' rights designed to facilitate the enforcement of other rights, and (E) a miscellaneous group. These are not watertight analytical categories – some of the rights to time off are applicable to trade union representatives, for example – but they help to organise the material for the purposes of discussion. Although it might seem logical to focus on more structural questions, such as the different ways in which statutory provisions on remedies are drafted, discussing the material by the type of right involved is much more useful when considering evaluative questions. Understanding what is at stake for the claimant is key to understanding issues such as what replicative remedies might be available and how the particular right in question might rank against others for the purposes of assessing quantum.

[37] *Vento*, above n 13.

[38] For example, Employment Relations Act 1999, s 11(3), for breaches of the right to be accompanied at a disciplinary or grievance hearing under s 10.

A. Time-Off Rights

There are many situations in which a working person (usually an employee) has a statutory right to time off work. The most obvious examples are the various rights to rest breaks during the working day and to daily and weekly rest periods under the Working Time Regulations 1998.[39] There are also numerous rights to time off in specific circumstances, such as for ante-natal appointments, emergency leave to care for a dependant, and time off for trade union representatives. The precise formulation of each right varies, and some are rights to paid time off whereas others are not. Where the right is to paid time off, the law typically provides a right to claim unpaid wages where the employer permits the working person to take the time off but refuses to pay them during that time.[40] This is a replicative remedy. In some cases, there is also a remedy if the claimant is subjected to a detriment beyond just being denied the time off, or unfairly dismissed by the employer for asserting their rights.[41] But my main concern here is with the remedy for not allowing the claimant to take the time off at all.

This is of interest from a vindicatory perspective because, while some claimants will suffer identifiable losses as a result of not being given time off, many will not. For example, an unreasonable refusal to grant emergency leave may mean that the employee incurs costs in making alternative provision, such as paying a professional carer or childminder to help. However, in other cases, loss is difficult to envisage. For example, someone who is refused time off for an ante-natal appointment does not experience any obvious quantifiable loss as a result of the employer's infringement of their right. Indeed, it seems likely that, in many cases, the only practical consequence of being refused time off is that the employee will have to undertake the relevant activity outside working hours. While this is obviously inconvenient and limits the employee's options for using their free time, it is not easy to conceptualise as a loss unless the employee can show that the time would have been used for financial gain, for example, by working in a second job. Of course, in some instances, the employee will be unable to undertake the relevant activity outside working hours – there may be no ante-natal appointments for times when the employee is not working, and many of the public duties protected in statute must be carried out at specific times – but, again, it is difficult to turn the employee's lost opportunity to undertake a valuable activity into a compensable loss.

The law adopts as many as six different remedial approaches in respect of time-off rights, which can be grouped together into three broad categories. In one

[39] Working Time Regulations 1998 (SI 1998/1833), regs 10–12.

[40] For example, the right to time off for employee representatives for consultation on collective redundancies or transfers under s 61 ERA 1996 should be remunerated in accordance with s 62, and a claim may be made under s 63(1)(b) and (5).

[41] See ERA 1996 ss 48 and 49. Note that some time-off rights have both a freestanding remedy for refusal and a detriment claim (eg WTR regs 30–31), whereas others have one or the other but not both.

group, the tribunal may award the employee a sum equal to the pay they would have earned during the time they would have taken off or, occasionally, double that sum. In the second group, the tribunal may award what is described as 'compensation', though this label is often open to question. There are at least three different sets of wording in operation to guide tribunals in their quantification of the award of 'compensation': 'just and equitable' on its own; 'just and equitable' having regard to 'any loss sustained by the employee which is attributable to the matters to which the complaint relates' and the employer's default; and 'just and equitable' having regard to the employee's loss and the employer's 'behaviour'. I explore below whether there is any significance in these different approaches to drafting. In the third group, the right to take time off is not expressly enforced in its own right, but there are actions available in the event that the employee is subjected to a detriment or dismissed for asserting the right.[42] Since 'detriment' is broadly construed in this context, these provisions are generally sufficient to cover a simple refusal to permit the employee to take time off, though such claims are rare and will not be discussed further here.[43] In any of these groups, it is conceptually possible for the statute to place some kind of limit on the maximum amount the tribunal may award. In the current law, there are examples of this in both the first and second groups. The table below gives an overview of the position.

(i) Group 1 – Pay for the Time the Claimant would have Taken

As the table illustrates, some time-off rights attract an award of pay (or double pay) for the time the claimant would have taken off had they been allowed to do so. This remedy is not compensatory because if the claimant was refused time off, it can generally be assumed that they worked during the relevant time and were paid accordingly (and would have other rights and remedies if they had not been paid). This was noted by the tribunal in *Hasler*, a case in which the claimant had been refused time off to look for work during his redundancy notice period:

> But [the claimant] has in fact been paid for every day during the period of notice at the appropriate rate: therefore any award we give must be in the nature of a bonus if you look at it from one point of view, or a penalty on the respondents from the other.[44]

Of course, the tribunal's choice of language is not particularly helpful for the reasons given above, and the better view is that the award of compensation is vindicatory: it acknowledges that the claimant's right to take time off has been infringed by the employer's unreasonable refusal.

Although the calculation of the award requires the tribunal to consider evidence as to how much time the claimant wanted to take off, this is not a particularly

[42] ibid. The principal example is s 47C ERA 1996, which deals with various types of family leave, including maternity, paternity, parental and adoption leave.

[43] See ch 7 of this volume.

[44] *Hasler*, above n 2, [5].

Table 1 Remedial approaches to breach of time-off rights

		Pay for the time	Double pay for the time	Just and equitable	Just and equitable; loss; default	Just and equitable; loss; behaviour
ERA 1996, s 50	Public duties				X	
ERA 1996, s 52	Work or training	X (maximum)				
ERA 1996, s 58	Pension scheme trustees				X	
ERA 1996, ss 55, 56, 57ZA and 57ZB	Ante-natal care		X			
ERA 1996, s 57A	Emergency leave				X	
ERA 1996, s 61	Workforce reps	X				
ERA 1996, s 63A	Training for young workers[45]					
ERA 1996, s 63D	Training			X (maximum)		
ERA 1996, s 80	Parental leave					X
ERA 1996, s 80F	Flexible working			X (maximum)		
ICER 2004, reg 27	Workforce reps	X				
TULRCA 1992, ss 168, 168A, 170	Union reps and members				X	
WTR 1998, reg 30	Rest breaks, rest periods				X	

[45] This provision applies only in Scotland and Wales.

difficult exercise, and the size of the award is relatively straightforward to calculate. Indeed, this compares favourably with the 'just and equitable' formulation in use in respect of other time-off rights.

However, a significant problem with this group of awards is that the sums of money involved are likely to be relatively small. For example, the right to time off to look for work after being served with a notice of redundancy under section 52(1) ERA 1996 is subject to a limit under section 52(5): 'The amount of an employer's liability to pay remuneration under subsection (1) shall not exceed, in respect of the notice period of any employee, forty per cent of a week's pay of that employee.' Although this is not subject to the statutory maximum limit on the amount of a week's pay, it applies regardless of the length of the notice period, and it is unlikely to be worth claiming. Similarly, although the award for ante-natal appointments is set more generously at double the pay the employee would have earned, it is unlikely that the time off involved would be substantial in any particular case.[46] In some cases, it is also possible to bring a claim for any detriment suffered as a result of the employee's attempt to take time off, which may make it more worthwhile to claim and may also allow for compensation on occasions when a loss has been suffered, but this does not diminish the point being made about the remedies for mere refusal.[47] Small awards indicate that the rights in question are not valued by the law and discourage claimants from attempting to enforce them.

(ii) Group 2 – Just and Equitable Compensation

In the second group of rights identified in the table above, the tribunal is directed to award a sum of compensation that is 'just and equitable', with subtle differences between the precise statutory formulations.[48] This expression is very familiar from the unfair dismissal jurisdiction and has the advantage of accommodating situations in which the employee has suffered a loss as a result of the employer's refusal to permit time off.[49] However, it is highly problematic in purely vindicatory situations because tribunals often struggle to make substantial awards on this basis in the absence of any loss.

The most common formulation uses the idea of a 'just and equitable' award but also directs tribunals to consider the employer's 'default' and the employee's 'loss'. Section 172(2) TULRCA 1992, which sets out the remedy for trade union representatives and trade union members who are denied time off under section 168, 168A or 170 is a typical example:

[46] ERA 1996, ss 55, 56, 57ZA and 57ZB.

[47] Above n 41.

[48] Some provisions use 'behaviour' instead of 'default', and some simply use 'just and equitable' with no further explanation. On the reasoning discussed in this section, all of these options permit vindicatory awards because none of them confine the tribunal to considering the claimant's loss. It is not clear whether any other distinction is intended.

[49] ERA 1996, s 123.

> The amount of the compensation shall be such as the tribunal considers just and equitable in all the circumstances having regard to the employer's default in failing to permit time off to be taken by the employee and to any loss sustained by the employee which is attributable to the matters complained of.

Of course, one immediate response to this drafting might be to insist that the award is not vindicatory at all, since it contains clear references to compensation and loss. However, there are two reasons for thinking that, while compensation may sometimes be a goal, it is not the primary purpose of these awards. First, it is clear that time-off rights do not always (or even often) give rise to losses, a point signalled by the use of the word 'any' in the drafting. Second, the reference to 'default' could be a signal that something else is going on. It is significant that the most familiar formulation of a 'just and equitable' compensatory award, in section 123 ERA 1996, only refers to loss. It may be tempting to conclude that a reference to 'default' or, in some other provisions, 'behaviour', indicates that one of the purposes of the award is to punish the employer for failing to allow the employee to take the time off. However, as I have explained elsewhere, it is unhelpful and overly simplistic to treat every breach of employment rights as the proper subject of punishment when vindication often provides a more satisfactory explanation of what is going on.[50]

Section 172 TULRCA 1992 has been the subject of some litigation. In *Skiggs v South West Trains*, the claimant trade union representative was unreasonably refused time off by his employer to carry out his trade union duties, but the tribunal did not award him any compensation, because there was no evidence that he had suffered any loss.[51] The EAT held that the tribunal had misdirected itself by holding that loss was the only basis for an award, noting the reference to 'default' in the subsection and the contrast with the approach in unfair dismissal cases.[52] The EAT also accepted counsel's submission that 'the absence of identifiable financial loss is likely to be the rule rather than the exception' in these cases because the claimant would normally have worked and been paid accordingly when denied the time off.[53] The EAT said:

> In our judgment, Tribunals can properly consider whether it is just and equitable to make some reasonable and proportionate award by way of reparation to the individual union official for the wrong done to him by the employer in preventing or impeding his proper union activities on behalf of his members, without infringing the principle that the purpose must be compensation to the individual, not the imposition of any form of fine or collective punishment on the employer.[54]

Again, the EAT's analysis is impoverished by its assumption that the only ways to explain awards are compensation or punishment, but the underlying idea that

[50] See ch 4 and 5 of this volume.
[51] *Skiggs v South West Trains Ltd* [2005] IRLR 459 (EAT).
[52] ibid [15].
[53] ibid [17].
[54] ibid.

there should be some vindication of the claimant's rights is clear enough from this quotation.

However, the reliance on 'default' in *Skiggs* does not always lead to the making of a substantial award. A good illustration is the *Miles* case, on regulation 30 WTR, which uses the same wording.[55] The case concerned a worker in a care home who worked 48-hour live-in shifts. Although he was permitted to sleep during his shifts, this counted as working time under the CJEU's decisions in *Jaeger* and *SIMAP* because he was required to remain at the employer's premises.[56] The employer was therefore in breach of the WTR because it had denied him his 11-hour rest period in every 24 hours under regulation 10. The EAT upheld the tribunal's decision to make a nil award. In simple terms, it appears that the tribunal thought that it was not the employer's fault that it had been in breach, because the rules were complicated and difficult to interpret prior to the CJEU's clarification of the position. While this makes sense if the purpose of the award is to punish the employer, it does nothing to reflect the fact that, objectively, the worker's rights had not been respected. The right was to a rest period, rather than to 'not be wrongfully denied a rest period'. Characterising all awards as either compensatory or punitive leaves a gap in cases in which the individual suffers no loss, but the employer's breach is not particularly blameworthy. This gap could be addressed by the express recognition of vindicatory awards.

(iii) Groups 1 and 2 Compared

The 'group 2' approach has the advantage over 'group 1' that any loss actually suffered by the claimant can be reflected in the award. This is particularly important in the context of family leave rights, such as the right to emergency leave under section 57A ERA 1996, where the employee who is wrongly denied time off might incur childcare costs. However, there is greater uncertainty attached to these awards (which may deter claimants from litigating) and, as *Miles* illustrates, the most likely risk in practice seems to be a low or nil award rather than a high one. Judges steeped in the common law tradition clearly find it difficult to make substantial awards in the absence of loss because of the fear that they are providing the claimant with a 'windfall' or imposing an unwarranted 'penalty' on the employer, or both.

What is more of a puzzle is what differentiates the two groups of awards. For example, employee representatives who are denied time off to perform their functions feature in both groups: workforce representatives under section 61 ERA 1996 or the Information and Consultation of Employees Regulations (ICER) 2004 are in group 1, whereas pension scheme trustees and trade union representatives are

[55] *Miles v Linkage Community Trust Ltd* [2008] IRLR 602.

[56] C-303/98 *Sindicato de Médicos de Asistencia Pública (SIMAP) v Conselleria de Sanidad y Consumo de la Generalidad Valenciana*, ECLI:EU:C:2000:528, [2000] ECR I-7963; C-151/02 *Landeshauptstadt Kiel v Jaeger*, ECLI:EU:C:2003:437, [2003] ECR I-8389.

in group 2. Employees who are refused time off work for what might loosely be termed 'outside' activities also feature in both groups: ante-natal appointments in group 1; training, parental leave and public duties in group 2. The potential for the employee to have suffered loss does not seem to be the explanation. There is no obvious reason why union representatives are more likely to have suffered loss than non-union representatives. And it is possible to envisage both loss and no-loss scenarios in relation to outside activities, for example, where the employee has to pay for a private ante-natal appointment to secure one outside working hours, or where the employee who is unable to carry out public duties suffers no loss other than missing out on a fulfilling voluntary activity.

(iv) Reform

There are three possible options for reform. One would be to develop a new statutory formula directing courts and tribunals to make a vindicatory award to reflect the seriousness of the breach of the worker's rights, plus a compensatory award where any loss has in fact been suffered. This would fill the gap between punishment and compensation identified above, whilst maintaining a discretion to accommodate different types of case. For example, WTR cases can involve employer default over a long period of time – in *Miles*, a period of eight months had elapsed since the claimant had first expressed concern about the care home shift system – and this could be reflected in a higher award. Another option, perhaps more appropriate for some of the more specific time-off rights, would be to use a statutory formula but to construct this more generously, for example, using a fixed sum or different numbers of weeks' pay, in order to show that the rights in question are valued and to offer more of an incentive to enforce them.

A third, more radical solution would be to consider making replicative remedies available for some or all of these rights. Time-off rights are often time-sensitive – the employee needs to take the time off on a particular date in order for it to be useful – and an award of a sum of money long after the event is of no practical value. Dangerous working patterns with no rest breaks or rest periods need to be changed, not allowed to continue for many months until a hearing. These are good examples of situations in which affected employees either need rapid access to the tribunal or the assistance of a labour inspectorate with the power to resolve problems quickly.[57]

B. Consultation Rights

The current law deals with an employer's failure to comply with a duty to consult in a variety of different ways, including criminal offences, regulatory interventions

[57] Although HSE enforces various limits under the WTR, it has no power over workers' entitlements, such as the rest periods or rest breaks considered here.

leading to civil penalties, and replicative remedies. However, the breach of some duties to consult – notably on collective redundancies and transfers of undertakings – may result in a financial award payable to the affected employees, usually expressed as a number of weeks' pay. These provisions are my concern in this chapter. In many cases, it is hard to see how this award might sensibly constitute compensation for loss. The outcome would often have been the same whether or not the employer had consulted the workforce, and any 'loss of a chance' analysis seems hopelessly speculative. It will be argued in this section that, although the courts themselves have tended to adopt the language of punishment or sanction to explain awards in this context, vindication provides a more convincing explanation for what is going on. I will also consider the utility of vindicatory awards relative to some of the other available options.

It is helpful to begin by outlining the relevant provisions. The least well-known is TULRCA 1992, section 70B, the employer's duty to consult on training with representatives of a trade union recognised via a method under Schedule A1. Where the employer is in breach of this duty, the trade union may apply to the tribunal, which must make a declaration and 'may' make an award of 'compensation to be paid by the employer to each person who was, at the time when the failure occurred, a member of the bargaining unit'.[58] This is subject to a maximum in section 70C(4) of two weeks' pay. Under section 188 TULRCA 1992, the employer is under a duty to consult on collective redundancies. Depending on the nature of the employer's breach, a claim may be taken to a tribunal by the employee representatives, the relevant trade union, or the relevant employees under section 189(1). If the claim is well-founded, the tribunal must make a declaration and may make a 'protective award', which is an award of remuneration for the employees who have been made redundant or whom it is proposed to make redundant.[59] The award is for a 'protected period' which

> is of such length as the tribunal determines to be just and equitable in all the circumstances having regard to the seriousness of the employer's default in complying with any requirement of section 188 … but shall not exceed 90 days.[60]

The remedy for a failure to inform and consult under the Transfer of Undertakings (Protection of Employment) Regulations 2006 (TUPE), regulation 15 follows a similar pattern. The tribunal must make a declaration and may order either the transferor or the transferee (as appropriate) to pay 'appropriate compensation' to the affected employees. Under regulation 16(3), this is defined as 'such sum not exceeding thirteen weeks' pay for the employee in question as the tribunal considers just and equitable having regard to the seriousness of the failure of the employer to comply with his duty'. In all three cases, a significant limitation on the practical effectiveness of these awards is that if the employer refuses to pay, it is up

[58] TULRCA 1992, s 70C(3).
[59] The reason for the choice of this terminology is unclear: *Susie Radin Ltd*, above n 8, [24].
[60] TULRCA 1992, s 189(4)(b).

to the *individual employees* to go to the tribunal to enforce them, even if the claim was originally brought by a trade union or employee representatives.[61]

The three provisions are similar in that they attract discretionary awards of pay for a period of time, albeit with different maxima of two weeks, 90 days or 13 weeks respectively. One further difference between them is that the award for a breach of TULRCA 1992, section 70B is subject to the upper limit on a week's pay in section 227(1) ERA 1996, whereas the other two provisions are not. The latter point has been the subject of some debate, because both TULRCA 1992, section 188 and TUPE invoke the provisions from ERA 1996 on the calculation of a week's pay for the purposes of making an award. However, they do not refer to section 227, and section 227 itself (which lists a number of provisions to which it applies) does not mention them. Thus, it has been held that the section 227 limit is not applicable in the absence of any express wording to that effect.[62]

Under TULRCA 1992, section 70C, the award is described as 'compensation' and there is no further guidance as to how the tribunal should decide whether to award the maximum of two weeks' pay or a lesser sum. This is highly implausible as a basis for this award. While a failure to *provide* training might give rise to some identifiable losses, a failure to *consult* on training is one step removed and seems unlikely to do so. To the best of my knowledge, this provision has never been the subject of litigation. Under section 189 and TUPE, tribunals are directed to determine the length of the protected period or the amount of compensation (respectively) in accordance with the familiar idea of what is 'just and equitable' having regard to the 'seriousness' of the employer's breach.[63] As discussed above, this reference to the employer's breach can be taken as a signal that it is appropriate to make an award even when the affected employees have suffered no loss. However, the basis for doing so has, once again, puzzled tribunals and courts because they are so used to thinking in terms of compensation.

It seems likely that the original framing of section 189 was intended to peg the awards in some loose way to the duration of the consultation period. Under the Employment Protection Act 1975, the maximum 'protective award' corresponded to the minimum duration of the consultation period, so for redundancies involving 100 or more employees, it was 90 days, but for redundancies of between 10 and 100 employees, it was 60 days.[64] If the employer failed to consult, it would be obliged to pay the employees for the time it would have taken to conduct the consultation exercise, an approach which has sometimes been adopted in other contexts at common law.[65] While this might suggest a compensatory purpose, on the basis that the employees would have been employed and paid for *longer* while the employer carried out the consultation exercise, this is not necessarily true in

[61] TULRCA 1992, s 70C(6), TULRCA 1992, s 192 and TUPE reg 15(10) respectively.
[62] *Zaman v Kozee Sleep Products Ltd (t/a Dorlux Beds UK)* [2011] ICR D5.
[63] TULRCA 1992, s 189(4) and TUPE, reg 16(3).
[64] Employment Protection Act 1975, ss 99(3) and 101(5).
[65] For example, *Gunton v Richmond upon Thames LBC* [1981] Ch 448.

practice. For example, the employer might have carried out the dismissals on the same date but been more organised about its legal duties in advance. Moreover, any notional connection was severed in 1999 when the legislation was amended to make the 90-day maximum protective award applicable in all cases, including those in which the employer would only have had to consult for a minimum of 30 days.[66]

The leading case on the remedy for a breach of section 188 is *Susie Radin Ltd*.[67] In that case, the tribunal found that the employer had completely failed to comply with section 188 and it awarded the maximum. The Court of Appeal upheld the tribunal's decision and offered guidance on how awards should be determined. It was held that compensation could not be the purpose because there was no mention of compensation or loss in the relevant statutory provisions,[68] and because the awards were collective in nature, in the sense that the same sum would be payable to all relevant employees regardless of their own particular circumstances.[69] In a short judgment, Longmore LJ also rejected the idea that the awards were for a lost chance of not being made redundant, because they were available even where consultation was 'futile'.[70]

Relying on some language from the ECJ,[71] Peter Gibson LJ, giving the leading judgment, described the award as a 'sanction' and offered the following guidance:

> (2) The tribunal have a wide discretion to do what is just and equitable in all the circumstances, but the focus should be on the seriousness of the employer's default.
> (3) The default may vary in seriousness from the technical to a complete failure to provide any of the required information and to consult.
> (4) The deliberateness of the failure may be relevant, as may the availability to the employer of legal advice about his obligations under s. 188.
> (5) How the tribunal assess the length of the protected period is a matter for the tribunal, but a proper approach in a case where there has been no consultation is to start with the maximum period and reduce it only if there are mitigating circumstances justifying a reduction to an extent which the tribunal consider appropriate.[72]

Again, the language of punishment emerges in this passage because the courts do not have any straightforward alternatives once compensation is ruled out as an option. The difficulty with punishment is that it tends to focus attention on the

[66] Collective Redundancies and Transfer of Undertakings (Protection of Employment) (Amendment) Regulations 1999 (SI 1999/1925), reg 5(4), and for discussion see *Newage Transmission Ltd v Transport and General Workers Union* (UKEAT/0132/05/MAA, 25 May 2005); *Cranwick Country Food Plc v GMB Trade Union* (UKEAT/0225/05/ZT, 6 September 2005).

[67] Above n 8.

[68] An attempt to reintroduce compensation by treating the absence of loss on the part of the employees as a 'mitigating factor' in favour of the employer was (rightly) rejected by the EAT in *E Ivor Hughes Educational Foundation v Morris* [2015] IRLR 696.

[69] Although the former does not apply to TULRCA 1992, s 70C, the latter clearly does.

[70] *Susie Radin Ltd*, above n 8, [49].

[71] ibid [28], and see Case C-382/92 *Commission v United Kingdom*, ECLI:EU:C:1994:233, [1994] ICR 664.

[72] *Susie Radin Ltd*, above n 8, [45].

employer's motivation and mental state, as point 4 in the passage quoted above indicates. However, proving the employer's mental state may not be easy, and from the employees' perspective, a total failure to consult is a serious breach of their right to be consulted whatever the underlying motivation. Vindication offers a more helpful approach because it allows courts and tribunals to vary awards in accordance with the seriousness of the employer's breach, assessed in terms of extent rather than motivation. Thus, from a vindication perspective, the maximum award would be appropriate in cases where the employer had wholly failed to consult, in accordance with point 5 above.

Indeed, the vindication view is borne out by some of the later cases in which the maximum has been awarded for a total failure to consult even where the employer's breach was not 'deliberate'. An example is *Ivor Hughes*, in which the governors of a failing private school decided to close it with the consequence that the school staff would be made redundant. The governors did not take any legal advice and failed to consult on collective redundancies because they were not aware of their legal obligation to do so.[73] It was appropriate to award the maximum in that case. In practice, reductions from the maximum have tended to occur only in cases where the employer has made some effort to consult but has not fully complied with the section 188 duties. For example, in *GMB v Lambeth*, the employer had initiated the consultation process but the union had not responded promptly to requests for meetings,[74] and in *Amicus v GBS Tooling*, perhaps more controversially, the employer had engaged in some consultation when it became apparent that it was getting into financial difficulties, even though it had failed to conduct any further consultation after the date on which its section 188 duties formally arose.[75]

The *Susie Radin* guidance has also been applied in TUPE cases. Although regulation 15 TUPE uses the term 'compensation' rather than the device of the 'protective award', the use of this terminology has been described as a 'misnomer'.[76] Instead, courts and tribunals have treated the two sets of provisions as having the same 'punitive' purpose because of the language of 'employer default' they both share.[77] Thus, the approach in TUPE cases is also to award the maximum in cases in which there has been a total failure to inform or consult, and to make a lower award where some effort has been made.[78]

Arguably, the 'gold standard' remedy for a failure to consult is the public law approach of quashing the offending decision and requiring the decision-maker to re-take it after conducting the required consultation exercise. This vindicates

[73] *E Ivor Hughes*, above n 68.

[74] *GMB v Lambeth Service Team Ltd* (UKEAT/0127/05/CK & UKEAT/0129/05/CK, 13 July 2005).

[75] *Amicus v GBS Tooling Ltd* [2005] IRLR 683 (EAT).

[76] *Shields Automotive Ltd v Langdon* (UKEATS/0059/12/BI, 21 March 2013), [11]. It was noted in *Sweetin v Coral Racing* [2006] IRLR 252 (EAT) that, in the unlikely event that a claimant could point to a loss, this should be reflected in any award under reg 15.

[77] *Sweetin*, above n 76, [30], and see also *Cable Realisations Ltd v GMB Northern* [2010] IRLR 42 (EAT).

[78] For example, *Todd v Strain* [2011] IRLR 11 (EAT).

the right to be consulted by being as replicative as possible and, while the decision ultimately taken will often be the same, there is always a chance that it might be influenced by the consultation responses. Of course, for this approach to be effective, it is important to be able to get to court relatively quickly and to have some reassurance that the decision will not be implemented while the dispute is ongoing. In public law settings, injunctions are available for this purpose, though public authorities often co-operate voluntarily. Although there are a variety of different ways in which employers' duties to consult are enforced, none quite captures this approach. Perhaps the closest are the options in ICER to seek an order from the Central Arbitration Committee or in the occupational pensions context to complain to the Pensions Regulator, both of which are enforced by penalty provisions, but in both cases there is no power to prevent the employer from proceeding with a decision on which it has not consulted.[79] As chapter four explained, a failure to consult on health and safety matters is a criminal offence, but while this might seem to be the best option because it carries the greatest threat to an employer, it is ineffectual in practice because it is so unlikely to be enforced.[80] Preventing employers from implementing decisions on which they have not consulted therefore seems to be worthy of serious consideration. Importantly, situations in which there is some kind of emergency – redundancies are necessary because the employer is becoming insolvent, for example – are already catered for in the section 188 duty itself.[81]

C. Freedom of Association

In the freedom of association context, there are two different types of vindicatory award: the fixed sum set by statute in cases where the employer has offered an inducement to workers to give up trade union membership or collective bargaining; and the minimum awards in certain blacklisting cases and dismissals on trade union grounds or for acting as a workplace representative. In all these cases, the sums of money involved are a bit more substantial, at least in relative terms, and are clearly intended to give expression to the seriousness of the infringement of the claimant's freedom of association rights.

The history of the provisions on inducements to give up trade union membership or collective bargaining under TULRCA 1992, sections 145A and 145B is well-known. They represent the government's response to the ECtHR's ruling in *Wilson v UK* that the UK was in breach of Article 11 for failing to provide a remedy

[79] Information and Consultation of Employees Regulations 2004 (SI 2004/3426), regs 10, 13, 15 and 17; Occupational and Personal Pension Schemes (Consultation by Employers and Miscellaneous Amendment) Regulations 2006 (SI 2006/349), regs 11 and 12, and reg 18.

[80] Health and Safety at Work etc. Act 1974, ss 2 and 33.

[81] TULRCA 1992, s 188(7).

when workers who refused to accept so-called 'personal contracts' not subject to collective bargaining were denied a pay rise.[82] The provisions have been strongly criticised for the complexity of their drafting and for the various possibilities this may create for employers to continue to engage in anti-union conduct.[83] However, in the event of a successful claim, a relatively strong remedy is available. Under section 145E(3), there is a fixed award of £5,128 (index-linked) for each affected worker. There is no provision for reducing the amount of the award for any reason. This is in addition to a right to retain any inducement paid or offered, such as a bonus or pay rise.[84] From the employer's perspective, the liability here is potentially substantial where large numbers of workers are involved, though of course not all workers may be willing to enforce their rights. Employers may be able to take advantage of this by, for example, offering inducements to smaller groups of workers who are less active in the union and therefore thought to be less likely to sue.

This award is clearly vindicatory in nature. Although there is, arguably, a long-term loss associated with not having terms and conditions determined by collective bargaining, because of the wage premium unions are generally able to achieve, there is no sense in which this provision is seeking to compensate for that loss. There is no need to demonstrate that the employer's attempt to get rid of collective bargaining in fact succeeded. In most cases, there will not be any individual loss for particular workers: the inducement itself is *ex hypothesi* a benefit rather than a detriment. The fact that the same award is made to all workers regardless of their own situation is revealing. Nor is there any clear sense that the award is punitive. While it might be said that all employers offering inducements are behaving badly, there is no sense of gradation in this award and no way for the tribunal to express stronger disapproval of some employers than others. This suggests that what the award is doing is simply vindicating the right not to have an inducement made. Whether the award is set at a high enough level to serve that purpose, given the pernicious effect of inducements on the right to engage in collective bargaining, is unclear. But it is considerably more generous than other vindicatory awards identified in this chapter.

In some other trade union settings, the statute provides for a minimum award. These minima generally exist as part of a compensatory award, but they are vindicatory in nature because they secure a basic level of payment to the claimant regardless of any losses actually suffered. Again, there is no scope to vary these awards to reflect the extent of the employer's wrongdoing. Under section 152 TULRCA 1992, which provides that a dismissal of an employee on trade union grounds is automatically unfair, there is a minimum basic award of £7,836, index-linked,

[82] *Wilson v United Kingdom* (2002) 35 EHRR 20.

[83] AL Bogg, 'Employment Relations Act 2004: Another False Dawn for Collectivism?' (2005) 34 *Industrial Law Journal* 72.

[84] TULRCA 1992, s 145E(4), and see also s 146(2C)–(2D).

by virtue of section 156. Importantly, this award is potentially subject to deductions under section 122 ERA 1996. While some of these are designed to prevent double recovery, others relate to the employee's conduct, so a deduction may be made if the employee has 'unreasonably' refused an offer of reinstatement under section 122(1) ERA 1996, or where the employee's conduct prior to the dismissal would make it 'just and equitable' to reduce the award under section 122(2). In the fraught context of a dismissal on trade union grounds, these provisions may be particularly difficult to apply. It is easy to see why, for example, an employee dismissed for trade union activities might not want to accept an offer of reinstatement, but they are then exposed to the risk that the tribunal will find their refusal to be unreasonable within section 122(1). These issues were discussed more fully in chapter seven. Interestingly, the deductions reintroduce an element of compensation into the minimum award by ensuring that, even though the award itself does not depend on proof of loss, proof that the employee has suffered *no* loss may trigger a reduction.

A similar provision applies where the employee has been dismissed because of being on a prohibited list (a 'blacklist') under section 104F ERA 1996, though curiously the minimum here is £5,000 and it is not index-linked, so the value of the minimum award is likely to diminish over time.[85] Importantly, the relevant Regulations protect working people against the use of prohibited lists at all stages of the employment relationship, and the minimum award applies in other settings too.[86] Thus, the minimum is available under regulation 8 for breaches of regulation 5 or 6 (refusal of employment or of employment agency services) and under regulation 11 for detriment under regulation 9. Again, it is potentially subject to deductions in respect of the claimant's conduct.

Statute makes separate provision for employees who take on representative roles in the workplace outside the trade union context. Under section 120 ERA 1996, there is a minimum basic award of £7,836 (index-linked) where an employee is dismissed for acting as a health and safety representative (section 100), a representative under the Working Time Regulations 1998 (section 101A), an occupational pension trustee (section 102(1)), or a representative for consultation on collective redundancies or a transfer of the undertaking (section 103). The minimum award is subject to the deductions set out in section 122. While some of these roles may be undertaken by trade union representatives – and in some of these settings, priority is given to representatives of recognised trade unions – their remedy in respect of unfair dismissal lies under section 152 TULRCA 1992, discussed above, rather than under section 120 ERA 1996.

The rationale for the use of minimum awards in these contexts is relatively clear. Employees have a well-recognised fundamental right to join a trade union and take part in its activities, and this is infringed where they suffer negative consequences in the workplace as a result of their trade union membership or

[85] ERA 1996, s 120(1C).
[86] Employment Relations Act 1999 (Blacklists) Regulations 2010 (SI 2010/493).

activities. Although, for many labour lawyers, non-union representation at work is 'second best' to trade union representation, there are clear benefits to any attempt to introduce an element of democracy into workplaces, and working people who volunteer for representative roles without the support a trade union can offer are particularly vulnerable to ill-treatment by employers. The use of a minimum award expresses the importance of the rights at stake and the wrongfulness of the employer's conduct regardless of any losses suffered by the affected individual.

However, there are some anomalies in the current position. The decision to provide for a minimum award in refusal to hire and detriment cases where a blacklist has been used, but not in refusal to hire and detriment cases for trade unionists under sections 137 and 146 TULRCA 1992, or detriment cases for workforce representatives under the various provisions of ERA 1996, is hard to explain. On one view, the harm involved in refusing to hire someone or subjecting them to a detriment because of their trade union or representative activities is much the same whether the employer found out about the activities through a blacklist or in some other way. And while it might make sense to say that a minimum award is not appropriate in, for example, detriment cases because of the variety of different harms that might be included, this reasoning does not appear to have dissuaded the government from providing a minimum award in blacklisting detriment cases. On the other hand, it might be argued that blacklisting is particularly pernicious because of the potential for multiple employers in a particular sector to participate. As the scandal of the construction industry blacklist (which led to the enactment of the 2010 Regulations) demonstrated, some workers found it impossible to obtain work in the industry over a number of years because a number of major employers in the sector were involved.[87] However, it is not clear why the wider unfairness of the situation should be treated as having an impact on the liability of one employer.

Another anomaly in the current law is the difference in the minimum award as between blacklisting and other cases, and the failure to index-link the award in blacklisting cases. These differences are difficult to explain and seem simply to reflect the fact that the 2010 Regulations were introduced separately with a failure to think about how to integrate them into the wider legislative context. This seems to be a particular problem when legislation is introduced to respond to a crisis or scandal of some kind. An identical, index-linked award whenever this approach is used would be preferable.

More broadly, it is worth considering how the treatment of freedom of association (and closely-linked rights) compares with the treatment of other fundamental rights in the workplace. On the one hand, it might be argued that in all cases where an employee has been dismissed in breach of a fundamental right, a minimum award should be payable to reflect the seriousness of the employer's wrongdoing regardless of the employee's loss. A clear list of rights would need to be developed to make this approach work, and this is, of course, easier in relation to rights such

[87] See K Ewing, *Ruined Lives: Blacklisting in the Construction Industry* (Institute of Employment Rights, August 2009).

as the right to equal treatment which is already protected by a specific legislative regime than it is in relation to rights that might be protected at common law or under the Human Rights Act 1998, or even in international instruments to which the UK is a party. On the other hand, it might be questioned whether the awards discussed in this section are sufficient to vindicate the rights they purport to protect. Although awards in discrimination claims are formulated as compensation for loss with no minimum, so there is always the possibility of a nil or low award, awards can be quite generous in practice. A key point of comparison is the treatment of injury to feelings. This is a recognised head of loss in discrimination cases and compensatory awards are made in accordance with three bands laid down in the *Vento* case.[88] The awards discussed here would be within the lowest of the three *Vento* bands, reserved for less serious or one-off employer default cases. From this perspective, the fixed sums available in freedom of association cases no longer seem quite so substantial.

D. 'Procedural' Rights

A small group of statutory employment rights deal with what might loosely be termed 'procedural' matters, such as the right to be accompanied at a disciplinary or grievance hearing, the right to a statement of reasons for dismissal, and the right to inspect minimum wage records. These rights are intended to support working people to secure fair treatment at work and to enforce their substantive employment rights. It is unlikely that a breach of any of these rights will cause the affected individual a loss in itself. In the case of the right to be accompanied, it might be possible to engage in a 'loss of a chance' analysis, but this would be speculative in most cases. In relation to the other two rights, the employer may be trying to conceal a breach of the right not to be unfairly dismissed or the right to be paid the national minimum wage (NMW), but while such breaches may make it more difficult for the employee or worker to enforce their rights, they will often not generate additional losses beyond the original infringement. Nevertheless, breaches of these procedural rights currently attract financial awards, so it seems likely that these are vindicatory in nature. I will explore these awards in greater detail before considering whether there are any more replicative possibilities that could be used instead.

A breach of the right to be accompanied under section 10 Employment Relations Act 1999 attracts an award, described as 'compensation', of up to two weeks' pay under section 11(3).[89] This is subject to the statutory maximum in section 227(1) ERA 1996. On one view, the maximum award is so low that it hardly seems appropriate to vary it, but the statutory wording leaves no doubt

[88] Above n 13.

[89] See also Employee Study and Training (Procedural Requirements) Regulations 2010 (SI 2010/155), reg 17.

that this is a possibility.[90] A vindication analysis would suggest that the award should be varied to reflect the seriousness of the employer's breach. For example, the maximum might be awarded where the employer refused altogether to permit the worker to be accompanied, whereas a reduction might be appropriate in cases in which the worker was allowed to be accompanied to the hearing but the employer did not permit the companion to perform the various functions set out in section 10(2B).

The two main EAT decisions construing these provisions, *Toal*[91] and *Roberts*,[92] involved workers who wished to be accompanied by a particular union official who was not acceptable to the employer. The employer asked them to choose another companion who then accompanied them to their hearings. The substantive issue before the EAT on both occasions was whether the 'reasonableness' of the worker's request to be accompanied under section 10(1)(b) could include an assessment of the reasonableness of the worker's choice of companion.[93] It was held that it could not: the right was to a representative of the worker's choosing, subject only to the limitations in section 10(3) as to the classes of person from which that choice could be made.[94] Thus, the employer was in breach. The fact that the workers had both agreed to be accompanied by another companion did not matter because, under section 203 ERA, they could not validly agree to waive the employer's breach. However, the EAT in *Toal* then went on to hold that the award under section 11(3) was described as 'compensation' and was thus intended to redress any losses suffered by the workers.[95] It was not designed to punish the employer. Because section 11(3) states that the tribunal 'shall' make an award, an award of a nominal sum, such as £2, would be appropriate where the worker had suffered no loss. Although the issue of quantum was remitted to the tribunal in both cases, the EAT in *Roberts* implied that a nominal award might be legitimate in cases in which the worker had suffered no prejudice because they had been accompanied by an equally-qualified, albeit second choice, representative.[96]

These two decisions are somewhat problematic. It is clear that in both cases, the EAT was struggling with the idea that the employer had no right to object to the worker's choice of companion, even though the drafting is relatively clear. While it is easy to see why an employer might not want a worker to be accompanied by a person who has been hostile or disruptive in the past, allowing employers to object to companions raises a whole host of other issues about the worker's right to choose a person they trust (which is surely at the core of the right) and the very real risk that unscrupulous employers might object to knowledgeable and effective companions, such as trade union representatives, in order to weaken the worker's

[90] *Heathmill Multimedia ASP Ltd v Jones* [2003] IRLR 856, [11].
[91] *Toal v GB Oils Ltd* [2013] IRLR 696 (EAT).
[92] *Roberts v GB Oils Ltd* [2014] ICR 462 (EAT).
[93] The ACAS code as drafted at the time suggested that it might.
[94] *Toal*, above n 91, [16].
[95] ibid [29]–[32].
[96] *Roberts*, above n 92, [23] and [25].

position. The focus on the use of the term 'compensation', which has been ignored in other contexts, means that few claimants will now receive the maximum award under section 11(3), which in turn makes it unlikely that this provision will be much enforced. Most importantly, the idea that the worker suffers no 'loss' when they are accompanied by a second-choice companion ignores the fact that the right is (expressly) a right to be accompanied by one's *chosen* companion. This goes to the core of the right and should be vindicated by means of an award, given that no other mechanism of redress is open to the tribunal.

Of course, an alternative solution would be a replicative award. The obvious option here is to force the employer to take the decision again with the worker accompanied by their chosen companion. The advantage of this approach is that the worker gets the benefit of the assistance the companion can provide. This may, in turn, affect the outcome of the disciplinary or grievance procedure by enabling the worker to present their case more clearly and effectively. In some instances, this could make the difference between being dismissed or keeping one's job. However, it would be necessary for an order of this kind to be made promptly so that the matter could be resolved for the benefit of both the worker and the employer.

The right to a written statement of the reasons for dismissal under section 92 ERA 1996 can be infringed in two ways: by an 'unreasonable' failure to supply the reasons in response to the employee's request within the 14-day deadline, or by providing reasons which are 'inadequate or untrue'. Under section 93, the tribunal must make an award of two weeks' pay (which is not subject to the limit in section 227) and may make a declaration of its findings as to the employer's reasons for dismissal. There is no discretion to refuse to make an award or to reduce it from two weeks' pay. A similar remedy applies to the right to require the employer to produce National Minimum Wage records under section 10 National Minimum Wage Act 1998. Under section 11, this remedy is expressed as payment of 80 times the hourly rate of the NMW in force at the time of the award. This formula produces two weeks' pay on the basis of a 40-hour week, and again there is no discretion to refuse to make the award or to reduce it. The formula reflects the fact that it would be inappropriate to use the claimant's actual pay as the basis for the award because of the possibility that this might be below the level of the NMW.

These two formulaic awards are good examples of vindicatory awards. There is no suggestion of compensating for loss at all, since the amounts are fixed regardless of the claimant's situation. Nor is there any suggestion of punishment: the remedies do not admit of any variation for more egregious breaches, even though it is clear that the employer's breach might be deliberate and calculating in some cases (knowingly giving a false reason for a dismissal in an attempt to avoid a claim for unfair dismissal, for example) and merely a result of ignorance or incompetence in others. The claimant's rights have been infringed and the award acknowledges this.

There are, however, two difficulties with these awards. First, although there is no discretion to reduce them, the sums involved are small and, in most cases, not worth pursuing as freestanding claims. It seems likely in practice that most are added on to substantive claims for unfair dismissal or non-payment of the

NMW. Second, a payment of a sum of money at a later date does not come close to replicating the right, and is no substitute for an order requiring the employer to produce reasons or to produce records. It is possible that the decision not to give tribunals an order-making power in these instances (reinforced by a financial award if the order is not complied with) is a tacit acknowledgement of the fact that the claimant is likely to bring a substantive claim.

The law's treatment of the right to a written statement of particulars of employment under section 1 ERA 1996 offers an interesting comparison. Under section 11(1), the principal method of dealing with an employer's failure to provide a written statement, or the provision of an incomplete statement, is to make an application to the tribunal 'to determine what particulars ought to have been included or referred to in a statement so as to comply with the requirements of the section concerned'. The tribunal's role is, in effect, to set out the relevant particulars in the way that the employer ought to have done. This approach is strongly replicative. There is no freestanding right to a financial award for a failure to comply with the written statement provisions. However, where a claimant succeeds in one of the substantive claims listed in Schedule 5 of the Employment Act 2002, and the employer is in continuing breach of the duty to provide a written statement, the tribunal must make an award of two weeks' pay in respect of that breach under section 38. This is either a freestanding award, where the claimant has won the substantive claim but received no award, or an increase to the award made in respect of the substantive claim. The tribunal has a discretion under section 38(5) to make no award or increase if 'there are exceptional circumstances which would make an award or increase under that subsection unjust or inequitable', or to make an award or increase of four weeks' pay 'if it considers it just and equitable in all the circumstances'. In all cases a week's pay is subject to the statutory maximum in section 227 ERA 1996.

Section 38 effectively acknowledges that a claimant would be unlikely to pursue proceedings for an award of two weeks' pay for a breach of the right to receive a written statement, but provides for the vindication of that right in the context of other litigation. I have been unable to find any discussion in the case-law of reasons for varying the award, though presumably there is a case for awarding the higher sum where the employer has failed altogether to provide a written statement rather than just providing an inadequate or incomplete one. It is very unclear on what grounds a tribunal might decide to use the discretion in section 38(5) to make no award at all.

Before leaving the topic of procedural rights, it is worth considering a broader possibility: the use of vindicatory awards in respect of procedurally unfair dismissals. Chapter seven explored some of the problems with the use of compensation as a remedy in this context. It is difficult to obtain substantial compensation for a procedurally unfair dismissal where the tribunal concludes that the employee would or might have been dismissed in any event.[97] This limits the enforceability

[97] See *Polkey*, above n 12.

of procedural rights in the dismissal context. Wider availability of awards for injury to feelings would help to secure some redress for claimants who do not suffer any economic loss under the current rules, but this would not necessarily be sufficient to deter employers from disregarding their procedural obligations. One possible option would be to provide for a vindicatory award. Indeed, it might seem that procedurally unfair dismissals are a classic case for this approach: the award would vindicate the claimant's right to a fair procedure in a situation in which there is little or no compensable loss. However, while this would enable claimants to recover a (probably modest) additional sum, I have resisted advocating for this position in strong terms, for a reason which has threaded its way through this chapter: vindicatory awards are often a rather 'lazy' solution to a problem. Replicative remedies, discussed in detail in chapter six, provide a much stronger and more effective echo of the original right.

The procedural rights are an interesting group offering a choice between replicative remedies and vindicatory financial awards. There is generally no sensible way of calculating compensation, and a punitive approach seems disproportionate. The preference for vindication over replication, with the exception of the written statement, shows that the law often chooses the easier option rather than doing what is necessary to put things right for the worker.

E. Miscellaneous

A final example of a vindicatory award is the provision in regulation 18(12) Agency Workers Regulations 2010 for a minimum award of two weeks' pay in respect of a breach of the equal treatment provisions in regulation 5.[98] The remedial approach taken in the Regulations is unnecessarily complex, as the analysis in the *Amissah* case shows, using as they do the language of 'compensation' when unpaid wages are often at stake, and containing apparently duplicative apportionment provisions.[99]

For present purposes, the minimum award is of interest. It is not compensatory in nature, since it requires no proof of loss, and it is not punitive, since it does not turn on the respondent's attitude. It can be reduced under regulation 18(13) where the tribunal considers that it would not be 'just and equitable' in view of the 'conduct of the claimant and the respondent', but the fact that the award can be reduced does not change its underlying nature. Parliament could have provided a discretion to make an award, but instead placed the onus on the respondent to argue that it would be unjust to award even the minimum under the circumstances. Thus, the minimum can be seen as a way of vindicating the claimant's rights. It is worth noting that the minimum is potentially available

[98] Calculated in accordance with Agency Workers Regulations 2010 (SI 2010/93), reg 19.
[99] *London Underground Ltd v Amissah* [2019] EWCA Civ 125, [2019] ICR 1155.

against both the agency and the end-user where the tribunal finds that both are liable.

The equivalent provisions for part-time workers and fixed-term employees, who also have equal treatment rights, do not provide for a minimum award, and it is not clear whether there is any particular reason for the decision to offer vindication in the context of agency work only.[100] In all three cases, it is possible that claimants may be owed little in the way of compensation, making litigation not worth pursuing. However, a vindicatory award of two weeks' pay, while it may be intended to remedy this, is likely to have limited impact in practice. Nor can it seriously be argued that the rights enshrined in the Agency Workers Regulations 2010 are somehow more in need of vindication than other types of rights.

III. Conclusion

This chapter has sought to demonstrate that the law makes surprisingly extensive use of awards that are best viewed as vindicatory: their aim is not to compensate the claimant or to punish the employer but simply to provide a meaningful public acknowledgment through a financial award that the claimant's rights have been infringed. These awards are not conceptualised as vindicatory by the law itself and a wide variety of approaches to their statutory drafting can be discerned. Although a sum of money or a formula for calculation fixed by Parliament is often a sign of a vindicatory award, it is not conclusive, and I have argued that some awards expressed using familiar compensatory language are more likely to be vindicatory than compensatory in practice.

The presence of an unacknowledged category of vindicatory awards in the law gives rise to both conceptual and practical problems. On a practical level, where judges have a discretion to determine the level of an award, they have found this task understandably very difficult. Where the statute specifies compensation, judges may make unduly low awards, because the claimant has not suffered any obvious losses and they are concerned not to provide a 'windfall'. Where judges have noticed that there are no losses and have invoked the idea of punishment instead, they have tended to focus on the employer's motivation (which may be difficult to discern) rather than on the seriousness of the infringement of the claimant's rights. Recognising a separate category of vindicatory awards would bring much-needed clarity to the law and would give the judiciary a better basis for exercising their discretion and explaining their decisions.

More fundamentally, the fact that vindication is not well understood stifles a much broader debate about the uses and misuses of this type of monetary award

[100] Part-time Workers (Prevention of Less Favourable Treatment) Regulations 2000 (SI 2000/1551), regs 5 and 8; Fixed-term Employees (Prevention of Less Favourable Treatment) Regulations 2002 (SI 2002/2034), regs 3 and 7.

in employment law. As I explained at the outset, there are two key questions to ask: is a monetary award the most appropriate remedy, and if it is, is it set at a justifiable level? Based on the analysis in this chapter, both of these questions can now be addressed.

There are a number of instances in which it is possible to envisage using a replicative remedy instead of a vindicatory award. For example, where the employer has failed to consult employees in a collective redundancy or transfer situation, the law could prohibit the redundancies or the transfer from taking place until the statutory consultation process has been completed. Where the employer has not afforded the individual a fair procedure prior to dismissal or not allowed them to be accompanied at a hearing, it could be forced to conduct a procedure or to repeat the hearing with the appropriate companion in place. However, there is a real nervousness about replicative remedies in employment law, stemming from concerns about business efficiency and managerial prerogative, which seem to have weighed heavily with governments of all political persuasions over the years. Of course, these are legitimate concerns but, as I argued in chapter three, they are often given too much weight. The failure to recognise vindicatory awards for what they are is particularly problematic in this context because it might be assumed that employees who are affected by employers' failures to follow procedures are 'at least' being compensated for their losses, whereas in fact they are receiving a random sum of money which may or may not be sufficient to make them feel that their rights have been vindicated. This is a particular concern in relation to smaller awards such as that for a breach of the right to be accompanied.

The quantification of vindicatory awards is not straightforward, as I explained at the outset. Very trivial sums are unlikely to serve any real vindicatory purpose and may even be perceived negatively by claimants, whereas extremely high awards risk bringing the law into disrepute. But it is not possible to be much more precise than that. In the employment context, there are a large number of trivial awards, particularly in relation to time-off rights. Conceptually, these awards devalue the rights they purport to vindicate, and practically, they make it unlikely that most potential claimants would seek to enforce their rights. One obvious way to deal with this would be to increase the sums of money involved to a more realistic level. It would also be beneficial to make greater use of fixed awards – rather than giving tribunals discretion – to reduce uncertainty for claimants, unless there is a risk of real injustice to employers. However, time-off rights are a good example of the way in which a system of statutory rights enforced through tribunals does not serve working people particularly well. A central characteristic of time-off rights is that they are time-sensitive: a person with an ante-natal appointment needs time off when the appointment is taking place, not a monetary remedy months or years later. The ability to get a quick resolution of the problem through expedited proceedings or by enlisting the help of a labour inspectorate would be invaluable here.

Not all vindicatory awards are trivial, though. In the trade union context, there are more substantial awards in blacklisting cases and in certain types of case involving trade union representatives. But these awards give rise to further questions about how they compare with other cases involving workers' fundamental rights. At one end of the spectrum, discrimination cases often involve the award of substantial sums of compensation, including awards for injury to feelings. Although the latter are compensatory in nature, the vindicatory awards considered in trade union cases come roughly in the middle of the lowest of the three *Vento* bands, for less serious, one-off infringements. This seems inappropriate. At the other end of the spectrum, it would be possible to identify a variety of other infringements of fundamental rights in the workplace that are not singled out for special treatment. For example, a dismissal in breach of an employee's right to privacy or freedom of expression would not currently attract a minimum basic award.

9

Conclusion

In this concluding chapter, I aim to draw out the book's key findings. The first section revisits the three questions set out in chapter three, and summarises some of the answers identified in chapters four to eight. The second section explores in more general terms some of the reasons why remedies fall so far short of the ideal, and what reforms might be required.

I. Lessons Learned

Chapter three identified three big questions about remedies in employment law. First, does each remedy fit the corresponding right? Second, do the remedies on offer meet the specific needs of employment law? Third, does the remedial regime reflect the relative importance of different employment rights? Without attempting to capture every element of the preceding discussion, I identify here some of the main conclusions which can be drawn from the analysis.

A. Fit

At the most basic level, the question of fit is a technical one: is there a logical relationship between the effect of the breach on the claimant and the remedy the law provides? Most of the time, technical fit is not a problem: compensation is a common remedy for many breaches of employment law, and this is appropriate because the claimant who has lost their job or been denied a promotion in unfair or discriminatory circumstances will have suffered recognisable financial losses for which they ought to be compensated.[1]

However, chapter eight identified a serious problem: the use of awards labelled 'compensation' in circumstances in which no loss is likely to be incurred. I argued that the correct classification of many of these awards is 'vindicatory': in other words, their principal purpose is to acknowledge that the claimant's rights have been infringed. The fact that the law does not recognise this concept is problematic,

[1] See ch 7 of this volume.

because it is difficult for judges to make these awards at all – or quantify them sensibly – when their purpose is unclear. There are unhelpful discussions about the appropriateness of punishing the employer or giving the claimant a windfall. In general terms, my preference is to replace small financial awards with replicative remedies wherever possible, so that working people's rights are upheld more effectively, but if vindicatory awards are to be retained, there is an urgent need to develop a new statutory formula to capture their purpose properly.

The question of fit can also be more complex. In some instances, there is a choice to be made: between a compensatory or vindicatory award, on the one hand, and a replicative remedy on the other.[2] There are a number of instances in which the law has chosen a monetary remedy when a replicative option would be much more appropriate. For example, vindicatory awards are currently used to enforce time-off rights, the right to be accompanied at a disciplinary or grievance hearing, and the collective redundancy consultation process under section 188 TULRCA 1992.[3] These would be much more effectively and appropriately enforced by orders requiring the employer to grant the time off, or to retake its decision after a fresh hearing or after conducting the required consultation. Of course, working people would need prompt access to legal advice and to a court or tribunal to make these options work, but as a matter of principle, they are a much better fit for the rights in question. Chapter six highlighted the power of replicative remedies in some of the (unusual) cases in which they have been used, including to enforce contractual commitments and statutory working time obligations.

Even where the law does choose a replicative option, it is often not implemented particularly effectively. Chapter six explored some of the problems with the use of injunctions at common law to enforce disciplinary procedures that might prevent termination. The courts have not consistently adopted an objective approach to mutual trust and confidence in these cases, sometimes allowing employers to claim that they cannot continue to employ a person even where there is no objective basis for this assertion. The *Jones* case provides a promising model for the future.[4] I also explained why re-employment orders under the statute law of unfair dismissal are not true replicative remedies, and are thus not particularly effective. Although commentators have often focused on tribunals' limited enforcement powers (which are clearly a problem), probably the most significant issue is that re-employment orders do not operate preventatively, to restrain a 'rights-threat'.[5] An order that can only be invoked after dismissal is bound to be less effective.

[2] Ch 4 also explored questions of fit, suggesting that some employment law offences currently in existence might not be defensible – such as those relating to agency work – but that there might be scope for new offences, notably for extreme examples of trade union discrimination.

[3] See ch 8 of this volume.

[4] *Jones v Gwent CC* [1992] IRLR 521.

[5] SA Smith, *Rights, Wrongs and Injustices: the Structure of Remedial Law* (Oxford, OUP, 2019), ch 6.

B. The Needs of Employment Law

In identifying the specific remedial needs of employment law, I focused on two questions in particular: do remedies recognise the non-financial, dignitary interests of working people, and do they deter employers, where possible, from non-compliance?

Predictably, two of the most obvious conclusions on these points emerged in chapter seven, on compensation, in which unfair dismissal naturally dominated the discussion. First, the law's failure to make compensatory awards for injury to feelings available in principle in all cases, including unfair dismissal, is a problem from the perspective of dignity, since it deprives tribunals of one of the most obvious ways of recognising the non-financial losses incurred by an employee who has lost their job in unfair circumstances. If they were available, such awards could be used to reflect the employee's loss of job satisfaction, social contact and career development, and to acknowledge any particularly bad behaviour by the employer during the dismissal. Second, the maximum limit on the compensatory award, although rarely an issue in practice, is hard to square with the idea of deterrence because it gives employers a clear indication of their maximum liability in an unfair dismissal claim, even where the employee can prove additional losses on the basis of rigorous rules. This encourages a cost-benefit analysis of the dismissal rather than compliance with the law.

But there are some less obvious, but equally significant, problem areas for dignity and deterrence in the law as it stands. One set of issues relates to the way in which employees are treated when they make claims for compensation or even for money owed to them by their employers. For example, chapter seven explored some of the ways in which normal employee reactions – getting annoyed during a disciplinary hearing, for example, or refusing to accept a re-employment offer from the employer – might be used to reduce compensation on grounds of contributory fault or failure to mitigate, even in quite marginal circumstances. Chapter six examined the two-year limitation period applicable to an unlawful deductions claim. These examples are problematic from a deterrence perspective. Working people's claims are undervalued, either by rules which make logical sense but are applied with insufficient care, or by rules which are deliberately designed to limit their recovery. Employers benefit from knowing that, even if they do not comply with the law, these rules will operate to reduce their liability.

Another difficult body of rules from the perspective of dignity and deterrence is public enforcement through the criminal law, explored in detail in chapter four. In theory at least, the use of criminal offences to enforce certain aspects of employment law marks them out as particular priorities for the deterrence of wrongdoing by employers. However, the reality can be rather disappointing, for two reasons. First, many public regulators are under-resourced and therefore unable to inspect employers, investigate problems and prosecute offenders to any reasonable level. This is so even if it is accepted that prosecution should be reserved for the most serious offenders as part of an escalating regulatory strategy. As chapter four explained, for example, cuts to the Health and Safety Executive's (HSE) budget and an outdated enforcement regime mean that health and safety law has a limited deterrent effect. Second, criminalisation often seems to be accompanied by a lack of consideration for the impact of offences on victims. In particular, agencies charged with enforcing the law often do not have any formal powers to help victims secure redress. The national minimum wage (NMW) regime is a positive counter-example, though careful thought would be required as to how best to extend this model to other areas.

Finally, chapter five identified some strategies designed to improve the law's deterrence effect which have not been particularly successful, such as the penalty regimes for 'aggravated breaches' of employment rights and for non-payment of tribunal awards. The idea appears to have been to increase the cost to employers of wilful disregard of employment law itself and the enforcement role of the tribunal respectively. However, neither scheme is particularly well-known or widely used, so in most cases, any penalty just adds to the overall cost of the employer's original breach, and is unlikely to have much impact on determined, deliberate wrongdoing. Penalties only make sense in the context of wider systemic reform to improve both knowledge about employment rights and access to the tribunal or another enforcement mechanism.

C. Priorities

In chapter three, I suggested that the law's priorities should be to ensure that work is free and rewarded, equal, decent, participatory and reliable. In some respects, the law goes some way towards achieving these goals. For example, the remedial regime gives high priority to discrimination claims, with no upper limit on compensation for discriminatory dismissals, and the possibility of awards for injury to feelings as well as for financial losses.[6] And although there is some scope for improvement, particularly in relation to civil penalties, the approach to NMW enforcement (a key element of decent work) does at least prioritise redress for workers and makes strategic use of the criminal law as a last resort.[7] However, there are some gaps, and I will highlight two here: the treatment of unfair dismissal (other than in discrimination cases), and freedom of association and related rights.

I recognise that the priority I give to 'reliable' work is controversial, particularly because many working people now have 'worker' rather than 'employee' status, and thus no access to unfair dismissal protections. Nevertheless, the fact that unfair dismissal is now the preserve of the privileged is a reason to broaden its scope, not a reason to limit the remedies available. There are two obvious areas in need of improvement, both of which I have already touched on in this chapter. First, the

[6] See ch 7 of this volume.
[7] See ch 4 and 5 of this volume.

provisions relating to re-employment are unlikely to work effectively unless they are made to work as truly replicative remedies, applying to restrain a threatened dismissal which is procedurally or substantively unfair, or both.[8] Although the law on injunctions has its problems, it provides a much better model than the statutory regime. Second, the restrictions placed on compensatory awards – the statutory maximum limit on damages, and the absence of any power to make an award for injury to feelings – should not apply to any dismissal claim.[9] Losing one's job is one of the worst things that can happen to a working person, whether or not the reason is tainted by discrimination, and the law should reflect this in the remedies on offer.

Another area requiring reform is the law relating to remedies for freedom of association violations.[10] The issue here is that the law has developed piecemeal over time, and sometimes in response to specific problems – such as the use of prohibited lists – and therefore lacks logic and coherence. Upholding freedom of association by protecting trade union members and, particularly, activists from discriminatory treatment by employers should be one of the law's top priorities, for obvious reasons. Minimum awards serve an important purpose in vindicating trade unionists' rights, but they do not apply consistently across all the hiring, detriment and dismissal provisions. Although the sums involved are not trivial, they compare unfavourably with discrimination claims on other grounds (where awards for injury to feelings alone can be substantial, under the *Vento* bands[11]) and some are not index-linked. In a dismissal case, the maximum limit on the compensatory award continues to apply, and perhaps most worryingly, there is the potential for deductions to be made on grounds of contributory fault.[12]

II. Directions for Reform

One way to conclude would be to develop a set of detailed proposals for reform. But there is little point in doing so in the absence of any apparent political appetite for change and, in any event, many of the reforms that would be required are implicit in the preceding discussion. Instead, I want to approach the issue of reform from a thematic perspective, by spelling out the three broad problems with remedies this book has identified: analytical failures, structural injustices, and imbalances between working people and employers. For reform to be effective, each of these sources of injustice would need to be acknowledged and rectified, alongside the enactment of specific legislative changes.

[8] See ch 6 of this volume.
[9] See ch 7 of this volume.
[10] See ch 8 of this volume.
[11] *Vento v Chief Constable of West Yorkshire Police* [2002] EWCA Civ 1871, [2003] ICR 318.
[12] See ch 7 of this volume.

A. Analytical Failures

One significant issue is that, particularly when new statutory rights are being enacted, policy-makers have simply not paid enough attention to the task of choosing an appropriate remedy for the right in question: analysing the options available and selecting the one most likely to be effective. Disputes about remedies rarely reach the higher courts, so there is limited input from the judiciary, and the analysis of statutory regimes (as opposed to the common law) is not a particularly fashionable area for scholarship.

This has resulted in a tendency to apply a 'default' compensatory award using the 'just and equitable' formulation whenever new statutory rights are enacted.[13] But it is always worth asking what loss, if any, the claimant is likely to have suffered as a result of the infringement of their rights. If economic loss is unlikely, a compensatory award will do a poor job of putting things right. Either the tribunal will notice the absence of any loss and refuse to make an award, or it will take pity on the claimant and make an award on an unprincipled basis. Although there are examples of private law wrongs, such as trespass, which may not give rise to any loss, the development of private law has been driven largely by litigants who have experienced a loss and are seeking compensation to put things right. Statutory employment rights, by contrast, can simply be put in place by Parliament to address a perceived problem in the workplace, without any thought to whether this problem causes working people a loss in the sense understood by the law. Of course, one response might be to say that statutory rights are pointless if a breach causes no loss, but this would eliminate a wide variety of important employment rights, such as rights to rest breaks or rest periods and, in many cases, rights to be consulted or to have a fair procedure. The key is to ensure that the remedy fits the right being enacted.

It is hoped that this book has made a significant advance in mapping out the remedial landscape of employment law, identifying what fits badly at present and what could be made to work better. Although the discussion has benefited enormously from comparisons with private law and engagement with some of the theoretical analysis in that field, employment law should have its own, distinctive approach to remedies.

B. Structural Injustice

Another important strand running throughout the book is that of structural injustice. This term, introduced in chapter two, is used by scholars to describe a situation in which the structures a society puts in place to deal with a particular

[13] See ch 8 of this volume.

issue are intended to operate fairly but, in practice, create opportunities for injustice and exploitation.[14]

The most obvious example of structural injustice in the context of remedies is, of course, the means put in place for obtaining them: the tribunal system. On a superficial level, this provides working people with a fair and impartial forum in which to set out the ways in which their rights have been infringed and to secure a remedy to put things right. However, as chapter two explained, there are many obstacles in the way of accessing the tribunal. The most basic problem is lack of access to legal or other advice, to enable working people to recognise that what has happened to them is wrong in the eyes of the law, to understand how to bring a claim, and to present that claim in a legally-effective manner. This is exacerbated by employers' much easier access to legal advice (which replicates the imbalance of power between the parties) and by long delays in the tribunal system, which cause many claimants to give up. And even if the claimant succeeds, the employer may refuse to comply with the tribunal's order.

It is not easy to untangle issues relating to remedies from these broader, systemic problems, but there are two points worth highlighting. First, there are many employment rights which are effectively rendered unenforceable by a combination of the complexity of bringing a tribunal claim and the limited nature of the remedy on offer.[15] Examples include rights to time off for particular purposes, consultation rights and rights to be accompanied at disciplinary or grievance hearings. Of course, statutory rights with trivial remedies can sometimes be enforced, for example, when the working person has multiple claims against the employer. But, in most cases, the claimant is likely to be advised that it would not be worthwhile to bring proceedings. While it is tempting to suggest that some of these awards should simply be increased, it is not clear how easy this solution would be to implement in practice. Empirical research would be required to determine the point at which it would be viable to bring a claim to obtain the remedy on offer. It is possible that this practical 'tipping point' might be thought to be disproportionate to other remedies for more serious infringements. Second, the fact that tribunals do not have the power to grant injunctions limits their ability to put things right for working people by getting employers to comply with their orders.[16] For example, in the unfair dismissal context, employers can easily disregard a re-employment order by paying additional compensation. As I argued in chapter six, the law could make much greater use of replicative remedies, for example, to enforce consultation rights, but this proposal would only work if tribunals were able to use the contempt powers of the courts. Arguments that this is

[14] L Barmes, *Bullying and Behavioural Conflict at Work: The Duality of Individual Rights* (Oxford, OUP, 2016); V Mantouvalou, *Structural Injustice and Workers' Rights* (Oxford, OUP, 2023).

[15] A point which became particularly apparent when fees were payable to bring a tribunal claim: A Adams and J Prassl, 'Vexatious Claims: Challenging the Case for Employment Tribunal Fees' (2017) 80 *Modern Law Review* 412, and the discussion of fees in ch 2 of this volume.

[16] See ch 6 of this volume.

inappropriate are becoming harder to defend now that tribunals are much more court-like and often, in practice, consist of an Employment Judge sitting alone, without lay members.[17] Of course, while these suggestions largely assume the continuation of the tribunal system in a similar form, more radical options could also be considered. These might include providing an easy-to-use online fast track for certain types of claim, or providing a wholly different enforcement mechanism, such as an ombudsman or labour inspectorate.

However, while it may be tempting to turn to public enforcement to overcome problems with the tribunal system, the current system of public enforcement is itself another example of structural injustice. It appears that the law has put in place a system to protect the most vulnerable workers by enforcing the law on their behalf, but in practice, the system is weak. As chapters two and four explained, the public agencies charged with enforcing the law have limited resources and thus limited capacity to investigate problems or to take action. I outlined the cuts to HSE's budget over many years, with the corresponding impact on levels of inspection, and the marginal impact of the Employment Agency Standards Inspectorate on the well-documented problems of the agency work sector, among other examples. Of course, public resources are highly constrained and many areas of public life are under-resourced, but there is a risk that maintaining a system of public enforcement that most employers will never encounter undermines any potential for a deterrent effect.

Some of the problems identified here, particularly those relating to remedies themselves, could be tackled by means of legal reform, but the deeper issues with both public and private enforcement require a significant investment of funds to put right. Some resources would need to be directed to the enforcement regimes themselves: to give quicker access to the tribunal, or to increase the numbers of inspectors in the various enforcement bodies. But it would also be sensible to invest in mechanisms that would tackle problems at an earlier stage: by ensuring that working people knew their rights and were able to raise concerns with their employers without necessarily escalating them to litigation.[18] Although it is beyond the scope of the present study, support for trade unions and advice services could play an important role here.

C. Imbalance between Working People and Employers

A third aspect of the problem identified by this book is, in my view, a failure to strike a fair balance between the rights and interests of working people and the concerns of employers. This goes beyond the (arguably) inadvertent examples of

[17] Though cf Law Commission, *Employment Law Hearing Structures* (HC 308, Law Com No 390, April 2020).

[18] See ch 2 of this volume.

analytical failures and structural injustices to something more intentional. I have already highlighted some of the ways in which the law downplays the need to protect working people's dignity, so I will focus here on the undue weight it gives to employers' concerns. As I explained in chapter three, the substantive law typically strikes a compromise between the interests of employers and the rights and interests of working people, so it is not at all clear why an employer found to be in breach of the law should benefit from further deference at the remedies stage.

One obvious example of undue weight given to employers' interests can be found in the various ways in which the law limits employers' financial liability in the event of a breach. The cap on the compensatory award for unfair dismissal is the most obvious illustration but, as chapter seven demonstrated, there are a number of other, more subtle, ways in which the law seeks to minimise the compensation payable. For example, an employer who has made an unfair selection of the claimant for redundancy may find that its liability is limited by a favourable assumption that it would have selected the same person for redundancy on a fair basis in any event. Nor is compensation the only area for deference. Chapter six explained the various limits on the recovery of unpaid wages in the unlawful deductions jurisdiction, which are stricter than those found in the general law. Even though the employer clearly owes the claimant money, any back-pay claimed via this route will be limited to two years, for no apparent reason other than to limit employers' liability. And because vindicatory awards are not recognised by the law, courts and tribunals have sometimes refused to make substantial awards where the employer's failure was inadvertent and therefore not deserving of 'punishment'.[19]

In a different way, employers are also treated with considerable generosity when discussing whether it is 'practicable' to re-employ an unfairly dismissed person, or whether there is 'trust and confidence' for the purposes of an injunction.[20] In the unfair dismissal jurisdiction, an employer may sometimes be allowed to assert that it no longer trusts the employee, even if it has failed to establish (often because of a poor investigation) that the employee did anything wrong. This may be enough to defeat a claim to reinstatement. And at common law, employers have sometimes been allowed to assert that they do not have 'trust and confidence' in the employee for the purposes of an injunction, even when the very object of the injunction would be to force them to investigate allegations of wrongdoing against that employee. Managerial prerogative carries very considerable weight in many of these cases. But when an employee refuses a re-employment offer in an unfair dismissal case, courts and tribunals are noticeably less sympathetic to the argument that they did not believe that the employer was being genuine.[21]

Arguments about the impact of workers' rights on managerial prerogative and on the financial health of firms are, of course, pervasive throughout employment

[19] See ch 8 of this volume.

[20] See ch 6 of this volume.

[21] *Wilding v British Telecommunications Plc* [2002] EWCA Civ 349, [2002] ICR 1079, discussed in ch 7.

law, so on one level, it is no surprise that they feature in debates on remedies too. However, they do need to be handled with care, for the reasons given in chapter three, and balanced against the interests of working people. To take the examples given here, there needs to be a very good reason for restricting a claimant's ability to recover money they are owed, and for denying a replicative remedy that would do a good job of upholding the claimant's dignity. Effective reform of remedies requires a better, fairer balance to be struck between the needs of working people and their employers. In other words, employment rights should be properly valued.

BIBLIOGRAPHY

Books

Adams, Z, C Barnard, S Deakin and S Fraser Butlin, *Deakin and Morris's Labour Law* (7th edn, Oxford, Hart Publishing, 2021)

Adlercreutz, A, and B Nyström, *Labour Law in Sweden* (3rd edn, London, Wolters Kluwer, 2021)

Ayres, I, and J Braithwaite, *Responsive Regulation: Transcending the Deregulation Debate* (Oxford, OUP, 1992)

Barmes, L, *Bullying and Behavioural Conflict at Work: The Duality of Individual Rights* (Oxford, OUP, 2016)

Bercusson, B, *European Labour Law* (London, Butterworths, 1996)

Bogg, A, J Collins, M Freedland and J Herring (eds), *Criminality at Work* (Oxford, OUP, 2020)

Burrows, AS, *Remedies for Torts, Breach of Contract, and Equitable Wrongs* (4th edn, Oxford, OUP, 2019)

Cane, P, *The Anatomy of Tort Law* (Oxford, Hart Publishing, 1997)

Choudry, N, et al, *Harvey on Industrial Relations and Employment Law* (London, LexisNexis UK, 1991, now online)

Collins, H, *Employment Law* (2nd edn, Oxford, OUP, 2010)

—— *Justice in Dismissal: The Law of Termination of Employment* (Oxford, OUP, 1992)

Davidov, G, *A Purposive Approach to Labour Law* (Oxford, OUP, 2016)

Davies, ACL, *Perspectives on Labour Law* (2nd edn, Cambridge, CUP, 2009)

Davies, PL, and M Freedland, *Labour Legislation and Public Policy* (Oxford, Clarendon Press, 1993)

—— (eds), *Kahn-Freund's Labour and the Law* (3rd edn, London, Stevens & Sons, 1983)

Deakin, SF and Z Adams, *Markesinis and Deakin's Tort Law* (8th edn, Oxford, OUP, 2019)

Dickens, L (ed), *Making Employment Rights Effective: Issues of Enforcement and Compliance* (Oxford, Hart Publishing, 2012)

Dickens, L, M Jones, B Weekes and M Hart, *Dismissed: A Study of Unfair Dismissal and the Industrial Tribunal System* (Oxford, Blackwell, 1985)

Duff, RA, *The Realm of the Criminal Law* (Oxford, OUP, 2018)

—— *Answering for Crime* (Oxford, Hart Publishing, 2007)

Farmer, L, *Making the Modern Criminal Law: Criminalization and Civil Order* (Oxford, OUP, 2016)

Feinberg, J, *The Moral Limits of the Criminal Law: Harm to Others* (Oxford, OUP, 1984)

Forsyth, CF, and IJ Ghosh, *Wade & Forsyth's Administrative Law* (12th edn, Oxford, OUP, 2022)

Fredman, S, *Human Rights Transformed: Positive Rights and Positive Duties* (Oxford, OUP, 2008)

—— *Women and the Law* (New York, OUP, 1997)

Freedland, MR, *The Personal Employment Contract* (Oxford, OUP, 2005)

Freedland, M, and N Kountouris, *The Legal Construction of Personal Work Relations* (Oxford, OUP, 2011)

Grabenwarter, C, *European Convention on Human Rights: Commentary* (Munich/Baden-Baden/Oxford, CH Beck/Nomos/Hart Publishing, 2013)

Husak, D, *Overcriminalization. The Limits of the Criminal Law* (New York, OUP, 2008)

King, J, *Judging Social Rights* (Cambridge, CUP, 2012)

Mantouvalou, V, *Structural Injustice and Workers' Rights* (Oxford, OUP, 2023)

McCrudden, C, *Understanding Human Dignity* (Oxford, OUP, 2013)

Peers, S, T Hervey, J Kenner and A Ward (eds), *The EU Charter of Fundamental Rights: A Commentary* (Oxford, Hart Publishing, 2014)

Robson, JM (ed), *The Collected Works of JS Mill, Vol XVIII* (London, Routledge, 1977)
Simester, AP, and A von Hirsch, *Crimes, Harms and Wrongs: On the Principles of Criminalisation* (Oxford, Hart Publishing, 2011)
Simester, AP, et al, *Simester and Sullivan's Criminal Law: Theory and Doctrine* (6th edn, Oxford, Hart Publishing, 2016)
Smith, SA, *Rights, Wrongs and Injustices: The Structure of Remedial Law* (Oxford, OUP, 2019)
Stevens, R, *Torts and Rights* (Oxford, OUP, 2007)
Tolley's Health and Safety at Work Handbook 2023 (London, LexisNexis, 2022)
Zakrzewski, R, *Remedies Reclassified* (Oxford, OUP, 2005)

Journal articles

Adams, A, and J Prassl, 'Vexatious Claims: Challenging the Case for Employment Tribunal Fees' (2017) 80 *Modern Law Review* 412
Adams-Prassl, J, 'Article 47 CFR and the Effective Enforcement of EU Labour Law: Teeth for Paper Tigers?' (2020) 11 *European Labour Law Journal* 391
Almond, P, and S Colover, 'Mediating Punitiveness: Understanding Public Attitudes towards Work-Related Fatality Cases' (2010) 7 *European Journal of Criminology* 323
Alston, P, '"Core Labour Standards" and the Transformation of the International Labour Rights Regime' (2004) 15 *European Journal of International Law* 457
Anderman, S, 'The Interpretation of Protective Employment Statutes and Contracts of Employment' (2000) 29 *Industrial Law Journal* 223
Anderson, B, 'Migration, Immigration Controls and the Fashioning of Precarious Workers' (2010) 24 *Work, Employment and Society* 300
Ashworth, A, 'Is the Criminal Law a Lost Cause?' (2000) 116 *Law Quarterly Review* 225
Baker, A, 'The "Range of Reasonable Responses" Test: A Poor Substitution for the Statutory Language' (2021) 50 *Industrial Law Journal* 226
Baker, CD, 'Employment Protection: Individual Rights' (1976) 2 *Industrial Law Journal* 65
Barmes, L, 'Common Law Implied Terms and Behavioural Standards at Work' (2007) 36 *Industrial Law Journal* 35
—— 'Judicial Influence and *Edwards v Chesterfield Royal Hospital NHS Foundation Trust* and *Botham v Ministry of Defence*' (2013) 42 *Industrial Law Journal* 192
Barnard, C, 'The Working Time Regulations 1998' (1999) 28 *Industrial Law Journal* 61
Barnard, C, A Ludlow and S Fraser Butlin, 'Beyond Employment Tribunals: Enforcement of Employment Rights by EU-8 Migrant Workers' (2018) 47 *Industrial Law Journal* 226
Becker, G, 'Crime and Punishment: An Economic Approach' (1968) 76 *Journal of Political Economy* 169
Beever, A, 'The Structure of Aggravated and Exemplary Damages' (2003) 23 *Oxford Journal of Legal Studies* 87
Birks, P, 'Rights, Wrongs and Remedies' (2000) 20 *Oxford Journal of Legal Studies* 1
Bogg, A, 'Express Disciplinary Procedures in the Contract of Employment: Parliamentary Intention and the Supreme Court' (2015) 131 *Law Quarterly Review* 15
—— 'Employment Relations Act 2004: Another False Dawn for Collectivism?' (2005) 34 *Industrial Law Journal* 72
—— 'Labour, Love and Futility: Philosophical Perspectives on Labour Law' (2017) 33 *International Journal of Comparative Labour Law and Industrial Relations* 7
—— '*Okedina v Chikale* and Contract Illegality: New Dawn or False Dawn?' (2020) 49 *Industrial Law Journal* 258
Bogg, A, and D Brodie, 'Every Little Helps: Permanent Benefits, Contract Interpretation, and "Fire and Rehire"' (2023) 52 *Industrial Law Journal* 246
Bogg, A, and S Green, 'Rights are not just for the Virtuous: What *Hounga* Means for the Illegality Defence in the Discrimination Torts' (2015) 44 *Industrial Law Journal* 101

Bridge, MG, 'Mitigation of Damages in Contract and the Meaning of Avoidable Loss' (1989) 105 *Law Quarterly Review* 398
Brodie, D, 'Legal Coherence and the Employment Revolution' (2001) 117 *Law Quarterly Review* 604
—— 'Mutual Trust and Confidence: Catalysts, Constraints and Commonality' (2008) 37 *Industrial Law Journal* 329
—— 'Specific Performance and Employment Contracts' (1998) 27 *Industrial Law Journal* 37
Busby, N and M McDermont, 'Fighting with the Wind: Claimants' Experiences and Perceptions of the Employment Tribunal' (2020) 49 *Industrial Law Journal* 159
Collins, H, 'Compensation for Dismissal: in Search of Principle' (2012) 41 *Industrial Law Journal* 208
—— 'The Just and Equitable Compensatory Award' (1991) 20 *Industrial Law Journal* 201
Collins, PM, 'Finding Fault in the Law of Unfair Dismissal: The Insubstantiality of Reasons for Dismissal' (2022) 51 *Industrial Law Journal* 598
Craven, R, 'The Legal and Social Construction of Value in Government Procurement Markets' (2020) 47 *Journal of Law and Society* 29
Davidov, G (ed), (2021) 37(2/3) *International Journal of Comparative Labour Law and Industrial Relations* (special issue)
Davies, ACL, 'Problems Continue in the Horticulture Sector: The Seasonal Workers Pilot Review 2019' (2022) 51 *Industrial Law Journal* 494
—— 'Stress at Work: Individuals or Structures?' (2022) 51 *Industrial Law Journal* 403
Davies, ACL, and L Rodgers, 'Towards a More Effective Health and Safety Regime for UK Workplaces Post Covid-19' (2023) 52 *Industrial Law Journal* 665
Dickens, L, 'Unfair Dismissal Applications and the Industrial Tribunal System' (1978) 9 *Industrial Relations Journal* 4
Ford, M, 'Employment Tribunal Fees and the Rule of Law: *R (Unison) v Lord Chancellor* in the Supreme Court' (2018) 47 *Industrial Law Journal* 1
Fredman, S, 'Reversing Roles: Bringing Men into the Frame' (2014) 10 *International Journal of Law in Context* 442
—— 'Women at Work: The Broken Promise of Flexicurity' (2004) 33 *Industrial Law Journal* 299
Fudge, J, 'The Spectre of *Addis* in Contracts of Employment in Canada and the UK' (2007) 36 *Industrial Law Journal* 51
—— 'Why Labour Lawyers Should Care about the Modern Slavery Act 2015' (2018) 29 *King's Law Journal* 377
Gardner, J, 'What is Tort Law For? Part 1: The Place of Corrective Justice' (2011) 30 *Law & Philosophy* 1
Genn, H, 'Do-it-Yourself Law: Access to Justice and the Challenge of Self-Representation' (2013) 32 *Civil Justice Quarterly* 411
Gilabert, P, 'Labor Human Rights and Human Dignity' (2016) 42 *Philosophy and Social Criticism* 171
Gobert, J, 'The Corporate Manslaughter and Corporate Homicide Act 2007 – Thirteen Years in the Making but was it Worth the Wait?' (2008) 71 *Modern Law Review* 413
Gold, A, 'Book Review of: Stephen A. Smith, Rights, Wrongs, and Injustices: The Structure of Remedial Law (Oxford University Press, 2019)' (2020) 79 *Cambridge Law Journal* 615
Guild, E, and AM Barylska, 'Decent Work for Migrants? Examining the Impacts of the UK Frameworks of Gangmasters Legislation and Modern Slavery on Working Standards for Irregularly Present Migrants' (2021) 1 *Global Public Policy and Governance* 279
Gutman, K, 'The Essence of the Fundamental Right to an Effective Remedy and to a Fair Trial in the Case-Law of the Court of Justice of the European Union: The Best Is Yet to Come?' (2019) 20 *German Law Journal* 884
Hardy, T, 'Creating Ripples, Making Waves?: Assessing the General Deterrence Effects of Enforcement Activities of the Fair Work Ombudsman' (2017) 39 *Sydney Law Review* 471
—— 'Digging Into Deterrence: An Examination of Deterrence-Based Theories and Evidence in Employment Standards Enforcement' (2021) 37 *International Journal of Comparative Labour Law and Industrial Relations* 133
Hardy, T, and J Howe, 'Creating Ripples, Making Waves? Assessing the General Deterrence Effects of Enforcement Activities of the Fair Work Ombudsman' (2017) 39 *Sydney Law Review* 471

—— 'Too Soft or Too Severe? Enforceable Undertakings and the Regulatory Dilemma facing the Fair Work Ombudsman' (2013) 41 *Federal Law Review* 1
Hepple, B, 'Back to the Future: Employment Law under the Coalition Government' (2013) 42 *Industrial Law Journal* 203
Hobbs, R, C Barnard and S Deakin, 'Opting Out of the 48-Hour Week: Employer Necessity or Individual Choice? an Empirical Study of the Operation of Article 18(1)(b) of the Working Time Directive in the UK' (2003) 32 *Industrial Law Journal* 223
Jolls, C, C Sunstein and R Thaler, 'A Behavioral Approach to Law and Economics' (1998) 50 *Stanford Law Review* 1471
Kirk, E, 'The "Problem" with the Employment Tribunal System: Reform, Rhetoric and Realities for the Clients of Citizens' Advice Bureaux' (2018) 32 *Work, Employment and Society* 975
Lewis, D, 'Re-Employment as a Remedy for Unfair Dismissal: How can the Culture be Changed?' (1999) 28 *Industrial Law Journal* 183
Mantouvalou, V, 'Are Labour Rights Human Rights?' (2012) 3 *European Labour Law Journal* 151
—— 'The UK Modern Slavery Act 2015 Three Years On' (2018) 81 *Modern Law Review* 1017
McMullen, J, 'The Resurgence of Proceduralism in Unfair Dismissal Law – The End of the *British Labour Pump* Principle' (1988) 51 *Modern Law Review* 651
Mulcahy, L, 'The Collective Interest in Private Dispute Resolution' (2013) 33 *Oxford Journal of Legal Studies* 59
Murphy, J, 'The Nature and Domain of Aggravated Damages' (2010) 69 *Cambridge Law Journal* 353
O'Higgins, P, 'Labour Is Not a Commodity – An Irish Contribution to International Labour Law' (1997) 26 *Industrial Law Journal* 225
Ormerod, D, and R Taylor, 'The Corporate Manslaughter and Corporate Homicide Act 2007' [2008] *Criminal Law Review* 589
Pearce, D, and R Halson, 'Damages for Breach of Contract: Compensation, Restitution and Vindication' (2008) 28 *Oxford Journal of Legal Studies* 73
Puttick, K, 'From Mini to Maxi Jobs? Low Pay, "Progression", and the Duty to Work (Harder)' (2019) 48 *Industrial Law Journal* 143
Robinson, P, and J Darley, 'Does Criminal Law Deter? A Behavioural Science Investigation' (2004) 24 *Oxford Journal of Legal Studies* 173
Roper, V, 'The Corporate Manslaughter and Corporate Homicide Act 2007: A Re-Evaluation 10 Years on from the First Case' [2022] *Criminal Law Review* 290.
Simpson, B, 'The Employment Act 2008's Amendments to the National Minimum Wage Legislation' (2009) 38 *Industrial Law Journal* 57
Steel, S, 'Damages Without Loss' (2023) 139 *Law Quarterly Review* 219
—— 'Remedies, Analysed' (2021) 41 *Oxford Journal of Legal Studies* 539
Steel, S, and R Stevens, 'The Secondary Legal Duty to Pay Damages' (2020) 136 *Law Quarterly Review* 283
Tilbury, M, 'Aggravated Damages' (2018) 71 *Current Legal Problems* 215
Varuhas, JNE, 'The Concept of "Vindication" in the Law of Torts: Rights, Interests and Damages' (2014) 34 *Oxford Journal of Legal Studies* 253
Weil, D, 'A Strategic Approach to Labour Inspection' (2008) 147 *International Labour Review* 349
Williams, K, 'Unfair Dismissal: Myths and Statistics' (1983) 12 *Industrial Law Journal* 157

Chapters in books

Aliverti, A, 'Doing the Dirty Job: Labour at the Intersections of Criminal Law and Immigration Controls', in A Bogg, J Collins, M Freedland and J Herring (eds), *Criminality at Work* (Oxford, OUP, 2020)
Almond, P, 'Workplace Safety and Criminalization: A Double-edged Sword', in A Bogg, J Collins, M Freedland and J Herring (eds), *Criminality at Work* (Oxford, OUP, 2020)

Atkinson, J, 'Human Rights as Foundations for Labour Law', in H Collins, G Lester and V Mantouvalou (eds), *Philosophical Foundations of Labour Law* (Oxford, OUP, 2018)
Barmes, L, 'The Contract of Employment and the Remedial Dimension', in M Freedland et al. (eds), *The Contract of Employment* (Oxford, OUP, 2016)
Bogg, A, and M Freedland, 'Criminality at Work: A Framework for Discussion', in A Bogg, J Collins, M Freedland and J Herring (eds), *Criminality at Work* (Oxford, OUP, 2020)
Bogg, A, KD Ewing and A Moretta, 'The Persistence of Criminal Law and Police in Collective Labour Relations', in A Bogg, J Collins, M Freedland and J Herring (eds), *Criminality at Work* (Oxford, OUP, 2020)
Colling, T, 'Trade Union Roles in Making Employment Rights Effective', in L Dickens (ed), *Making Employment Rights Effective: Issues of Enforcement and Compliance* (Oxford, Hart Publishing, 2012)
Collins, H, 'Justifications and Techniques of Legal Regulation of the Employment Relation', in H Collins, PL Davies and RW Rideout (eds), *Legal Regulation of the Employment Relation* (Alphen aan den Rijn, Kluwer Law International, 2000)
—— 'Theories of Rights as Justifications for Labour Law', in G Davidov and B Langille (eds), *The Idea of Labour Law* (Oxford, OUP, 2011)
Davies, ACL, 'Migrant Workers in Agriculture: A Legal Perspective', in C Costello and M Freedland (eds), *Migrants at Work: Immigration and Vulnerability in Labour Law* (Oxford, OUP, 2014)
Deakin, S, 'The Contribution of Labour Law to Economic and Human Development', in G Davidov and B Langille (eds), *The Idea of Labour Law* (Oxford, OUP, 2011)
Dickens, L, 'Introduction', in L Dickens (ed), *Making Employment Rights Effective: Issues of Enforcement and Compliance* (Oxford, Hart Publishing, 2012)
Dukes, R, 'Hugo Sinzheimer and the Constitutional Function of Labour Law', in G Davidov and B Langille (eds), *The Idea of Labour Law* (Oxford, OUP, 2011)
Ford, M, 'The Criminalization of Health and Safety at Work', in A Bogg, J Collins, M Freedland and J Herring (eds), *Criminality at Work* (Oxford, OUP, 2020)
Freedland, M, and C Costello, 'Migrants at Work and the Division of Labour Law', in C Costello and M Freedland (eds), *Migrants at Work: Immigration and Vulnerability in Labour Law* (Oxford, OUP, 2014)
Green, S, 'Wage Theft as a Legal Concept', in Bogg, J Collins, M Freedland and J Herring (eds), *Criminality at Work* (Oxford, OUP, 2020)
Mantouvalou, V, 'Human Rights, Labour Rights, and Criminal Wrongs', in A Bogg, J Collins, M Freedland and J Herring (eds), *Criminality at Work* (Oxford, OUP, 2020)
—— 'In Support of Legalisation', in C Gearty and V Mantouvalou, *Debating Social Rights* (Oxford, Hart Publishing, 2010)
McCrudden, C, 'Procurement and Fairness in the Workplace', in L Dickens (ed), *Making Employment Rights Effective: Issues of Enforcement and Compliance* (Oxford, Hart Publishing, 2012)
Meeran, G, 'The Employment Tribunals', in L Dickens and A Neal (eds), *The Changing Institutional Face of British Industrial Relations* (Alphen aan den Rijn, Kluwer, 2006)
Sullivan, GR, 'Workplace Welfare and State Coercion', in A Bogg, J Collins, M Freedland and J Herring, *Criminality at Work* (Oxford, OUP, 2020)
Tombs, S, and D Whyte, 'Reshaping Health and Safety Enforcement: Institutionalising Impunity', in L Dickens (ed), *Making Employment Rights Effective: Issues of Enforcement and Compliance* (Oxford, Hart Publishing, 2012)
Weiss, M, 'Re-Inventing Labour Law?', in G Davidov and B Langille (eds), *The Idea of Labour Law* (Oxford, OUP, 2011)

Reports/Guidance/Press

Cabinet Office, *Procurement Policy Note 06/20 – Taking Account of Social Value in the Award of Central Government Contracts* (September 2020)

Crown Prosecution Service, *The Code for Crown Prosecutors* (October 2018)
Department for Business and Trade, and Department for Business, Energy and Industrial Strategy, *National Living Wage and National Minimum Wage Government evidence on enforcement and compliance 2021/22* (April 2023)
Department for Business and Trade, Department for Business, Energy and Industrial Strategy and HMRC, *National Minimum Wage: Policy on Enforcement, Prosecutions and Naming Employers who Break National Minimum Wage Law* (June 2022)
Department for Business, Energy and Industrial Strategy, *Employment Tribunal Naming Scheme Guidance* (December 2018)
—— *Employment Agency Standards (EAS) Inspectorate: Annual Report, 2020 to 2021* (June 2022)
—— *Enforcement of the National Minimum Wage in the Social Care Sector* (July 2017)
—— *Survey of Employment Tribunal Applications: Findings from the 2018 Survey* (BEIS Research Paper Number 2020/007, July 2020)
—— *Trade Union Statistics 2021* (May 2022)
—— *Establishing a New Single Enforcement Body for Employment Rights: Government Response* (June 2021)
Department for Business, Innovation and Skills, *Ending the Employment Relationship Consultation* (September 2012)
—— *Resolving Workplace Disputes* (January 2011)
—— *The Payment of Tribunal Awards: 2013 Study* (London, 2014)
Department for Trade and Industry, *Fairness at Work* (Cm 3968, May 1998)
Donovan, Lord, *Report of the Royal Commission on Trade Unions and Employers' Associations 1965–1968* (Cmnd 3623, 1968)
ECHR, *Guide on Article 4 of the European Convention on Human Rights* (August 2022)
Employment Agency Standards Inspectorate, *Annual Report 2020–2021* (June 2022)
Ewing, K, *Ruined Lives: Blacklisting in the Construction Industry* (Institute of Employment Rights, August 2009)
Gangmasters and Labour Abuse Authority, *Annual Report and Accounts 1 April 2021 to 31 March 2022* (HC 915, December 2022)
—— *Code of Practice on Compliance, Enforcement, Labour Market and Modern Slavery Investigations* (October 2018)
Genn, H, and Y Genn, *The Effectiveness of Representation at Tribunals: Report to the Lord Chancellor* (Lord Chancellor's Department, 1989)
Hampton, P, *Reduction in Administrative Burdens: Effective Inspection and Enforcement* (UK Government, 2005)
Health and Safety Commission, *Annual Report and the Health and Safety Commission/Executive Accounts 2001/02* (HC 1202, October 2002)
Health and Safety Executive, *Annual Report and Accounts 2019/20* (HC 442, July 2020)
—— *Annual Report and Accounts 2022/23* (HC 1599, July 2023)
—— *Enforcement Policy Statement* (October 2015)
Home Office, *Modern Slavery: Statutory Guidance for England and Wales and non-Statutory Guidance for Scotland and Northern Ireland* (30 January 2023)
Independent Anti-Slavery Commissioner, *Annual Report 2021–2022* (2022)
International Labour Organization, *General Survey on Labour Inspection* (2006)
—— *Guidelines on General Principles of Labour Inspection* (2022)
Law Commission, *Aggravated, Exemplary and Restitutionary Damages* (No 247, 1997)
—— *Criminal Liability in Regulatory Contexts* (No 195, 2010)
—— *Employment Law Hearing Structures* (No 390, 2020)
Low Pay Commission, *Compliance and Enforcement of the National Minimum Wage* (September 2023)
—— *National Minimum Wage: Low Pay Commission Report 2022* (January 2023, CP 758)
Ministry of Justice, *Tribunal Statistics Quarterly, April to June 2020* (December 2021)
—— *Tribunal Statistics Quarterly, July to September 2022* (December 2022)

—— *Tribunal Statistics Quarterly, April to June 2023* (September 2023)
Poinasamy, K, and A Bance, *Turning the Tide: How Best to Protect Workers Employed by Gangmasters, Five Years after Morecambe Bay* (Oxfam, 2009)
Presidential Guidance, *Employment Tribunal Awards for Injury to Feelings and Psychiatric Injury Following De Souza v Vinci Construction (UK) Ltd* [2017] EWCA Civ 879 (September 2017)
—— *Employment Tribunal Awards for Injury to Feelings and Psychiatric Injury Following De Souza v Vinci Construction (UK) Ltd* [2017] EWCA Civ 879 (Sixth Addendum to Presidential Guidance Originally Issued on 5 September 2017) (March 2023)
Resolution Foundation, *Enforce for Good: Effectively Enforcing Labour Market Rights in the 2020s and Beyond* (April 2023)
Senior President of Tribunals, *Consultation on Panel Composition in the Employment Tribunals and the Employment Appeal Tribunal* (February 2023)
Sentencing Council, *General Guideline: Overarching Principles* (October 2019)
—— *Sentencing Guidelines for Corporate Manslaughter* (February 2016)
—— *Sentencing Guidelines for Gross Negligence Manslaughter* (November 2018)
—— *Theft Offences: Definitive Guideline* (February 2016)
Taylor, M, *Good Work: The Taylor Review of Modern Working Practices* (July 2017)
Trades Union Congress, *P&O Ferries Mass Sackings – One Year On* (17 March 2023)

INDEX

www.ingramcontent.com/pod-product-compliance
Ingram Content Group UK Ltd.
Pitfield, Milton Keynes, MK11 3LW, UK
UKHW020248290926
15470UKWH00002B/813

9 781509 955268